Contents

*Dedicated to gardeners everywhere
who take these disasters
and improve on them.*

Kauai

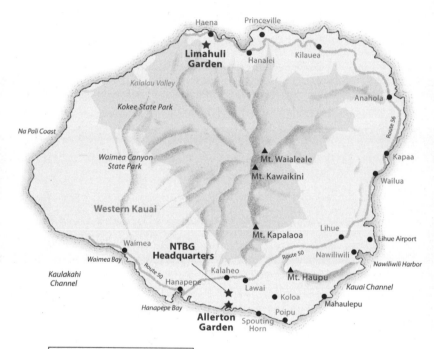

Haena
Princeville

★ **Limahuli Garden**
Hanalei
Kilauea

Kalalau Valley

Kokee State Park

Anahola

Na Pali Coast

Route 56

Waimea Canyon State Park

▲ Mt. Waialeale
▲ Mt. Kawaikini

Kapaa

Wailua

Western Kauai

▲ Mt. Kapalaoa

Lihue

Lihue Airport

Waimea
NTBG Headquarters

Route 50
Nawiliwili

Waimea Bay

Kalaheo

Nawiliwili Harbor

Kaulakahi Channel

Route 50
Hanapepe
Lawai

▲ Mt. Haupu

Koloa

Kauai Channel

Mahaulepu

Hanapepe Bay

★ **Allerton Garden**
Spouting Horn
Poipu

THE HAWAIIAN ISLANDS

Kauai

Niihau
Oahu
Molokai
Lanai
Maui
Kahoolawe

Pacific Ocean

Hawaii

PART ONE

Discovery

CHAPTER ONE

Solitary Expeditions

SLOWLY I TURNED the corner onto my perfect little street of stone houses and picket fences already
steeped in the long shadows of early evening. I parked my Toyota, then picked a path through the tricycle and other toys left
on the sidewalk by the neighbors' children. There was no hurry.
I had no plans.

Inside, my reading corner waited, a lady's wing chair in wool
plaid pulled close to the white brick fireplace. Passing into the
narrow galley kitchen, I gathered the makings for a simple
meal, a standard entry in my repertoire of Single Working Girl's
Twenty-Minute Dinners. Green salad, leftover balsamic vinaigrette. I set a pot of water on to boil for angel-hair pasta, peeled
garlic cloves, and chopped parsley. On second thought, I turned
off the water and went upstairs. Blue and white toile papered
the renovated bathroom and dressing room in an eighteenth-
century pastoral scene. I switched on a brass student lamp in the
darkened study. Twin green globes cast ponds of light on a wall
of photographs: smiling family members and friends; vacation
shots from hiking the Alps; skiing in Italy; watching the races at
Saratoga Springs. All evidence of a full, happy life, right?

I kicked off high-heeled pumps and hung up my tailored suit while I drew a hot, foamy bath in the claw-footed tub, then got in for a soak. Even that didn't take the edge off an evening with too much free time. Wrapped in a silk dressing gown, I went back downstairs and launched a CD of John Coltrane's *My Favorite Things*. In a nightly ritual, I dared myself to light the fire with a single match, touching the flame to four corners of crumpled newspaper. Satisfied that it caught, I set a tray with cloth napkin and silver, then brought it back to the fireside. I studied the flames. *My God, I'm going to spend the rest of my life here.* Restoring this English-style ramshackle cottage until it was as trim as a sailboat had consumed nine years. But I had tired of playing house. A child of preppy, Connecticut suburbia, I had settled for more of the same in the happily-ever-afterdom of suburban Philadelphia. For most of my neighbors and peers, lawyer husbands and above-average children had replaced the circle pins and penny loafers we had worn with brutal conformity as teenagers.

While many women my age rushed about, drawn and quartered between big lives of child-rearing and high-powered jobs, I found myself underemployed and sliding into midlife with not much to show for it. Now forty-four, I'd been divorced for almost fifteen years. My last great love affair had died more than a year ago. I couldn't quite escape an ingrained sense that a solitary woman was a misfit, a dried-up celibate or eccentric, or worse yet, too unattractive to find a presentable mate.

I once deemed my work as a reporter for *The Philadelphia Inquirer* the apogee of existence. Now corporate profiteering and betrayal had slithered into our midst. It no longer seemed fun or noble. Healthy, over forty, either single or with children who had flown the nest, many of my colleagues faced similar midlife angst, professional and personal. Our well-developed careers had gone flat. What to do now with our brightly educated minds, expensively toned bodies, and elongated life spans that promised another thirty or forty years of active life? Was plastic surgery to be the last frontier? Recently a recurring nightmare plagued me, waking me with a Delphic warning: *You are doomed to a life of small luxuries.* Not lavish, big spending bursts of vacation houses, big cars, and jewels, but just enough for comfort.

Roosters haunted me like the Ghost of Christmas Future. During the years when my girlfriends and I had hunted antiques stores and flea markets to fill up our newly purchased houses, we noticed rooster knickknacks everywhere. Rooster coffee mugs, rooster salt shakers, rooster napkin holders, rooster-anything-you-can-imagine. "Look, another item for the rooster shop we're going to open when we're old and retired," we'd joke. The roosters became emblematic of all the useless junk that Americans buy and all the wasted hours middle-aged women fill with aimless shopping for more useless stuff. Opening a rooster knickknack shop was the last thing I'd ever do, I vowed.

I had read many of the writings of psychologist Carl Jung, who devoted much of his study to the midlife crisis. He felt the suffering at that age held potential for change. Adults dedicate the first half of life to building fortune, family, and career. Jung theorized that at midlife those pursuits lose their power of attraction, and personal values shift into reverse. What was once important dims, while new pursuits and a growing spirituality loom on the horizon. Fail to pay attention to the warning lights of depression and anxiety, and you risk sinking into a quagmire of regret and resentment. Thousands of us baby boomers are re-inventing ourselves, we're told. But I had yet to find any instruction books. How to begin when you're frozen by inertia? When fear paralyzes? "We would rather be ruined than changed, We would rather die in our dread," wrote W. H. Auden.

The telephone ring interrupted my gloomy ruminations. I rushed to the kitchen wall phone and stood listening while Dr. William Klein cheerily announced that he was coming to Philadelphia for meetings. He invited me to dinner Sunday night. "We'll go someplace fancy," he promised. Bill Klein was an erudite botanist, one of my favorite sources. Over the years, I enjoyed our infrequent lunches that probed the realm of ideas.

I hung up the phone, went upstairs, and pulled on a pair of faded green Army fatigues and one of Dad's old sweaters with holes in the elbows. I rummaged under the sink for a flashlight, then escaped outside to the garden. With its damp scent of recent rain, the cold night air made me shiver. A nearly full moon washed the garden in light and shadow. I trained the light beam on top-heavy, wobbling daffodils. Every autumn I had dug in more bulbs, more varieties, until now hundreds lit the small yard: sunset oranges of the giant Fortissimo; creamy Ice Follies; a few collectors' pinks such as Salome, with its whisper white petals and apricot centers. I searched for perfect blooms. Not those past their prime, marred by creeping translucence along crinkling petals.

I carried an armload of flowers into the kitchen. A few dots of black dirt speckled an insouciant Las Vegas blossom. Once I watched champion daffodil grower Kathryn Andersen use the tip of her tongue to gently lap away splashes of dirt from prize

entries. Anything stronger could nick or dent the flower. I tried
it. The petals felt as soft as baby skin but had a crisp taste of
celery. Gardening always cheered me up.

BUYING AN OLD HOUSE had unleashed a pent-up de-
sire. That first winter I read garden books late into night. Weekends I haunted nurseries, just to look at the plants and smell
loamy earth. I signed up for a night course in landscape design
at the nearby Morris Arboretum. Although a novice, I chose
one of the most difficult and labor-intensive projects: an English
perennial border, to match my English cottage. I lusted after
towering blue delphiniums, pink snapdragons, lavenders, and
heathers.

My small cottage garden occupied only about four hundred
square feet. It begged to be called postage-stamp in size. Worse,
a fortresslike hedge of arborvitae surrounded the perimeter.
"Get rid of it," advised the landscape instructor. I looked at him
as if he were an anarchist. But I came to realize that if I was
to get anywhere, I had to clear-cut the whole yard, analyze the
site for light and shade, drainage and soil conditions, and then
start anew.

I chopped down each tree with a hatchet. Even with goatskin
gloves, my thumbs ached. A dated gardening book, a gift from
my mother, advised double-digging eighteen-inch trenches,
English-style, then filling the furrows with cow manure. Two
truckloads of organic humus and sand added height. I liked the
physical work of bending muscles to the task and learning to use
a shovel. Lured by the magical alchemy of the garden that trans-
forms manure and garbage into roses, I saved coffee grounds and
vegetable peels as precious nutrients for the compost heap. The

mindless weeding and meditation on each task transformed my small plot into a place to forget daily cares. Minutes disappeared into hours without notice. Sometimes I'd garden as the moon came up, trying to squeeze in a few last tasks.

That first spring, every inch of the yard exploded into lavenders, nasturtiums, and lilies. Brooding, black-red Don Juan roses and nude-colored New Dawn pink climbers veiled the second-story balcony. A really good garden requires an almost religious adherence to its theme. I couldn't resist growing American-as-pie zinnias by the score or cramming dinner-plate-sized dahlias into the back of the border, ignoring one English garden writer's dismissal of dahlias as "so vulgar."

I cared not. The garden became a place of abandon for me, a joy of fantasies.

Dr. Klein had introduced me to the notion of the garden as an intellectual journey, a physical record of the history of civilization. From him I learned that medieval monks cultivated medicinal herbs in the first botanical gardens. For thirteen years, Dr. Klein had directed the Morris Arboretum of the University of Pennsylvania, transforming it from a weedy and forgotten Victorian botanical garden into a thriving educational center with new buildings, explosive plans, and thousands of visitors. "If Bill Klein had been a plant, he would be a pachysandra," I had written in a profile of him for the *Inquirer*. "Invasive and slightly out of control." One of those rare scientists who knew how to spin a story, he enlisted people to his cause. Some found the ebullient, verbose botanist rather alarming. And like all visionaries who goad for more and more progress, he eventually found himself out on a limb. Just as university regents were about to impose budget controls to rein in his little Eden, he quit to become the director of Fairchild Tropical Botanic Garden in Coral Gables, Florida.

I kept in touch after he left Philadelphia, and flew down to Miami to write a story for the newspaper shortly after Hurricane Andrew blew apart much of south Florida. The storm toppled Fairchild Garden's collection of rare palms and turned its manicured grounds into a snarl of overturned trees. Many staff members lost their own houses, yet they showed up to work long days for Dr. Klein. As he walked through the rubble, Dr. Klein promised, "Fairchild will rise again. It's the nature of gardeners to take these disasters and improve on them."

His garden reopened to the public in thirty days. "It was nothing that General Patton couldn't have done," he insisted. The performance earned him a reputation in the garden world as the hurricane-fixer. But he quarreled with Fairchild Garden's intrusive board of directors, complaining that they were always leaning over his shoulder, hampering his plans, restricting his vision. So he jumped at the chance to become executive director, CEO, and president of the National Tropical Botanical Garden on the Hawaiian island of Kauai. "As soon as I heard that the board of trustees lived five thousand miles away and met only twice a year, I knew it was the place for me," he confided. Now aged sixty-two, he planned to stay until retirement, transforming his last garden institution into his masterwork.

Sunday evening I studied my closet full of clothes, looking for something suitably dressy for a pricey dinner. I had a classy wardrobe, thanks to hand-me-downs from my sister who lived in Milan with her Italian clothier husband. I chose a tailored navy blazer and slacks, with a silk top draped into a V-neck, a chunky gold ring set with an emerald-cut green tourmaline, flashy earrings to match, and navy heels.

I always enjoyed the sunset drive down to Center City along the Schuylkill. Rowing sculls skimmed the river, bathed in the same golden light Thomas Eakins painted more than a century ago. I regarded Philadelphia as just the right size. Big enough for a world-class orchestra, great restaurants, and museums, small enough that I could drive home in thirty minutes.

When I entered the noisy lobby of the nondescript Hershey Hotel on South Broad Street, I did not see any sign of Dr. Klein. Finally he appeared, dressed in rumpled pants, wrinkled sweater, and a green baseball cap. He looked kind of schlumpy, balding with professorial wire-rim glasses and a girth of extra pounds he was always trying to lose. "Where should we go?" he asked. I groaned silently. He had forgotten his promise of an upscale meal. I slipped off my too-fancy earrings and hid them in a pocket, then suggested Upstares at Varalli, a casual Italian restaurant across the street. I tried to suppress my irritation. By the entrée, I regained enough humor to ask about life in Hawaii. "Mah-velous, mah-velous," he said expansively. "You should see my office. I can see whales breaching in the distance out one window. The other looks out onto a hillside where cows graze."

"Sounds like the boondocks," I said. "What are you doing on the East Coast?"

"Looking to hire somebody to help me raise money, actually," he said. "Are you interested?" He threw it out so casually that I didn't see the barbed lure.

"Oh sure," I said. "It probably doesn't pay anything."

"Actually, it does."

I said quickly, "I'll never leave journalism."

He looked away, eyelids dropping over half-closed eyes.

TWO WEEKS LATER, I waited on the couch outside the executive editor's office, surveying the familiar newsroom landscape. I had spent years here on midnight deadlines and frenzied story chases. Cheap metal desks jammed against one another, cluttered with newspapers and file folders. A plastic shark head hung over one desk. The newsroom had served almost as a college dorm for my generation of journalists who spent most of their professional lives at *The Philadelphia Inquirer.* Truthfully, it was better than college — a couple hundred of the best young journalists in the country, all intensely inquisitive and engaged, had fought and schemed to get here. We were drawn by the newspaper's legendary editor, Eugene L. Roberts, Jr., who valued creative writing and investigative reporting and gave reporters enough time and money to pursue their best work. Despite the dedicated individualism of journalists, we all drank the same elixir, a heady promise that we were building a great newspaper. The stories produced in those years soared, uncovering police brutality, budget excesses at the Pentagon, chaos at the IRS, and deep narratives of ordinary lives made brilliant. Then the apparatchiks and bean counters took over and corporate greed became the dominant goal. Roberts couldn't fight off Knight Ridder, the newspaper chain owners, and even he left.

A newspaper resembles a grand opera company, with its repertoire cast and fierce competitions, endless fallings-out and countless love affairs. Once it slips, it can never attain those high notes again, and you spend the rest of your life remembering.

Now, editors relegated more and more reporters to the Shit List. Including me, I feared. Whether covering New Jersey gambling, corruption at city hall, or cultural institutions, I could dig out stories. But in the new era, support was vanishing for that kind of reporting. A couple of years ago I had volunteered to create the Home and Design section. An odd choice for a hard news and investigative reporter, but I saw it as a refuge that also offered a chance to write about architecture and gardening. It worked for a while. The new section editor didn't know anything about home or design but delivered pep rally speeches in Dale Carnegie platitudes: *We're going to be number one in the country! We're building a team!* Lately I had to fight off news-you-can-use stories. I got away with turning down an assignment to write a shopper's guide to summer fans. But when I refused to write puff pieces promoting real estate for sale, I ventured into insubordination. I asked for a transfer, reactivated a campaign to go overseas, to cover science, to do anything to get out of Features.

The secretary signaled me to go into the executive editor's office. Max stood poised before an antique worktable, his carved mahogany desk and bookcase behind him. Its sumptuous decor had the odd style of a turn-of-the-century robber baron. Max's starched blue oxford shirt was rolled up to the elbows as he ruffled papers, ostensibly busy. He glanced sideways at me and said, "Sit down, Lucinda, this will only take a minute." He remained standing. Max was handsome, in a rich kid's preppy Harvard way, with dark hair curled over chiseled features. Charming and so fresh-faced that I instinctively smiled and forgot to be wary.

He never met my eyes and continued to leaf through papers.

Okay, I would not have to write about real estate, but I could forget about going abroad. Or anywhere else. I wasn't going anywhere. He ran through a list of trumped-up offenses. "That's a bunch of crap," I said. I may have sounded tough. But as I stood, I felt like I teetered on a tightrope. As I walked out the door I knew I had reached a dead end.

Enough of my friends had signed on to *The New York Times* and *The Washington Post* that I might be able to land at either one. Nausea swept over me, and an icy sweat slid down my spine and withered my spirit.

TEN DAYS LATER, I woke up at 3 a.m. and sat upright in bed. Why not take that job in Hawaii?

Why the *hell* not?

I switched on the lamp and moved across the hall to the study. I pulled down an atlas and turned to the Hawaiian Islands. Dozens of tiny specks and dots of land formed a chain that started in the mid-Pacific and stretched northwest for 1,500 miles. The Hawaiian archipelago is the most isolated place on earth, in terms of distance from continents. Los Angeles lies 2,550 miles away; Tokyo 3,860, with nothing in between.

The southernmost Big Island (Hawaii) anchors the chain. Ovals and amoeba shapes of Maui, Lanai, Molokai, and Oahu bunch together like a closely strung necklace. Smaller, circular Kauai lies farther north and west, distanced from the rest.

As an adventure, it struck me as suitably remote and exotic, but not all that daring. My own grandmother, Otelia Breck, risked more when she traveled from Germany to Ellis Island in 1909 at age twenty-four, alone, unattached, with no English and little money. Plus, the top honeymoon destination in America couldn't be too wild and woolly. I feared drinks with umbrellas and tourist hulas. But I *had* dreamed of living in the pastoral countryside, with a pared-down life far from suburban materialism and out of reach from corporate America.

Nature—rugged, ferocious, and raw—always had a restorative effect on me and quieted my inner storms. Henry Beston, in the foreward to a new edition of his classic book, *The Outermost House: A Year of Life on the Great Beach of Cape Cod,* wrote famously of our need to return to nature. "Nature is part of our humanity, and without some awareness and experience of that divine mystery man ceases to be man. When the Pleiades and the wind in the grass are no longer a part of the human spirit, a part of very flesh and bone, man becomes, as it were, a kind of cosmic outlaw, having neither the completeness and integrity of the animal nor the birthright of a true humanity."

I wanted my journey to the outermost island to bring me closer to that divine mystery. A time for serious reflection, for stilling the unease over what I had not accomplished in the first half of life and for discovering what I wanted for the second half. A chance to revise my biography.

As I continued my research over the next few days, I discovered that Kauai was nicknamed "the Garden Island." Considered by many to be the most beautiful of the islands, it was also the greenest. A year-round population of fifty thousand barely filled its 550 square miles, much of it impenetrable jungle or sheer cliffs. The inaccessible Mount Waialeale, claimed to be the wettest spot on earth with 624 inches of rainfall per year, dominated the interior. Lavish amounts of water, sun, and fertile soil provided ideal growing conditions. Yet Hawaii was America's imperiled Eden. Called "the Extinction Capital of the World," Hawaii had lost more plant and animal species than any other place in America, with many more wavering on the brink. Five hundred and forty U.S. plant and animal species had now become extinct—almost half, or 250 of those, had occurred in Hawaii. I wanted to get there before the cosmic outlaws had taken them all.

All these troubles made Hawaii a botanist's paradise, a microcosm for carrying out important, planet-saving work. If we can't save 550 miles, how can we save the rest of the earth?

Dr. Klein's National Tropical Botanical Garden was grander and more extensive than I had realized. An empire. On the island of Kauai, there were two NTBG jewels: the imposing Allerton Garden, one of the great garden estates of the world; and the Limahuli Garden and Preserve, a one-thousand-acre treasure of native species and ancient remnants of a Hawaiian settlement. On the tip of Maui, the NTBG managed the most sacred site in all of Polynesia, Piilanihale *heiau*—a sixteenth-century war temple where human sacrifices were thought to have occurred. Two preserves on the Big Island were untouched expanses of open territory. On the mainland, the NTBG owned the elegant Kampong in Coconut Grove, Florida, home and estate of plant explorer David Fairchild.

Granted a rare charter by the United States Congress in 1964, the Garden's mission was to serve as a national resource to preserve Hawaii's threatened tropical flora. Yet Dr. Klein sketched a portrait of a closed, reclusive institution. For several years as a cultural reporter, I had chronicled the transformation of the quirky Barnes Foundation, the repository of the world's foremost collection of French impressionist and postimpressionist art. It was preposterously located in a mansion just outside of Philadelphia. Founded by eccentric Dr. Albert Barnes, whose prescient collecting taste was unfortunately accompanied by bombastic ravings about art education, his foundation was run by cultlike followers who operated it like a private club. From what I learned through Bill Klein, Allerton Garden might rival the Barnes Foundation in its determination to remain hidden. His mission to turn Allerton and the other sites into true public gardens appealed to me. It might be fun to work from the inside for once, instead of trying to burrow my way in as a journalist. Dr. Klein didn't resemble a fairy godmother, but perhaps he was.

I had never seriously contemplated leaving journalism or the *Inquirer;* I imagined I would grow old there, perhaps die with a half-written story still in the computer. But now that I had made the decision to leave I saw it as inevitable. James Michener in *Hawaii,* his wonderful if sometimes fictionalized history of the islands, concocted what to me was an entirely believable tale of why natives of Bora-Bora left their home around A.D. 800 to sail five thousand miles north, thrusting into the unknown, eventually landing in Hawaii as the first settlers. Michener wrote that powerful and greedy high priests imposed worship of a new god on the Bora-Bora populace as a thinly disguised grab for political power. The priests killed anyone who questioned the new order. The rebellious King Tamatoa watched with horror as his best warriors were slain. He realized he had to leave. Michener wrote, "He saw, as if in a revealing vision, how foolish he had been to combat the will of the inevitable. New gods were being born, and new gods conquer; but what Tamatoa did not realize was that the contentment of soul which his confession induced was merely the prerequisite for a decision toward which he had been fumbling for some months."

Journalism as I knew it would not recover for at least another generation or two. A vast bloodletting had just begun. News chain owners and their bean counters and finance directors triumphed in ascendancy, looting news outlets for greater and greater profits. Perhaps worse, during these fat times while newspapers were making a killing, no serious research or development was undertaken to plot the future of what we'd soon be calling "dead-tree journalism." As the newfangled Internet came barreling down the track, our leaders' solution was to give its news away on free Web sites. And once that happened, they couldn't figure out a way to get it all back, even to save their skins. Why buy the cow when you can get the milk for free?

Yet leaving brought a sense of failure. I felt akin to Michener's Tamatoa as he led his people into exile: "No man leaves where he is and seeks a distant place unless he is in some respect a failure; but having failed in one location and having been ejected, it is possible that in the next he will be a little wiser. . . .

"Only if they had been craven could they have swallowed their humiliation and remained on Bora Bora; this they would not do. It is true that they fled into the dark, but each man carried as his most prized possession his own personal god of courage."

Circumstances have to pile on top of one another, pushing us out from the comfortable heap and forcing us either to act decisively, or quietly accept what is unacceptable and slowly fade away. Moving to another place would not be enough. I needed a new vocation, one that would capture me as fiercely as journalism once had. Perhaps the garden would become my calling. If not, I sensed it would at least provide a place to heal.

Was this not destiny, after all, that my path that had begun in a garden of English perennials should lead to the Garden Isle?

DESPITE MY GROWING EXCITEMENT, preparations for leaving Philadelphia plunged me into deep anxiety. Job, career, house, comfortable niche of friends — I had put them all on the line. I comforted myself that true adventures come without safety nets. "If not now, when?" was a question that we women of a certain age use to justify an extravagant purchase. Not many role models stood out for me to follow. In her revelatory book, *Writing a Woman's Life,* Barnard professor Carolyn Heilbrun traced how many women of accomplishment — Virginia Woolf and Colette, for example — did not come to their most serious endeavors, their awakening to their true selves and voices, until after they turned fifty. Those late bloomers also had to forge ahead into terra incognita, avoiding the only real narratives society offered them — either the marriage story that ends when the prince and princess walk down the aisle, or the erotic tale, in which characters like Madame Bovary flout social conventions for passionate affairs, only to be punished by early death, ostracism, or suicide. Not much of a choice. Even now, in twenty-first century America, we are still trying to figure out our own narratives for aging. Heilbrun wrote about the challenge. "As we age, many of us who are privileged . . . those with some assured place and pattern in their lives, with some financial security — are in danger of choosing to stay right where we are, to undertake each day's routine, and to listen to our arteries hardening. . . . Instead, we should make use of our security, our seniority, to take risks, to make noise, to be courageous, to become unpopular."

I remembered an old garden proverb: Why not go out on a limb? That's where the fruit is.

As I packed, I heard warnings. *There's nothing to do in Hawaii. It's a place where you turn on the television and watch basketball in the afternoon. Food is bad. Architecture uninteresting. No suitable men.*

It may be good for the soul to dispossess every few years, but it takes fortitude to dismantle a house and confront your unfilled hopes and intentions, assigning them destinations: Put into storage on the East Coast; pack for Hawaii; discard.

Waterford crystal I'd received as wedding presents and used once a year. Good riddance!

The canning jars bought at the height of vegetable production in my garden. Never again. Out!

The plaid wool armchair next to the fire. Storage.

The embroidered baby's quilt I stitched in college, so sure then that I would have a babe in arms of my own someday. Someday hadn't come and I had never gotten around to finishing it. Storage.

I felt as if I were throwing out a hope chest.

Friends threw a good-bye luau, complete with roast pig. Girlfriends danced a hula enacting the story of Lucinderella as she bid *Aloha Oe* to traffic jams and meddlesome editors. They prepared the traditional send-off gift, a mock front page. Headlines read WHIRLWIND LUCINDA KAUAI BOUND; ISLANDERS BEWARE, FLEESON EN ROUTE.

My charming little house sold after only one day on the market. The small profit paid off all my credit card debt. I had no mortgage, no bills, no husband, no reason to stay. The question became not how could I leave, but why had I remained so long? I didn't fit, never had, and more important, didn't want to anymore. I was a woman who lived alone although I wasn't sure that was a choice made by inclination or fate. I was going to a Pacific island to start all over again.

CHAPTER TWO

Treasure Island

OR THE LAST twelve hundred years, the small Hawaiian Island of Kauai has been luring adventurers to its crystalline bays and rain-forested mountains. It was the first of the islands settled by voyaging Polynesians, and the first landfall of Captain James Cook. Called "the Separate Kingdom" by the Hawaiians because a treacherous one-hundred-mile channel protected it from invasion by King Kamehameha's canoeing warriors, Kauai has kept this discrete status. Commuter jets from Honolulu make the trip in twenty minutes. As my plane passed over the white-flicked channel below, the Garden Island rose sharply from the waves, a fertile universe, primordial and undisturbed. Towering green sugarloaf mountains loomed over the rocky southern shore, indented here and there with crescents of pure white sand. Mist shrouded higher peaks in the distance. I sensed the quickening of pulse, the leap of spirit that comes with the beginning of an adventure. It would be impossible for anyone to approach a small island from the air without feeling its call of mystery, perhaps risk and danger. Or treasure.

As we neared, the plane banked around a mountain hump, so close I felt I could reach out and touch its sharp cliffs, defined like a contour map that fell off sharply without mercy into the turmoil of crashing waves. We approached a toy-sized harbor surrounded by a rolling carpet of a seaside golf course and a patchwork quilt of agricultural fields.

As we disembarked into a hick-town terminal, languid slack-key guitar music twanged over the airport PA system. Resort employees in gaily printed aloha shirts hung purple orchid leis on many passengers.

No one greeted me. My arms felt heavy, as if swimming through the moist air laden with thick, pungent scents of tropical flowers. Five minutes, and I felt sticky with perspiration. A sullen driver appeared, the husband of a Garden employee pressed into duty to drop me at my new house. He walked ahead of me to the car, reluctantly carrying one of my three heavy suitcases. Dr. Klein had gone to San Francisco for meetings but had sent ahead house keys to the cottage where I could live, rent-free. Unexpectedly, he had thrown in a company car as part of the deal.

We drove without conversation through the county seat of Lihue, now a dilapidated main street with more than half of its businesses empty or boarded up. Three years earlier, the worst recorded hurricane in Hawaiian history had swept over the island. Recovery from Hurricane Iniki was obviously incomplete. We headed west on the two-lane Route 50, the island's one and only highway. Banks of silver and green sugarcane waved on either side of the road.

After about thirty minutes we passed a century-old factory building, whose roof had caved into a tawdry ruin. "Old pineapple cannery," the surly driver explained. Huge, towering trees draped with thick jungle vines blocked the late-afternoon sun. As we turned onto a narrow, serpentine road, a curtain of vines parted to reveal a cemetery of junked cars and washing machines corroded by rust. After another sharp curve, we pulled into a dirt driveway to begin a long, slow uphill climb. Giant feathery bamboo trees enclosed the drive, their soaring branches meeting to form a Gothic tunnel. As the car ascended through the bamboo arches, I felt as if I were entering the nave of a filigreed green cathedral. So perfect was the Gothic illusion that I found myself listening for anthems and the crescendo of organs.

We burst from the tunnel's cloistered light into the hot tropical sun onto an immense open plateau of green lawn. Bent palm trees dotted the verdant expanse like hoops on a giant croquet field. I glimpsed a one-story cottage at the far end, perhaps a quarter of a mile away. As we neared I saw that the house perched on stilts, one edge overlooking a jungle ravine, so that a wide expanse of windows opened straight into treetops. It had a childlike appeal, like a grownup's tree house. Spiky bromeliads, staghorn ferns, and orchids sprouted from forks in surrounding trees, casting the house in calming shade.

The driver set my bags on the front porch and sped off. I unlocked the glass door and stepped in. A rush of musty overheated air enveloped me. As I struggled to open a locked window, a flesh-colored lizard dropped onto my head.

Eeek! It fell to the floor and slithered away. Gecko.

The cottage's main room was a huge expanse walled with banks of windows, although dirt filmed the panes. Scratches in the black-painted wood floors revealed undercoats of many colors, like a Jackson Pollock canvas. A sagging couch and a couple of rickety tables seemed sad and forlorn. In the kitchen, rust spots erupted on the door of an old refrigerator. Inside, an assortment of jars and bottles looked ancient and moldy. Ugh. I pulled open a creaky drawer to find silverware, rusty from tropical moisture.

Down the hall in the bathroom, two mouse-sized roaches skittered across the floor. A pile of unsavory-looking sheets and towels lay crumpled on a bottom shelf. I turned on the faucet in a plastic lavender-tinted tub. A trickle of brown water dribbled out, accompanied by a loud clanging and knocking.

Get out! Run! Get some cleaning supplies, some new sheets, some air!

Outside, an old rusty Volkswagen Golf sat parked in the dirt drive. So this is the promised company car. No air-conditioning, I discerned with disappointment. As I reached up to adjust the rearview mirror, it came off in my hand like a cheap toy. *Someday this might seem funny,* I thought. At the moment, though, I felt trapped in a Goldie Hawn movie.

Dr. Klein had frankly described the house as unoccupied for two years, and promised the Garden would fix it up. But the damage looked too extensive. And expensive.

Hoping to get some immediate supplies, I drove to the nearest supermarket, Sueoka's in Old Koloa Town, which sent me further into shock. A bewildering mishmash of goods, many labeled in foreign languages, were piled high along crowded aisles of Korean, Japanese, Chinese, and Filipino foods. An incongruous selection of Portuguese delicacies was tucked amid large shelves of Polynesian and Hawaiian specialties. What strange land had I fallen into?

I had wanted pastoral country, the real Hawaii, but this might be *too* real.

I AWOKE IN A PANIC in the middle of the night. The air seemed to vibrate with weird noises, a confused cacophony of moans, low groans, and creaks that filled the terrible black outside the cottage. *Ooooh, oooh, ahhh, ahhhh, oooooooh.* Are there monkeys in Hawaii? The sinister black seemed so thick that I had to grope for a light switch, and sighed to see that the clock read 3 a.m. My mind raced to what a horrible fix I had gotten myself into. I knew that I couldn't sleep again, so I set up the laptop on the dining room table and began to write:

I rushed pell-mell into this momentous change and I am stuck with it, alone in the jungle, marooned in a filthy and dilapidated house. I am overwhelmed with loneliness and the feeling of having made bad choices in life. Here I am, footloose and unmoored. Why did I take this job? I have been so wrapped up in the romance of moving to Hawaii that I did not analyze the full impact of picking up and moving 5,000 miles away.

CHAPTER THREE

This Is the Boondocks

*A*FTER A SOLITARY weekend, on Monday morning I hurried the Volkswagen Golf into the Lawai Valley below the cottage and around a hairpin curve, barely missing a dusty pickup truck driven by a leather-colored cowboy. Three happy dogs of indiscriminate breeding rode in the open back, heads into the wind. A banana plantation grew around the corner from the cottage, its long canoes of leaves upturned like celery bunches. Squawking broods of feral chickens materialized out of the brush, dowdy hens with trains of chicks, or solitary cocks. Sorrel-colored cows grazed the rolling green hillsides. Jeez, this really *is* the boondocks.

The Garden offices were only a five-minute drive from the cottage but still difficult to find at the end of a residential road. Not a single helpful sign pointed the way. I approached the entrance gate. A forbidding placard hung crookedly on a metal gate:

NTBG HEADQUARTERS

A RESEARCH AND EDUCATION FACILITY

PRIVATE PROPERTY. NO TRESPASSING.

No wonder they have trouble attracting visitors. They scare away anybody who can actually find it. I parked and walked up a sidewalk between two low garden beds contained by sharp-edged lava rock, then paused at the head of a terrace to inhale the beauty of the setting. Minimalist and modern, the Garden's cement headquarters banked into the earth like a gunnery pillbox, partly cantilevered over the steep-walled Lawai Valley. Standing here, it felt almost possible to lift off into the air with the white tropic birds and swoop over the valley and out to the crinkled blue Pacific in the distance.

An imperious rooster eyed me from the lawn, cocking a russet head and rustling gorgeous green tail feathers, as lustrous as those plucked by Scarlett O'Hara to adorn a bonnet. In front of the sliding glass front doors to the Garden office lay a tumble of shoes: ladies' pumps, sandals, a pair of large sneakers. One quickly learns in Hawaii that the iron in the ubiquitous red dirt stains the floors, so people take off their shoes before entering private homes. Apparently, the Garden office followed the custom. I slipped off new rubber-treaded hiking sandals and slid open the door.

A sleek blond secretary nodded coolly: "Oh, there you are. Hello."

Beyond her I could see into Dr. Klein's empty office, with its three walls of glass that looked out to that panoramic view. A slab of koa wood served as a conference table, set over a jewel-toned Oriental rug. Administrative offices and an open area for clerical staff extended in the other direction. Four women sat at teak desks facing the windows to the valley. Two rose to greet me with excitement. Cindy, a slight woman about my age, had handled fund-raising operations alone for many years and was now to be my assistant. Teri, my secretary, was a small woman in her fifties with short platinum blond hair. She fluttered around and ushered me into my office. The room was big enough, although it faced away from the valley, to the parking lot.

Apologetically, Teri gestured at stacks of beat-up cardboard boxes that dominated the room. "We're so short of storage space that we're using this office to keep our materials," she said.

I, too, had a spiffy teak desk, although my office chair listed when I sat down. Except for my own staff, nobody else said hello. "Did everyone welcome you?" demanded Dr. Klein when he telephoned from San Francisco later that morning.

"Err. Yes."

"I thought they'd present you with flowers."

"Nothing like that."

"How was the cottage? Everything there to suit you?"

This one I couldn't bluff. "Well. Not really."

"What's wrong?" he asked with alarm.

I paused, then said flatly, "It's filthy."

"Get out of there," he cried. "I'll get the staff to book you into a bed-and-breakfast. Now I'm really angry. I ordered everything to be put in good shape for you." When I put down the receiver, I was buoyed with relief that I didn't have to spend another night in that cottage. I turned to settling into my office. The boxes had to go. I needed a comfortable desk chair, a worktable, and chairs. I gave a quiet but celebratory yelp of glee, crumpled up scrap paper into a ball, and aimed for the wastebasket. Missed.

Although my windows looked out on the parking lot, they also gave me a terrarium-like view into a bed of tropical plants, which appeared gigantic and extraterrestrial to my temperate-zoned eyes. Clusters of maroon flowers emerged from the center of a five-foot-tall plant. Two hummingbirds beat rapidly in and out of its juicy petals. A lucky omen?

THAT AFTERNOON, I STOPPED by the cottage on the hill to collect my suitcases. A dented sedan sped up the bamboo tunnel and parked. A wizened, ancient Filipino darted out of the vehicle, eying me with suspicion. A cigarette dangled from his lip, seemingly glued in place. Thinning hair was brushed back with old-fashioned cream. His T-shirt blared the name of a rock group while his jeans hung low on his hips, showing a bit of flat belly. He had a helper with him, a sullen, shirtless young man with homemade tattoos on both arms.

"I'm James," said the older man, in a none-too-friendly tone. I realized he was the caretaker. I had heard that James had worked for thirty-eight years as the house servant to Robert and John Allerton, the Chicago millionaires who had built the Kauai estate that became the centerpiece of the botanical garden. Now retired, James looked after this little cottage as a part-time job. "Been a lot of break-ins," James informed me. "No one here in day, people get into the house. Not too safe." During the two years the house had been empty, he said, a television set, a china closet, and other valuables had disappeared. What would happen, I silently worried, to my computer equipment, television, and sound system?

I asked James about the monkey noises at night. "No monkeys in Hawaii," he snorted. "That's bamboo rubbing together." I listened, and could hear faint creaks and pops that in stronger wind had sounded like a horde of chimpanzees. James offered to show me the property, and as we walked up a small hill and down the long lawn, I grew intimidated. It was a much larger canvas than my tiny Philadelphia garden.

One of the Garden's wealthiest patrons had donated the cottage and its five acres of land for staff use. Her identity was kept secret, although Dr. Klein said that at one time she had been identified as one of the six wealthiest women in America. James informed me, "She used to fly to the island in her private plane and put the pilot up in a hotel while she stayed in the cottage. She liked to get away from it all."

Because she hadn't visited the place in years, James worked without supervision. At one time, the hilly property had been planted in pineapple, which had sucked up the soil's nutrients and left it dry and empty. "Everything you see, I put in," he said proudly, with a sweep of an arm. "Botanical garden gave me nothing. I brought all myself. Trees, plants, cuttings." The result was what is sometimes called Apache landscaping—a patch of this, a patch of that. No guiding design prevailed, but the sheer amount of plant material impressed me. Manila palms acted as sentries along the curving dirt drive. A hedge of hibiscus sprouted huge, aromatic blossoms in oranges, reds, and pinks. Gaudy birds-of-paradise soared nearby. A line of scraggly macadamia trees dangled nuts. Other bounty included a lychee tree and a dozen or so large mango trees. Rock-edged circles held deep purple bromeliads. Giant versions of what I recognized as schefflera, grown as houseplants back home, formed a long allée along the drive. Here they produced upturned clusters of red spokes covered with knobby purple seeds. "Octopus trees," James called them, and I saw how the spokes resembled tentacles and suckers.

The plateau surrounding the cottage fell off on all sides into steep ravines. Dense, impenetrable hedges of ferns and shrubs edged the lawn, in effect creating a high-topped fortress. Relentlessly the sun beat down. But the cottage itself was cool, and if you opened all the windows it would catch the cross breezes. The vastness of the property and its wondrous seclusion tempted me. From the front porch, one could not see another house. It was as if I were in a sanctuary.

IN THE OFFICE the next morning, I sensed a transformation from yesterday's Sleepy Hollow doze. Dr. Klein had returned. The office staff walked more briskly and sat at their desks with more purpose. Dr. Klein's habit was to rise at 4:30 a.m. and work at home for several hours, making telephone calls to the East Coast or working out on his NordicTrack with a book balanced in front of him. An extreme extrovert, he seemed to require those hours of dark, solitary quiet before the rest of the world intruded. After he arrived at Garden headquarters in late morning, secretaries, botanists from the science building, and garden foremen streamed in and out of his office. As he and I met intermittently throughout the day, I felt reassured. Everyone addressed him as Dr. Klein and, although I decided I'd continue to call him Bill to his face, I already found myself referring to him in the third person by his formal title. It suited him.

By 7 p.m. that second day on the job, everyone else had gone home. I bent over my computer, working on a to-do list, when I looked up to see Bill standing in my office door. "Lucinda's still here!" he said, padding into the room in stocking feet, a wide grin on his face. "Working late, I see. Well, I always tell my staff that there are twenty-four hours in a day. You are welcome to work day and night. How do you like your new office?"

"Great. I even have hummingbirds outside my window."

"There are no hummingbirds in Hawaii," he said definitively.

"Really? C'mere. What's buzzing around that big plant that looks like some kind of spider lily?"

He walked over and gave a cursory glance out the window. "*Sphingidae*. Sphinx moths. That's a Queen Emma's Lily. *Crinum augustum*. Lucinda, you should bone up on these tropical plants."

I appraised the fat-bodied moths and wondered whether the climate fostered gigantism. "Give me a break," I said. "First I'll learn the pedigrees of the Garden's big donors. Then I'll work on Hawaiian names. Then maybe I'll get around to tropical flora. God, Bill. There's a lot to do."

"Lucinda, this is an opportunity for you to have an impact. Larger institutions may be more developed, but here you can shape something, have a say in how it grows. Remember *Henry V*."

I knew the Shakespeare play, a favorite of his, chronicling the battle of Agincourt in 1415. The French outnumbered the English by ten to one. At dawn before the battle, young King Henry wanders among his British troops and overhears one soldier wishing aloud for more confederates. Later, the king exhorts his comrades in the famous St. Crispin's Day speech: " 'The fewer men, the greater share of honour.' " Dr. Klein began reciting. " 'We few. We happy few, we band of brothers.' I wouldn't wish for a single man more."

CHAPTER FOUR

They're All Lost

W AIMEA ARBORETUM AND Botanical Garden on the north shore of Oahu struggled to stay out of bankruptcy. Designed as sort of a botanist's version of Disneyland, the tourist attraction could not compete with the surf at Waikiki, the USS *Arizona* Memorial at Pearl Harbor, or even Honolulu's Ala Moana shopping center, until recently the largest in the world. Without much success, Waimea Garden operators tried to lure paying visitors with a nighttime luau featuring dancers in grass skirts who ran through the grounds carrying lighted torches, then dove from a cliff into a pool.

Dr. Klein sent me here — a short plane ride away — to check out the competition. Wasn't much, I thought, as I made my way to a shabby trailer and office of the garden's chief botanist, Keith Woolliams. A slight, white-haired Brit, Woolliams remained ghostly pale despite spending decades in the tropics. If he had lived a century ago, he'd be wearing a pith helmet. Now his white-collared shirt drooped and his knobby knees under khaki shorts showed nary a glimpse of a tan. His English accent, honed while training at the Royal Botanic Gardens Kew, boomed strong as he used Latin nomenclature for plants. Yet he delivered a dismal message. "The botanists know that all the Hawaiian plants are lost," he said quietly.

"Lost?" I sputtered.

"Nothing can save them," he said.

We walked to his greenhouse, a stifling hot enclosure roofed in hard green plastic. With my reporter's curiosity I had begun to research the looming extinction crisis that threatened all of Hawaii's native species: plant, animal, insect, and mollusk. But I had not perceived the future as so bleak.

Woolliams ticked off the problems. Hawaii has only about a thousand native plants. Eighty-nine percent of them are endemic—found only in the islands. If a species dies out here, there is no other population elsewhere to provide a genetic safety net. Compare this to California native plants, of which 30 percent are endemic, or Florida natives, of which only 5 percent are endemic plants, and you begin to sense the wonder, weirdness, and utter fragility of the Hawaiian flora.

While only about one hundred—10 percent—of the Hawaiian plants have become extinct, the situation is far worse than that figure suggests. About a third of the native species consist of only one hundred individual specimens, often far fewer. A couple of the rarest orchids live deep in the rain forest with a grand total population of about five plants each. Even without the clanging alarm bells ringing over global warming, scientists predict that perhaps two-thirds of the Hawaiian plant species could disappear by the end of the century.

The geography of the Hawaiian Islands accounts for much of the problem. Under the ocean more than seventy million years ago, volcano eruptions built towers of lava until the peaks jutted above the water, forming islands. Eons of hurricanes and rainfall eventually broke down the lava to black soil. Plant colonizations came slowly. Seeds and wisps of root hopped from landfall to landfall across the Pacific, eventually arriving in Hawaii, borne by bird, adrift wave-tossed flotsam, or blown by storm. Only one species made it every twenty thousand to thirty thousand years.

Once rooted, plants evolved with specialized traits required by the island ecology, where high mountains rose precipitously from beaches, and rain forest or bog at one level turned into dry forest only a few hundred feet lower, and around the corner, wind-tormented drought. Small islands often harbored seven or more different climates. Some plants existed in only one valley, or two.

Peace reigned, at first. Just as in the original Garden of Eden described in the Book of Genesis, God gave the native foliage no thorns or thistles. Nor did the plants develop other warrior characteristics, such as toxic secretions to poison encroaching vegetation or ward off predators. They didn't need defenses in the early days of Hawaii because the islands were too far away for any land mammal migrations; the fauna consisted of only a few snails, a long-distance bird, or a seal. The ultimate hot-house varieties, native Hawaiian plants could survive only in paradise.

So when intruders arrived, the natives could put up little resistance. Polynesian voyagers brought new food crops of taro, coconut, and yam, paper mulberry for fiber to make clothing, and pigs for slaughter. Captain Cook discovered what he named "the Sandwich Islands," in 1778, and let loose some of his own pigs, which intermingled with the feral Polynesian variety. The American missionaries, mostly Presbyterians and Congregationalists from Connecticut and Massachusetts, started arriving in 1810, as did the sailors from all over the globe who stopped in Hawaii to resupply their ships for whale hunts. Traders raped the forest, mining it for the native sandalwood, coveted in the Orient for its spicy scent. They took it all, leaving none to survive. Highland forests turned into clear-cut wastelands. And then the onslaught really began.

In the last 150 years, an eye blink in geological time, plantation owners consumed thousands of acres for sugar and pineapple crops, using up most of the dry forest that had fringed the mountainous islands and depleting the soil. The plant species that had thrived were pushed to small pockets and ledges. Droves of tourists started discovering Hawaii in the 1930s, and in galloping pace over the next decades built hotels, condos, shopping centers, and highways, eradicating more of the specialized habitats with devastating consequences. But it was what the incoming settlers brought with them that delivered the coup de grace. Escaped barnyard goats proliferated in the mountains and mowed down plants in quantity. The growing pig population rooted deep trenches, throwing up plants with abandon, not discriminating between the rarest of orchids or commonest of weeds. Banana poka, yellow ginger, strawberry guava, and other imports spread rapidly through forests, sturdy, aggressive, and better equipped for battle. Like all incoming carpetbaggers, the newcomers' greatest offensive tactic was their ability to steal. They grew tall, robbed sunlight from those below, sent down deeper roots that sucked up nutrients, and crowded out the delicate Hawaiian varieties.

Airline passengers coming or leaving the Hawaiian Islands are prohibited from transporting any plant material; Department of Agriculture agents X-ray all baggage to ensure that no seeds or other possible contaminants are carried in. But the horse has long escaped the barn.

Now botanists count more than eight thousand nonnative, or imported, plant species growing in Hawaii, about one hundred of which are so out of control that they have consumed tens of thousands of acres. It's the story of all Hawaii, mirroring the horrifying tale of the native Hawaiian peoples themselves. When the missionaries and sailors arrived, they found a civilization of more than three hundred thousand people—by some accounts, as many as one million. Within fifty years, measles, smallpox, syphilis, and other Western disease reduced the population to thirty thousand.

Now I was the new import, the interloper.

I felt deflated by Keith Woolliams's doomsday message. Perhaps his own losing effort to keep Waimea Garden solvent colored his view? Overwhelmed, sinking, he obviously couldn't take on the fight to right the botanical health of the Hawaiian Islands. Surely not everyone would go quietly into the night?

After bidding Woolliams good-bye, I emerged from his office into the blinding sun and headed off to the main attractions at Waimea Garden. I walked up the paved paths past a grove of heliconia, the waxy torches of crimson and sunset pink ginger. I bent to read a label and saw they had originally come from Brazil. Further along the curved path, I marveled at a drift of orchids, flashy purple, pale green, and snowy white. Also imports, from India, New Zealand, and Brazil. A thicket of birds-of-paradise, the flame orange and blue blooms that resembled a plumed heron's head and beak? South Africa. Showers of cerise bougainvillea? Brazil again. The treacly sweet smelling groves of plumeria, whose blooms form the five-dollar leis bestowed on incoming tourists? Central and South America.

All the showy tropical flowers that we foreigners thought spilled from every corner in Hawaii were imports. Venus flytraps to hook the tourists. The average visitor to Hawaii rarely sees a native plant.

I STILL NEEDED a place to live. In those first disconnected weeks, I moved from one bed-and-breakfast to another. The Volkswagen's static-filled radio could not pick up National Public Radio. The B and B rooms had no radios, either. *The New York Times* was flown in only on Sundays. I had rarely felt so isolated, so cut off from what was happening in the larger world. Each morning at dawn, I'd put on my gym clothes and drive to Poipu Beach to either work out at the Hyatt hotel's health club or run along the coastline. I liked that hour, when the night sky streaked pink. One morning as I turned down Koloa Road, the VW Golf silently died.

I walked to work that day. When I arrived, I asked about getting another vehicle to tide me over until the Golf could be fixed. I was handed the keys to a late-model Mazda sedan unused except for a daily run to the post office. I got in and saw, blissfully, that it had air-conditioning. I tuned into NPR to hear Cokie Roberts reporting from the White House. "I love you, Cokie!" I yelled.

Later that afternoon, I told Dr. Klein how happy I was to be able to listen to mainland news again. "I'm surprised," he said, puzzled. "We had that Mazda put in shape for you before you came."

"The Mazda?"

"You know, the gray Mazda."

"No, I've been driving an old VW."

"How did that happen? You weren't supposed to be getting that old thing."

First the house, inexplicably filthy. The junker car. My office mates continued to treat me with subzero indifference, and I realized I was undergoing a form of hazing. It felt petty to even notice their snippy salutations, the poor welcome, the fact that nobody except Dr. Klein invited me to lunch. I was the hired gun, yet it seemed like every time I looked up from my desk, somebody was in my office complaining that I hadn't followed "proper organizational procedure." Employees weren't supposed to use the Allerton beach. They couldn't visit the garden on weekends. Volunteers couldn't explore the back hills and trails. One day I taped an urgent note to Dr. Klein's door so he would see it when he came in, only to find it ripped down. "The Garden doesn't do that," one of his assistants informed me. The bald-headed finance director hired to sort out the tangled books was particularly pained by my presence. Before I arrived he had been the most senior staff member; now there were two of us in what Dr. Klein grandly titled "the senior management team." As I investigated my budget numbers, I realized that the finance director had assigned me impossible fund-raising goals, doomed to fail. I put an end to that. I don't work for you; I work for Dr. Klein, I told him, and knew I had made an enemy.

This was an institution peopled with staff who had been at the Garden for years, sometimes decades, free to do what they wanted at their own pace. Dr. Klein was changing things, but slowly. My task was to raise money but also to put the place on the map by bringing people in, defining the Garden's image, promoting it. It would require a fundamental shift in outlook. I wasn't sure we could pull it off.

I STARTED ANSWERING ads in the local newspaper and looking at modern apartments in the Poipu area, with its luxury hotels, condo villages, and fake stone waterfalls. This was Tourist Hawaii, a pampered retreat that most visitors to Kauai never left. The places I could afford didn't have great views and were packed together so closely that I'd have to draw the curtains for privacy. With their hotel-room decor of bland pastels, they could be in Miami or San Diego.

When I returned to the Garden office after one discouraging housing search, I went into the quiet library to have a discreet chat with Rick Hanna, the Garden's librarian, resident computer expert, historian, marine biologist, but most important to me, potential friend. He, too, was a refugee of sorts, having migrated from California to Honolulu in the 1970s. When a relationship broke up at the same time a job at the University of Hawaii library went sour, he applied to the Garden as a fluke. Handsome, in his late forties, he had a lean athlete's frame and dark curly hair that I had heard attracted a series of blondes. Still, I sensed that if I needed to know something about the Garden's history or some arcane fact about Kauai, Rick would give a straight answer.

I asked him what he thought I should do about my housing dilemma.

He counseled considering a salvage job before I gave up on the cottage. "Some of these plantation cottages are really fabulous when they're fixed up. You ought to go talk to Michael Faye out at the Waimea Plantation Cottages. He's become a real expert on the plantation cottage style. He restored a whole settlement of them and turned them into a high-priced resort." The Fayes, he said, were an old, established family on the island's west side, where they owned a lot of land and had been involved in ranching and sugar enterprises for a hundred years.

I mused, "The condos I've seen are modern and nice, but so generic they could be located anywhere. The cottage would be a chance to experience something really Hawaiian."

"Yes," he agreed. "This is your chance."

As I FOLLOWED Route 50 westward, the landscape became hotter, drier, dustier. I passed a sign identifying a red dirt road that led to where Captain Cook took his first step in Hawaii. On January 20, 1778, on his third voyage around the world, Cook had sailed his ship *Resolution* into Waimea Bay. The gentle islands were among the very last place on earth still undiscovered by Western navigators. Thousands of curious natives — most of the women naked — paddled hundreds of canoes into the bay to greet him, mistaking him for a white god in plumed hat.

Smoke rose across the horizon and drifted across my windshield in a thick fog. A temporary road sign warned: CANE BURNING, LOW VISIBILITY NEXT FIVE MILES. Stray cinders swirled everywhere. In preparation for harvest, plantation workers burned sugarcane to draw the plant juices up into the stalks, later to be pressed to extract the juice in the nearby mill, then boiled into syrup and dried into a granular state. Sugar had made fortunes in the islands. Now the cane fields were fast disappearing as even such stalwart clients as Pepsi and Coca-Cola switched to corn and beet syrup. Tourism reigned these days. Almost one million tourists arrived on Kauai each year, drawn by its rugged, unspoiled beauty, the famous wave breaks known throughout surfdom, the Na Pali Coast hiking trail, called one of the ten best in the world by some guidebooks, and the stretches of empty white-sand beaches. Hollywood had long ago discovered the island and frequently used it as a backdrop when a tropical setting was needed. A colony of movie stars lived on the north shore, giving Hanalei and Haena the status of Vail or Aspen.

Yet Kauai still lagged behind the other resort islands in their mad rush into tourism development. Hurricane Iniki had pushed the island back even further. Residents would later recall these early post-Iniki years as halcyon days, when you could buy an ocean-view condo for under $100,000, before tour companies unleashed all-terrain vehicles to jar the countryside, before *USA Today* named Poipu as the best beach in America, before several hundred surfers met in the ball field at Koloa Park to try to stop the advent of a surfing world championship that would attract too many competitors to their favorite haunts. That would come later.

All the islands seemed to have a village named Waimea (*wai* means *water* in Hawaiian), and Kauai's Waimea looked like a sleepy, small Texas cow town, circa 1950. False-fronted Old West-style stores lined the main road. Half a dozen jacked-up, high-rigged pickup trucks and four-wheel-drive Jeeps were parked outside a grocery store. As I left the town's outskirts, I approached a grove of several hundred coconut palms. A white-railed entrance bore the sign WAIMEA PLANTATION COTTAGES. AN AUTHENTIC SUGAR EXPERIENCE. I parked in the shade of a palm and mounted wooden stairs onto a shaded veranda with wicker armchairs. A receptionist called Mike Faye on his cell phone and, after a short wait, a tanned man with laughing eyes, black hair, and full mustache came into the lobby. He picked up a master key and led me out to the lawn through an avenue of palms leading to the ocean. Tin-roofed cottages painted in pastel blues and greens were sprinkled throughout the grounds, each set at an angle and screened by ferns and bamboo palms.

Sounds from the highway dropped off. A sprinkler pulsed. A parrot squawked. I sensed this was a place where one could close the door and forget about stress, appointments, or anything purposeful for a long while. Faye had furnished the cottages with Morris chairs, rattan furniture, and ceiling fans that re-created an atmosphere of 1930s plantation life. Except for the bathrooms. Showers were the size of small rooms, with big, fat nozzles raining like waterfalls in a tropical forest. No need for a curtain, you just stood in the breeze and got wet. I was charmed.

"How did you work out this style?" I asked.

"We had fifty cottages to work on," Faye said. "One late night a bunch of us were sitting around a bonfire, drinking beer and singing ancient songs from the 1920s and 1930s. I thought, 'This is the real Hawaii. How do we capture this feeling?' The cult of old houses has never been strong in Hawaii. Everything is modern. But I always had a feeling for these old cottages." He hunted down vintage plantation camp houses all over the island, pulled them apart, trucked them here, and reassembled them with modern amenities.

As I confided my quandary over whether to renovate the cottage, Faye suddenly turned, recognition on his face, "When I was growing up, my family had a ranch in the Lawai Valley, where I would go on weekends to fool around with horses. Now, where is this house?"

"On Lauoho Road. You know, around the corner from the banana plantation and up the hill through a bamboo tunnel?"

"Yeah, I know it. On Halloween, my friends and I went trick or treating on horseback around there, so we knew all the houses. But we never went up to that one. There was something about it, so removed from everything else, that was kind of spooky." *Great,* I thought, *I've got the neighborhood haunted house.*

I wanted nothing to do with renovations. I knew all about the dust, the upset, the workmen traipsing through the house early in the morning or not showing up for weeks until I wanted to strangle them. The projects that didn't turn out quite right and made my blood boil every time I looked at them. Never again. And yet I remembered that wondrous privacy of five acres. I asked him, "So? Do you think I should do it?"

He just pressed his lips into a straight line. Slowly he nodded his head.

CHAPTER FIVE

The Secret Garden

*U*uu-ghha, *uuuuu-gghaaa,* the horn blared like a submarine's dive signal as a cartoonish vehicle bore down on us with threatening speed. Dr. Klein drove the fanciest of the Garden's three antique touring cars, a restored, silver-gray 1947 Dodge land sampan once used as a public taxi on the Big Island. The Rube Goldberg-like contraption had a long snout festooned with acres of shiny chrome. A surrey-style roof provided shade for open-air seating. None of us at the Garden entirely trusted Dr. Klein behind the wheel, as he usually got so involved delivering the botanical lecture of the day that he paid scant attention to the road. He screeched to a stop where I waited with half a dozen prospective donors invited to a late Sunday afternoon barbecue. Few could resist a private, after-hours invitation to Allerton Garden. I ushered the guests up onto rear leather benches. We jostled against one another as the sampan careened out of the parking lot, seemingly on two wheels.

At the end of the public road, two massive brick King Kong gates barred our way. Dr. Klein cheerfully refused all offers of help, hopped down to unlock the gate, drove through, then hopped back down again to lock it behind us. We followed a red dirt road through two more locked gates, along the edge of a field of tall sugarcane. Then we entered a lane enclosed by hedges of thorny night-blooming cereus vine that blocked any view.

With a dramatic flourish, Dr. Klein drew to a stop before an opening in the dense foliage. A steep cliff fell away before us, revealing a hidden cove of blue waters veiled by bending palms and the chartreuse lawn of the Allerton estate. Bathed in late afternoon sunshine, there stretched before us a strange other world, isolated and enclosed by jagged lava cliffs surrounding the valley. Two of the guests gasped, as people always did at their first sight of Lawai-Kai. It was an iconic vision of a rich man's paradisiacal hideaway—calm, inviolate, alluring in its secretiveness.

Subdued by the breathtaking beauty, we were quiet for the rest of the descent, veering away from the ocean into the forest. We passed through a narrow rock canyon where air roots from a giant banyan tree above brushed our roof, then through a plumeria grove that wrapped us in its musky scent. On the valley floor, Dr. Klein parked the sampan at Pump Six, a red barnlike building that once housed irrigation pumps for the old sugar plantation that had filled the valley before the botanical garden was established. We'd ferry the picnic supplies to the beach in electric golf carts.

Dr. Klein opted to walk, leading what I privately called "the Big Donor Tour." Tonight's guests included a wealthy couple targeted for the Garden's $1,000-per-year Fellows Society; a couple of local businessmen; a visiting scientist. Not really A-list, but Dr. Klein gave them the million-dollar treatment: his lecture on the history of gardens; his views of landscape design; his plans for turning NTBG into not only a tourist attraction but a preeminent center for botanical research. To fuel his ever-expanding enterprises, Dr. Klein adopted the P. T. Barnum approach to fund-raising. The moneyed were no different than others, he theorized, and what they really missed was passion and the chance to do something important. He was selling dreams.

For the staff, long neglected and ignored, Bill became their uber-mentor, encouraging them to reach for new aspirations. He invited them to dinner, sponsored study trips to mainland gardens to broaden their outlooks, and advised further education for some. "Gardens are for growing people" was a Klein motto. While much of the Garden staff worshipped him as the long-sought savior who could shake up the place and turn it into a showplace, others resisted his plans for change. "You're turning it into a Disneyland," accused one of the intransigents in a meeting. "Visitors will tramp over the plants and ruin our scientific collections," they complained. In a rare fit of temper, Dr. Klein had turned an apoplectic red to address them, "This is our future, folks. We need to bring in people or the Garden will die."

He seemed to befriend any and all, promiscuously. A visiting scientist, author, or other personage with even the shakiest of credentials could wangle a free tour and lengthy discussion with him. I protested after one late Friday night when he pressed me and several other staff members into entertaining a couple of bozos from L.A. — filmmakers, they claimed. But he was unrepentant. "Make friends, because come a hurricane, you're going to need them," he insisted.

Our group trailed behind him as we walked into the tropical fruit orchard planted by the garden's creators, Robert and John

Allerton, soon after they arrived from Illinois in 1938. Gnarled orange and lemon trees grew in profusion, but also cherry trees. Cannonball-sized pomelos resembling thick-skinned grapefruit littered the ground. Dr. Klein reached up and plucked a waxy yellow star fruit, took out his penknife, and cut samples for the group. Munching the crisp applelike slices, the guests were literally eating out of his hand.

We meandered down a cinder-covered pathway, past a cast-iron shell urn that marked the entrance to Allerton Garden. The light changed, the temperature dropped, and a green gloom enmeshed us in a sense of lost antiquity. High Java plum trees soared above, dwarfing our mere human forms. No matter how many times I came here, I was never quite prepared for its arching vastness. As we strolled, we passed the Thanksgiving Room, the first of what the Allertons called their "garden rooms." An opening in the far leaf wall revealed the white latticework of a whimsical gazebo and another, more secret, garden beyond. The story was that Robert and John Allerton had invited guests to a casual picnic on Thanksgiving Day, then ushered them here for a surprise formal banquet.

The two Allertons, almost Victorian in formality, were the best of hosts. They famously induced guests to choose from their extensive costume collection of silk Chinese robes and skullcaps, gold-threaded saris from India, Japanese kimonos, or the Bali dancer's spired headdress that made the Allertons giggle when the women unknowingly chose it, a prostitute's gilded finery. Looking into the shadowy, green-walled room, I imagined long tables garbed in white linens, silver candelabra, and dark-skinned butlers serving from lavish trays. I could almost see specters of costumed guests, glasses in hand, gliding among the tables, laughing.

I discerned a hint of camp at Allerton, a humor that stops just at the edge of bad taste. The Victorians built garden follies—fake Gothic castle ruins, grottoes, and forest huts—to create an atmosphere of a lost world. Allerton Garden is a Victorian folly, but with a wink. Coy cupids and naked stone gods spy on visitors along the garden walks.

The Allertons were gay, although the Garden's official histories never acknowledge that fact. Garden tour guides don't even use the code phrase "long-time companions." I thought the subterfuge silly and arcane. But it was a different world when the Allertons arrived on Kauai, bought the property, and spent their last decades carving this wonderland out of the jungle. Robert, the wealthy heir to one of Chicago's stockyard fortunes, had entered middle age when he met John Gregg, a twenty-two year old orphan. Employing a protective camouflage, they posed as father and foster son. Their Hawaiian garden became their refuge and hideout. So the NTBG still calls them father and son, the elaborate masks they selected.

Nothing else in Hawaii even begins to match Allerton Garden, with its amphitheater-like valley into which the two gentlemen poured gleanings from their travels of the world—sculpture from Italy, China, and Thailand, and plants from tropical zones everywhere.

When Robert died in 1964, his obituary noted that few on Kauai really knew him. Yet for years the locals whispered stories about these two odd gentlemen. Cane workers spotted them from the cliffs above and reported that the Allertons wandered around naked. They threw parties, sometimes for men only, and they dressed up. I may have been plunked into paradise, but I couldn't suppress the reporter in me. I sorted through archives and quizzed Rick Hanna, who as Garden librarian was resident collector of Allerton memorabilia, looking for clues about who they were and how they lived. I couldn't understand why two refined, cultured men had abandoned Chicago for a rural sugar plantation island. The common wisdom holds that Hawaii is a place for people who are running away from something.

Since John Allerton's death in 1986, the estate remained remarkably unchanged. Criminally so, I thought. A maximum of fifty people came for escorted tours each day, so few that their presence in the immense grounds was hardly noticeable. I privately felt it was a miracle that even fifty showed up. Many tourist maps of Kauai did not note the garden's presence. Wherever I went on the island, I was met with ignorance about its existence. "Oh yeah, isn't that private, for rich *haoles* (white people) from the mainland?" people asked.

I followed behind as Dr. Klein led our guests past a gurgling cascade of water that spilled over a wall of lava rock into a deep pool. Climbing up a narrow stone staircase, we came to the most photographed of the Allerton garden rooms. Diana, Goddess of the Hunt, watched over a mossy reflecting basin wearing a blank smile frozen in stone. A white wooden temple unveiled alcoves displaying fey stone statues of naked adolescent boys. "Water is the soul of a garden," Dr. Klein told the group. "The Allertons had astutely organized the estate around dozens of natural and man-made springs, beginning with the Lawai Stream that runs down the middle like a spine." We stood at the edge of the Diana Room and looked out over the stream to a grove of stately fifty-foot-tall royal palms that rose like Egyptian columns. "Fresh water from the hills above the valley," continued Dr. Klein, "feeds the many fountains, pools, and dripping rock walls. It was with these fountains that the Allertons allowed their imaginations, as well as their classical inclinations, to run riot."

Then down the steps and onto some of the other tour highlights: the Three Pools; the Shell Fountain that spilled water from giant shell to giant shell down a fern-shrouded hill; the Mermaid Fountain with its bronze nymphs poised at either end of an undulating shaft of water that glinted in the golden afternoon sun. Tourists liked to hide between the giant roots of a Moreton Bay fig, the cozy nooks used in the movie *Jurassic Park* as a nest for dinosaur eggs to hatch.

"In no way does Allerton Garden resemble a natural Hawaiian landscape," lectured Dr. Klein in the voice of a professor who retained a childlike enthusiasm for his subject. "It is an unleashed fantasy of nature, a Chicagoan's view of a paradisiacal jungle. It is jammed with tropical greenery and flowers from all over the world."

I lagged behind the group but could hear his voice: "An obscured view heightens the mystery. The genius of Allerton Garden lies in its vistas enticingly veiled from view, its miles of paths and worn stone staircases that beckon to hidden trails and valleys. . . . "

Almost nobody builds gardens this size anymore. The grand du Pont gardens of Winterthur and Longwood Gardens and the Filoli estate south of San Francisco are able to keep their gates open only because they are tax-exempt institutions supported by a paying public. To aspire to garden on this scale requires not only a great fortune, but patience. The designer must put aside his need for hurry and self-gratification, and look ahead one hundred years to forecast how his plan will look in full maturity.

The Allertons' vision will only be sustained if kept alive by our staff gardeners. For without them, predators would take over. Even so, a few plant tendrils spilled over the walls. Dr. Klein fingered a curl of vine, and even from a distance I saw his eyes twinkle. I knew what was coming—one of his favorite lines. He delivered it perfectly. "In the best gardens, like this one, God seems to be winning a little."

Dr. Klein seemed happiest when he was here in his domain, expounding on what the garden meant to us humans. To him, the garden was the supreme achievement, a work of art and a place for serious scientific inquiry. Within its green boundaries it housed painting, sculpture, mosaics, and fountains. Its transformational quality inspired music and served as a setting for its performance. A Noah's Ark, he called it, as the garden collected some of the earth's most endangered flora and was also a laboratory for studying biology, evolution, and the very mysteries of life.

The group moved ahead and disappeared out of sight around a bend in the path. The visitors were enthralled by Dr. Klein and wouldn't miss my absence for a while. I loved this time in the garden, when the staff had all gone and silence descended. All I could hear was a whisper of palm fronds. The tension between voracious jungle and managed design on such a large scale felt almost like a physical presence, and quite overwhelming. The very same philodendron vines grown as houseplants on the mainland here produced gargantuan, elephant-eared ropes, barely caged behind rock walls. I had seen gardeners hacking the growth back with machetes that seemed too puny for the task. I crunched along the cinder path to my favorite spot, a maze of tropical blooms in the Cutting Garden. Tall spears of pink and crimson torch gingers created a fragrant, impenetrable jungle. Near the ground, waxy orange heliconias sprouted like Martian mushrooms. As I penetrated further, I saw a beefsteak heliconia hanging overhead, its blood-red mass the size and shape of a rack of ribs. Try working *that* into an arrangement.

Early in my tenure at NTBG, I gleefully came here, machete in hand, greedy to pick my fill. Before I could produce even one slim vaseful of gingers and heliconias, I had to hack away a forest of tall spears. I never did it again.

The Lawai Stream widened and pooled along the approach to the Allerton guesthouse. Its two-story veranda and white columns could have been lifted intact from a Mississippi bayou. Since Hurricane Iniki, Rick Hanna lived here in solitary splendor, as permanent resident and part-time watchman. Tucked into a cleft in the rock hill, the guesthouse had been spared by the hurricane but offered few amenities. The kitchen consisted of a refrigerator and hot plate, with running water for washing dishes provided by an outside garden hose. No television or radio reception. Rick parked his car, a creaking old Dodge Dart he called Martha, a mile away at Pump Six and used a handcart to carry groceries and laundry. But in return he resided within a stone's throw of Lawai-Kai as lord and overseer of the most luxurious location I'd ever seen.

Bob the peacock spread his glinting feathers for me as I neared. Bob had probably lived on the Marriott hotel grounds twelve miles away, but had been whirled to Allerton Garden by the hurricane and elected to remain. Rick named him after the garden founder and fed him cat food.

"Anybody home?" I hollered.

"Yeah," a deep voice answered. Rick lounged in a tipped-back chair on the porch, reading a faded, cloth-covered book, an old adventure story from the 1930s. "I'm working my way through the Allertons' library. Going for a swim?"

"Yeah."

"Good. I'll go with you."

I climbed up to the porch and followed him through a rusty screen door, then turned right to the guest room. The furnishings hadn't been changed in decades. Four-poster twin beds were covered with frayed patchwork quilts. A navy Oriental rug was worn to its white thread backing. Once in my swimsuit, I strode out to the beach, then took a running start to break through the surf. The bottom quickly dropped off. I was out of my depth at once.

Rick cut laps back and forth across the cove. I bobbed languidly in the smooth rolls and surveyed the remains of the Allerton estate house, the white Colonial mansion. The hurricane had struck it head-on. Winds greater than 120 mph had picked up a quartet of life-sized classical statues representing the four seasons, hurling them like battering rams and slamming them into beams until the house was brought to its knees. The decapitated statue heads rolled back and forth like wrecking balls, shredding paintings and furniture. Three feet of sand surged into the house, destroying the rest.

Next door to the collapsed great house lay the remains of Queen Emma's Cottage. In 1870, the young widowed queen had come from her Honolulu palace to Kauai and stayed in this two-room frame house, part of a large, royal encampment. The storm flattened it, too, so it looked like Dorothy's Kansas house dropped into Oz. For years the NTBG's lawyers and the insurance company squabbled over a settlement to rebuild both structures. Dr. Klein had broken that logjam, too, and architects now drafted reconstruction plans.

By the time I toweled off and dressed, our party was spread out over the Allerton house lawn. Everybody held a drink and scooped chips into a fresh tropical salsa made from chopped papaya, mango, red pepper, onion, and cilantro. A couple of guests played a desultory game of croquet with Rick.

Dr. Klein's wife, Janet, had marinated ahi steaks in ginger teriyaki and had baked hot curried fruit and iced chocolate brownies. Janet appeared content in Hawaii. Silver streaked her short dark hair, and when she laughed, her long silver earrings jingled—a gift from her husband, she said proudly. She wryly called herself a camp follower, traveling in her husband's wake, raising their four children, acting as hostess, serving as a quiet moon to his resplendent sun. Now the kids were on their own. A gifted botanical artist, she spent days bent over a magnifying lamp, painting portraits of Hawaii's endangered plants. As usual, Dr. Klein commandeered her into doing all the picnic shopping. She complained of having to make the long drive to Cost-U-Less, a discount store in Kapaa, north of Lihue. "What's the big deal?" I asked. It's only fifteen miles away. "It's the island effect," she said. "After you've been here for awhile, your world seems to shrink and driving even to Lihue seems too far."

As the sun descended to the ocean horizon, Dr. Klein and Janet began a practiced tuna duet, placing the thick steaks in a wire basket, then over banked coals. Janet set a timer to measure

the minutes before flipping the fish, as ahi is divine if left almost, but not quite, raw in the middle. Surrounded by a semi-
circle of guests, Dr. Klein hurtled full-throttle into a discourse
about aliens, the invasive plant species blamed for pushing out
the native flora. Botanists hotly debate the topic, arguing over
the definition of *native,* a distinction particularly difficult in
Hawaii, where all plants originally arrived as colonists. Are native species those that existed before Captain Cook arrived or
before the first Polynesians came in their voyaging canoes? Some
botanists take a long view, that it's part of the natural order for
new invaders to take over until a balance prevails. Others hold
that the aliens represent all the troubles man has unleashed with
his infernal tinkering.

Dr. Klein was philosophical: "Do you realize that all of the
Hawaii plants evolved from just two hundred and ninety different species? They came to Hawaii where they were set free in
a superb environment, to adapt and flower out to hundreds of
different forms, each acclimating to its own microclimate. I say
that is why we can't get too upset about recent invaders. All of
the plants in Hawaii were invaders of some sort. Can you imagine, being cut loose from all your past ghosts and demons and
given perfect conditions to thrive and just take off?"

I laughed. "Sounds like us, Bill."

One of Hawaii's frequent rainbows poured down to Lawai-
Kai. The luminous bands of colors were unusually bright. As
the arc moved toward us, we stood still, entranced.

Dr. Klein announced merrily, "This is the pot of gold!"

CHAPTER SIX

They Were One of Us

*I*N THE GARDEN library, I found a typewritten transcript of a tape-recorded conversation with John Allerton in which he described in detail how he and his adoptive father stumbled onto what would become their home for the rest of their lives. The transcript was useful in creating a picture of their early life, which I began to amplify by talking with James, my own gardener at the cottage, and anyone else I could find who knew the Allertons.

The two men were in the habit of making long winter cruises to exotic parts of the world, particularly the South Pacific and Southeast Asia. Returning home from Australia in 1938, they had time to kill, stuck in Honolulu for three days before their ship sailed back to America, then home to Illinois. Why don't you go see the old McBryde place on Kauai, a friend suggested. The property had been on the market for the three years since sugar planter Alexander McBryde had died.

Robert and John boarded a small plane to cross the rough one-hundred-mile channel that kept Kauai separate from the other islands. Robert, sixty-five, was intrigued. With his hair swept back, he was quiet and reserved and wore a pressed shirt and tie. John, thirty-seven, drove. Often laughing, John was more fun, more outgoing. He pulled the old Packard to a stop on the valley floor, and they got out. They walked onto the expanse of almost fluorescent green grass, under bending palms. The dark Victorian house wasn't much. Knock it down, John the architect suggested. A few Hawaiian tenants up the stream grew taro, watercress, pumpkins, and lotus roots. They could be removed, said Robert. You could build gates at the cliffs and no one could come in. They gazed back toward the head of the stream, up the valley that was enclosed by jungle and another wall of rock. It was its own world here.

Back in the rented car, they headed to Hanalei to see the old town and famous bay. After a half hour of silence, Robert ventured that it might be nice to have a winter place where they could stay instead of traveling all season. Yes, agreed John. He turned the automobile around and went back.

"This is going to be my paradise," Robert Allerton said. He wrote a check for fifty thousand dollars, and bought eighty-six acres and one of the most private coves in all Hawaii.

When they returned to Kauai later that year, Robert placed an ad in *The Garden Island* newspaper to announce that the beach was now private. No trespassing, it warned. For further protection, Robert leased two beautiful bays, extending his property almost to Spouting Horn, the ocean blowhole in Poipu. At the eastern entrance to the estate, the Chicagoans erected what we now call "the King Kong gate," with brick piers and swinging doors of Chinese red.

They sawed up McBryde's house and made a big bonfire. John sketched plans for a more open dwelling. "I want to see ocean and sky from every window," Robert directed. John designed a flat concrete-slab floor level with the ground, so that there seemed to be no barrier between the outside and in. He had been intrigued by a photo of the headmaster's house at St. Paul's School in New Hampshire, Robert's alma mater. That house incorporated a large veranda under the roofline, so that the structure resembled a giant porch. John copied the idea for the Kauai house, laying it out in an L-shape around an open courtyard, encasing the rooms behind long, screened lanais.

"We thought the best idea was to fit in with the style that was on the island, and of course the first architecture that was here in Hawaii was what the missionaries brought with them from Cape Cod, so it necessarily meant a clapboard type of house," John explained in that taped conversation. "So when anybody asks me what this style of architecture is, I always say, 'It's early missionary.'"

Simple and open to the sea breezes, the main house grew grand because of John's flair with elaborate carved moldings. Working with a lumber mill in Waimea, he designed classic Georgian scrolls, lavish curved cornices, and wide baseboards. He paneled the library with intricate moldings and mantel, all painted in deep red. When finished, the room looked as if it could have been imported intact from Connecticut. Along the lanai surrounding the house he designed multiple sitting alcoves, small conversation groupings, so that Robert, nearly deaf without his hearing aids, could more easily socialize.

They renamed the beachfront property Lawai-Kai. There is no literal translation for their invented name, except that it conveyed a meaning of plenty. Plenty fish, plenty in the valley.

FOR THEIR FIRST two years on the island, building the house and starting a garden consumed them. They didn't even bother to visit the two main sights on Kauai—the gorgeous red-banded Waimea Canyon or the castellated cliffs of the Na Pali Coast. They didn't want anything to do with local life, and the locals left them alone. The two men stayed only a few months each year, arriving on Kauai shortly after Thanksgiving and returning to Illinois in April to see the daffodils bloom.

Everyone on the island knew the Allertons were very, very rich. But odd. Almost a joke. It wasn't just that two men lived together or that they were *mahu*—the Hawaiian word for *gay*—or that they were rumored to be nudists. What made the Allertons laughably different in their early years on the island was their Deco furniture and modern art, their mainland taste, and the fact that they were rarely seen.

Robert and John remained so shut off from the rest of the island that when the Japanese attacked Pearl Harbor in Honolulu, the Allertons didn't know about it for a full day. Most of Kauai had prepared for some sort of outbreak, and residents jumped to assigned posts shortly after the December 7, 1941, bombing began at 8:30 a.m. By 11:45 a.m., all of Kauai had sprung to action. Within hours, sewing machines across the island hummed with the sound of women stitching bandages and uniforms. Provisional police declared martial law and appropriated radio station KTOH as the emergency communications center until the Army in Honolulu ordered all stations off the air at 1:30 p.m.

The military immediately ordered a strict blackout throughout the islands. Civilian wardens patrolled, ready to arrest violators. But no one told Robert and John, still newcomers. Finally somebody telephoned them after dark and said, "I hope you're not showing any lights."

"What for?" John asked.

"Don't you know war was declared?" the caller demanded.

Had the Germans invaded? John worried. "Who are we at war with?" he asked.

All civilian air flights off Kauai were cancelled for two years. Shipments from Honolulu were suspended. The Allertons could have wangled special privileges if they had wanted or, at the least, could have taken a military ship to Honolulu, and from there, sailed or flown back to Illinois.

Robert insisted on staying.

In the two weeks after Pearl Harbor, the Kauai chapter of the Red Cross received a large contribution of two hundred dollars donated, according to a front-page article in *The Garden Island* newspaper, by a "Mr. Ellerton." Despite the misspelling, the local gentry quickly identified him and asked Robert to head the Red Cross fund-raising campaign. He agreed. With quiet efficiency, he raised a record seventeen thousand dollars—an amount that earned him election to the post of chairman of the entire Kauai chapter of the Red Cross. Robert pressed Flora Rice, the wife of his lawyer, to act as his spokesperson, so he could remain behind the scenes. John, younger and more fit, joined the Kauai Volunteers Regiment as a captain.

Military commanders considered rural and unpopulated Kauai, the most northern of the main Hawaiian islands, a likely site for a Japanese invasion. Hundreds of Army soldiers and Navy seamen landed within weeks. The Army identified Lawai-Kai, facing south and offering a flat-bottomed bay and beach, as a prime landing spot. Soldiers dug a watch camp into the beach and another on top of the cliff. They strung dozens of rolls of barbed wire across the bay.

All of Kauai went into high alert in the weeks preceding the
June 4, 1942, Battle of Midway. Extra hospital beds and supplies
were prepared and nurses were called to emergency duty. Only
years later would the people of Kauai learn that the American
military had cracked the Japanese code, allowing a strategic attack on the Imperial Japanese Navy. The rout was so complete,
with so few American casualties, that no wounded ever arrived
on Kauai. The Battle of Midway not only effectively eliminated
the core of the Japanese Navy; it removed the Hawaiian Island
chain from any real danger of invasion. For the rest of the war
Kauai offered an exotic idyll for those stationed there, peace-
fully coexisting with the doting populace.

Throughout the military occupation, Kauai families eagerly
invited soldiers home for dinners, picnics, and dances. The
"Tired Pilots" program had begun on Oahu as a way for the
locals to host aviators at their homes to give them some R & R.
Robert and John quickly volunteered to host their share. They
held concerts on the lawn for servicemen, a hundred at a time,
who sat in their dress khakis with arms folded over knees,
shaded by coconut palms. The barbed wire off Lawai-Kai
trapped seaweed and debris, becoming so tangled and thick
with vegetation that it blocked the ocean view. But the wire
barriers floated on rafts, and those who knew how could part
them to swim. Lawai-Kai became a beach spot for off-duty of-
ficers. The Allertons invited them for lunch, for luaus, for quiet
strolls in the garden. A steady parade of crisp Navy whites and
Army tans came and went.

For the Allertons, not only was it patriotic, it was exciting.
James Michener would later write about the pent-up sexual-
ity of young military men cast adrift on a tropical island, in

his *Tales of the South Pacific,* later made into the Rodgers and Hammerstein musical. The 1958 movie version was filmed entirely on Kauai, including a scene shot in Allerton Garden in which Lieutenant Cable and his Polynesian lover, Liat, raced laughingly through the jungle.

The steamy, sexy vibrations that electrified the Allerton estate in the war years were likely of an entirely different nature. The war changed everything for gay men and women alike. Before, they had mostly lived their lives in isolation, only a few urbanites finding companions in shrouded nightclubs. The draft brought gay servicemen and women together in droves to share their stories and experiences. The war turned into a watershed event for gay identity. Emboldened, they started to come out of the closet.

During those war years, Kauai plantation society courted the Allertons, inviting them to their black-tie yacht club parties, family weddings, and cocktail parties. In turn, the Allertons welcomed them to Lawai-Kai, becoming entwined with the island wealthy. Before Pearl Harbor, they had been outsiders. After the war, the islanders agreed: They were one of us. Charmed by the summers as well as the winters in Hawaii, the Allertons decided after peace was declared to move full-time to their Kauai estate. They never mentioned to anyone that Illinois was becoming inhospitable to "their kind" and remained somewhat mysterious. "You could only get so close," one acquaintance told me, "and then a wall went up."

CHAPTER SEVEN

Mission

*M*IKE FAYE HAD promised that the cottage would be ready in six weeks, but after two months, renovations continued to drag on. The Kleins invited me to use their *ohana* (Hawaiian for *family,* also used to describe a mother-in-law suite) with its own entrance through their garage. Their house itself was built like a ship, with a two-story prow pointing to a distant ocean view. In the back courtyard, a red lightbulb lit a steaming hot tub so it bubbled like a volcano. I imagined Dr. Klein boiling there in royal splendor. Behind his back I called him "the Grand Poobah," for all his treasured executive perks: the reserved parking space in the headquarters' parking lot, his secretary and assistant to keep his calendar and arrange his travel like a *Fortune* 500 chieftain, and his frequent reference to himself in the third person as "the executive director."

For dinner I often fetched takeout from Kalaheo Steak House. After my usual order of prime rib and salad, I sometimes fed bits to a friendly stray cat that had taken up residence on my door stoop. I had a weakness for tiger-striped cats and starting calling him Sam. No matter what time I arrived home, he waited for me. One early evening, I lifted him as I closed the apartment door behind me. He laid his head against mine and purred. "Okay, Sam, that's enough," I murmured. "See you later."

I drove back to Garden headquarters for some after-hours work. The full moon lit my way as I went through the usual rigamarole—unlocking the padlocked gate to the entrance, swinging open the gate, driving through, stopping, relocking the gate behind me, parking in the dark. I groped my way along the unlit lanai, used my key to open the front door, and rushed to punch in the security code—P-L-A-N-T—before the alarm sounded and summoned the police. The lights in my office formed a small island in the black night. It gave me the creeps sometimes to work here alone, but the lack of interruption meant I could focus on the papers, files, and reports spread out in stacks on my desk and across the carpet.

I searched for something to write about the Garden. Dr. Klein had already rushed us into a $10 million fund-raising campaign. He had gone through the prescribed step of commissioning a feasibility study to assess a target goal. He drafted a master plan detailing conceptual blueprints for each of the five sites. Not only did he envision improved roadways and trails, but a new entrance to Allerton Garden, a $1 million science building, new greenhouses, and several new endowed chairs to bring in top scientists. He freely adopted Chicago architect Daniel Burham's motto as his own: "Make no small plans; they have no power to seize men's minds." From the beginning of my tenure at the Garden, various trustees would pull me aside to urge: Rein Klein in! There's a guy who could spend $100 million and it wouldn't be enough, commented one.

Bill functioned as the star, the front man who stroked the donors, while I cleaned up behind him as a glorified aide-de-camp. It fell to me to make rational sense of his grandiose projects, to put prices on them, then wrap them up in attractive packages. And I struggled. What could I say about the Garden, an institution that had sold itself on its potential for thirty years? Other botanical gardens around the country operated as big businesses, with multimillion-dollar-per-year gift shops, rental fees for weddings, symphony evenings, lectures, and full education programs. We had none of those.

What is a botanical garden? The name has been applied to gardens ranging from extensive research facilities associated with major universities and botanical institutes to tiny municipal parks that support little or no scientific activity. Many public and private "display gardens" — such as Allerton Garden — contain superb plant collections but do not provide labeling or maintain records on the plants in their collections.

The official definition comes from the *Botanic Gardens Conservation Strategy,* published in 1989 by the World Wildlife Fund and the International Union for Conservation of Nature and Natural Resources. It states that a botanical garden contains "scientifically ordered and maintained collections of plants, usually documented and labeled, and open to the public for the purposes of recreation, education and research."

NTBG didn't do well by those criteria either. Bill Klein had asked an old Air Force buddy and fellow botanist, Dr. Richard Mandell, to come out and survey the NTBG collections. He found that two-thirds of the plant holdings in the garden had lost their labels, had disappeared, and/or were of unknown provenance.

I flipped through a thick file. In 1989, the Garden won a prestigious John D. and Catherine T. MacArthur Foundation grant to botanize the islands, that is, send field researchers out to find out what plants and how many grew there. Botanical records for Hawaii date back to 1779, when amateur botanist David Nelson sailed with Captain Cook and collected samples, which he took back to England. But for the next two hundred years, much of the islands' difficult terrain lay unexplored by botanists.

All of the Garden's five botanists and horticulturists in the Plant Science Department functioned as field collectors. Two of them, Steve Perlman and Ken Wood, used climbing equipment to scale vertical cliff ledges and rock columns, reaching habitats and ecosystems never examined before by any man, much less a botanist. The last of the completely untouched Hawaiian landscape survives only on these breathtakingly narrow snippets of land and ledges, undisturbed by encroaching agriculture or feral pigs or goats.

Perlman and Wood produced impressive results. They discovered twenty-nine new plant species and rediscovered another twenty-two thought to be extinct. At the bottom of a page summarizing the Garden's explorations, I found a short paragraph set off, in smaller, agate type:

> Since 1990, NTBG has conducted 893 field expeditions throughout the Hawaiian Islands, atolls, and promontories. This is the most comprehensive survey of the Hawaiian Islands ever undertaken.

Eureka!

As I dug further, I discovered another unheralded factoid buried in Garden reports: A part-time nursery worker named

Kerin Lilleeng-Rosenberger had developed growing methods for more than 75 percent of all native Hawaiian plants, another feat never before accomplished.

I could see a narrative: The Garden's daring explorers climbed remote regions of Hawaii to search for plants once thought extinct. They discovered lost species and brought back rare seeds to the botanical garden. There, the pioneering horticulturist coaxed life from them in experimental growing techniques. In the botanical garden, rare plants flowered in protection, ready to repopulate the earth.

Our north shore garden, Limahuli, was already attracting attention for its conservation efforts. I had immediately liked its young director, Chipper Wichman, who envisioned that the entire one-thousand-acre Limahuli Valley could be protected in its nearly pristine state, then used as a repository for rare nursery seedlings. Chipper, a boyish, lanky man in his forties, had shown such promise that Bill Klein further encouraged him as his logical successor to the entire NTBG empire.

ONE PLANT IN PARTICULAR, *Brighamia insignis,* showed how a brave plant hunter could single-handedly save a species. Steve Perlman had rescued this strange-looking plant with its bulbous base sprouting an elephant-skinned pole topped by a cabbage-like burst of foliage. In order to flesh out my story line, I frequently walked down the lanai to the Science Building to catch Perlman. I learned to look for piles of mud-stained backpacks outside his office, indicating that he had returned from a collecting trip.

"To me, *Brighamia* is a world class–looking plant," Perlman enthused when I found him one day in the Garden's herbarium, the seed and dried specimen repository that always smelled of formaldehyde. "They get a huge water storage base. They're six feet tall. The leaves are nothing much, but the flowers are." The *Brighamia insignis* species on Kauai sends out waxy clusters of tubular flowers, lemon in color. On the sea cliffs of Molokai, its other primary habitat, another variety produces cream-colored flowers. "Put it all together, it's a really spectacular-looking plant," he said. "I really like it."

Perlman had arrived on Kauai in the 1970s, drawn by the surfing, a sport that almost took his life. A monster wave at Polihale Beach broke his neck a couple of decades ago. He recovered, and although he has since broken other small parts—toes, fingers, and a cracked rib—it never deterred him from either riding waves or climbing treacherous slopes.

He first worked on Kauai as a nurseryman on a private estate, spending his spare time hiking the island and learning its terrain. As he became enamored of the native Hawaiian plant story, he studied horticulture at Kauai Community College and enrolled in the first class of student interns at the Garden, then named the Pacific Tropical Botanical Garden. When the Garden hired him, he apprenticed himself to staff botanist Derral Herbst for field collecting trips. Herbst, more stout, didn't like to climb trees or cliffs, so Perlman scrambled up them. Fashioning a homemade harness and knotted ropes, he would attach one end to a sturdy tree at the top of a cliff, then rappel down. As he became more skilled and learned to use professional climbing gear, he embarked on his own field investigations, employing mules, boats, and helicopters to drop him off on islets and rock pinnacles to reach those inaccessible nether regions.

Now in his forties, Perlman had grown only more impassioned, if possible, about his mission to botanize the untrammeled islands of the Pacific. Sun had bleached his fringe of blond hair to almost white, in sharp contrast to a tan that seemed to seep down to the bone, making his blue eyes appear the color of lake ice. If he could choose, he'd spend most of his time in the field. Few can keep up with him on his explorations, or want to, as many trips involve weeks of rough camping. "A lot of people can hike two or three days, but it's the fourth or fifth day on a trip that is the tough one," he says.

I remembered my first botanizing trip, to the New Jersey Pine Barrens with Philadelphia botanist Ernest Schuyler, to research a story about a rare disappearing but nondescript grass. We tramped for hours through a hot haze of golden grass marshes, discovering sundews — insect-catching bog plants — and a myriad of grass sedges that all looked alike to my novice eye. After hours we sat down in the shade to rest, me fidgeting all the while. "You're going to have to learn patience," Schuyler told me.

Perlman first saw *Brighamia insignis* through binoculars as he stood, looking up, from the bottom of vertical sea cliffs on Kauai's Na Pali Coast. Two thousand feet above him, at the very edge of a rock ledge, a magnificent six-foot-tall specimen swayed back and forth on its bowling-pin-shaped base. Excited, Perlman shared his discovery with Harold St. John, chief botanist at Honolulu's Bernice P. Bishop Museum. St. John suggested trying to grow it, so in order to collect seeds, Perlman scrambled up the cliff and rappelled down into a drift of more than one hundred *Brighamia* plants. An intimate love affair began.

Throughout his career, Perlman regularly visited *Brighamia* populations. A few developed seeds, which Perlman collected and sent to botanists at the Royal Botanic Garden, Kew; to Rancho Santa Anna Botanic Garden in California; and to Fairchild Tropical Botanic Garden in Florida. The botanists wrote back that they were successfully growing *Brighamia*.

But Perlman noticed that many of the *Brighamia* plants growing in the wild never produced seeds. They flowered, then the blossoms seemed to melt away without a trace. Fortunately, the plants were able to produce stamen heavy with golden pollen. So Perlman stepped in as surrogate father. He used a paintbrush, an old breeder's trick, to transfer pollen from the stamen on some plants into waiting pistils of others. A month later, he returned. It had worked. The plants developed fruit that ripened to seeds, giving him more to collect. He brought them back to the botanical garden.

French collector Jules Remy first documented the genus *Brighamia* in 1851 on the islands of Niihau, Kauai, Molokai, and Maui and named it after William Tufts Brigham (1841–1926), a geologist and early collector of Hawaiian plants. Although one of the large Lobeliaceae family in Hawaii, *Brighamia* is the only lobelia with a succulent stem and ancillary inflorescences, or soft branches, that carry erect flowers. The weighty base allows it to rock in the wind. The succulent green leaves feel somewhat rubbery and store water during drought. Horizontal roots can penetrate deep crevasses in a sheer rock face.

The mere sight of a tall *Brighamia* can inspire awe but also a smile, because of its almost comical swollen base. In 1919, the botanist Joseph Rock recorded some specimens growing fifteen feet tall. More commonly it reaches three to six feet.

Perlman theorizes that very large moths once penetrated the six- to eight-inch-long flowers to serve as pollinators. Large sphinx moths—similar to those I thought were hummingbirds in my first days on Kauai—are likely candidates. Collectors used to commonly net Kauai's legendary green sphinx moth as it fluttered along the Na Pali Coast and across the high forests of Kokee State Park. But in the last fifty years, only twenty or so have been caught. Perlman believes that as *Brighamia* retreated to cliff edges, sphinx moths no longer ventured into the unprotected open where they could be snatched by aggressive cardinals or white-eyes. Without its natural pollinator, the *Brighamia* withered away.

By this time Perlman had tracked *Brighamia* onto the highest sea cliffs in the world, on the smaller island of Molokai, home of the infamous Kalaupapa leper colony. There he found the *Brighamia rockii* (named after Dr. Rock) species. Again he used his paintbrush.

Perlman had seen reports by botanists working in the early 1900s that *Brighamia* also grew on Haupu, the mountain hump that looms over Kauai's south shore. For six years, he looked for them without success, hiking all around its foothills, even hiring a helicopter to drop him off at the summit.

One Sunday in the early 1980s, he attended a party at the Lihue home of Chipper Wichman's grandmother Juliet Rice Wichman, one of the early Garden trustees and an avid plantswoman. Perlman confided to her his quest to find the lost *Brighamia* on Haupu. She remembered a long-ago party held near the canoe club on the Huleia River, in 1917. A couple of boys from the Lydgate family paddled directly across the river and hiked partway up Mount Haupu. After about an hour, they returned holding big poles of plants—*Brighamia*!

Perlman immediately decided to retrace their route. He went to the canoe club, paddled a straight line across the river, and headed up a mountain gorge. Half an hour from the river, he approached a cliff, hiked around a corner, and found a small grove of *Brighamia*. That's how botanists work. Like detectives, they pore over the field notes of other botanists and herbarium records and pursue oral histories in order to track down plant populations.

Year after year, Perlman returned to the Haupu *Brighamia* drift of about a dozen plants. They served as the breeding stock for our botanical garden. Hurricane Iniki wiped them all out. One small plant survived alone in the Haupu gorge for a few years, but then it died. He used to get seeds from a few plants on Kauai near the ridge above Mahaulepu and the Kipu Kai gap, also on the south shore, but those plants also vanished after the hurricane.

Brighamia colonies are crashing all over Hawaii.

Perlman is the first to admit that it's an uphill battle to convince people of the need to save rare and nearly extinguished plants. His local friends look at the Kauai jungles and don't see that the island's plants are in danger. It's all green, they say, not realizing that most of it nowadays is alien *scheffleras,* guavas, and other imports. In frustration, Perlman finally started to tell his friends that the native Hawaiian plants taste good in stir-fry, like bok choy. Only that convinced them that the plants were worth saving.

Selling the public on conservation of endangered species has never been easy—that's why a big mammal like a whale or giant panda gets to be the poster child for such campaigns. The plant people have tried to construct a worldwide database for tracking plant populations and storing seeds, but not much has been done for Hawaii, where scientific collaboration seems almost nonexistent and tropical seeds are too pulpy to last very long. Botanists in general have typically been a timid lot, usually confined to their dusty herbariums. That was the beauty of Bill Klein—he realized that only by engaging a wider public would anything really be accomplished. He saw the botanical garden's real role as education. "People only will make an effort to save something they care about, and to care about it, they have to know about it," he'd say.

Plants provide everything we humans need—the oxygen to breathe, crops to eat, grain to feed animals, even the fossil fuels we so greedily consume. There are many examples of obscure tropical rain forest plants that have proved to contain ingredients for valuable medicines or other uses. A native Hawaiian cotton plant, for instance, can't be spun into cloth, but was so disease resistant that commercial growers hybridized it to produce a stronger cotton.

The need to preserve the inhabitants, plant or animal, on Earth should be obvious enough; they exist, whether we humans have use for them or not. Who knows what we'll discover about them in the future? When tinkering with the machinery, don't throw any pieces away.

In my mind, just the very beauty of each species demands divine protection. We probably wouldn't miss the elimination of a trombone or two in a two-hundred-piece orchestra. But if you take away the oboes, then lose the violas, misplace the winds, and remove the cymbals, you begin to hear a meager, dull band instead of a symphony.

Over the last twenty years, Perlman has pollinated by brush at least one hundred *Brighamia* plants. His collected seed yielded thousands of plants grown in the Garden nursery that have been sent to other Hawaiian botanical gardens.

A lot of people became familiar with *Brighamia*'s dramatic story thanks to the film *Hidden Hawaii,* which played at the Waikiki IMAX theater in Honolulu for more than a decade. The filmmakers pushed Perlman to exaggerate his cliff climbing, portraying him stretched spread-eagle across rocks and dangling more precariously from precipices than his usual cautious style. Now you can buy a T-shirt with a picture of the semi-ugly little cabbage plant, a symbol of plant rescue.

But the publicity hasn't helped save the plant.

"Pretty soon, all *Brighamia* will die out," says Perlman. "They are going very quickly and probably will be extinct in the wild in twenty years."

PART TWO
Digging In

CHAPTER EIGHT

Chicken Skin

*N*IGHTS IN THE Kleins' *ohana,* I delved into the literature of Hawaiiana. I plowed through the journals of Captain Cook's voyages aboard his ships, *Discovery* and *Resolution,* then attacked Jack London. London first visited Hawaii in 1904, then returned several times with his second wife, Charmian. They frequented Waikiki, where London learned to surf. Incongruously, he lived on Oahu when he wrote "To Build a Fire," his most famous short story about death in Alaska's Arctic tundra. Mark Twain's *Letters from Hawaii* recounted his own travels throughout the islands in 1866. Writing dispatches for *The Sacramento Union,* Twain bought a sorry-looking horse to ride up the volcanoes, tried his hand at surfing, and ate poi at luaus. Back then, Hawaii was a mythic land, occupying a position in the American conscious as a faraway paradise of savages and bare-breasted beauties.

But it was Isabella Lucy Bird to whom I kept returning. Bird grew up a semi-invalid and amateur botanist, the spinster daughter of an English clergyman. A spinal deformity required her to lie down much of the time, and depression sometimes kept her in bed all day. In 1872, the year she turned forty, she sailed on a recuperative cruise to the South Seas. A typhoon damaged her ship, and it limped into Honolulu Harbor. While the ship underwent repairs, so did she. For six months she explored the islands on horseback in what became a life-changing experience, then a book published under the title *Six Months in the Sandwich Islands.* Throwing off the restraints of a refined Victorian lady, Bird trekked by mule up the icy mountainside of Mauna Loa on the Big Island. She galloped the coast of Kauai at midnight, alone, and visited its enchanted rain forests. No camping in huts or long rides were too rough.

Many of her detailed accounts describing the Hawaiian flora and its lush jungle landscapes rent with pouring waterfalls were still accurate more than one hundred years later. Her writing helped me imagine nineteenth-century Hawaii, as well as understand it today. But it was her life story that intrigued me. I had only its briefest outlines. She never returned to Hawaii but went on to travel through Korea, Persia, Japan, and elsewhere, becoming the foremost British woman travel writer of her era.

"Her last years were sad, indeed," wrote Terence Barrow, Ph.D., in the foreword to a 1974 paperback edition of her Hawaii book. Barrow recounted how Bird had married after Hawaii, but her husband died within five years. She lived out the next decades in loneliness, he said. Even with this sketchy information, I questioned whether we were hearing Barrow's personal views on the suitable life for ladies, or Isabella's own assessment. Any woman who had thrown off the shackles of convention, galloped alone at midnight through jungle ravines, and then went on to travel for the next thirty years on the back of yak, pony, mule, or stallion did not strike me as a woman paralyzed by early widowhood and sentenced to bleak loneliness.

Sad, indeed, eh? I rankled at this presumption that the most celebrated female travel writer of the nineteenth century lived unfulfilled, despite her unorthodox success. Or was it precisely *because* of her unorthodox life you drew this conclusion, Mr. Terence Barrow, Ph.D.?

Isabella herself gave no hint of self-analysis in her writing; self-disclosure was not the Victorian style. Perhaps because of this lack of information, my imagination filled in the blanks. Here was a woman in profound midlife crisis who, after forty years of refinement, abandoned her corsets and petticoats to plunge headfirst into the tropics. She had not chosen an easy path, or one free from conflict and ambiguity. What made her take such a leap? It became my habit to pick up *Six Months in the Sandwich Islands* and read Isabella's description of each place I visited. I found myself comparing then and now. While she described Hawaii of a century ago, I wanted to report on its contrasts, the modern next to the archaic.

I kept wondering, *Isabella, what happened to you?*

DAVID CHANG WAITED in the Koloa library parking lot, his face tight with irritation, almost tapping his foot because I was ten minutes late. About my age and graying at the temples, he was collecting an oral history of Koloa, so I wanted to consult him about Isabella Bird's sojourn in the area. Trying to conscript him as an ally, I pulled out a photocopy of an 1868 map I had found at the Kauai Historical Society. "I'm trying to figure out exactly where Isabella Bird traveled during her four weeks on Kauai," I ventured. "She sailed in at Koloa Landing in 1873 and was met by Dr. James Smith."

"Back then Koloa Landing was the third largest whaling port in all of Hawaii," offered Chang, warming up. Now only a concrete boat ramp remains, where outrigger canoe clubs put their crafts into the water and snorkelers dive in the thirty-five-foot-deep water.

"Dr. Smith must have brought her to Koloa on the old Hapa Road," I said, tracing on the map the route of a now unused dirt track. Dr. Smith lived up the road in what Isabella described as a large adobe structure with a heavy thatched roof next to the old Koloa Church. The doctor put her up in a white thatched guest cottage overlooking Waikomo Stream.

Chang pondered, "The church has been rebuilt, but it's been on the same spot since 1835." We walked up the road and crossed the street to the church grounds to find the bend in the stream she had described. No solid evidence of a cottage. But we rummaged through dead leaves and found a pile of broken bricks, stucco, and stones of an old hearth. It could easily date to the 1870s.

One local history book asserted that Isabella rode through the lands now owned by the botanical garden. On another trip, she trekked west to the town of Hanapepe. Chang provided confirmation. "Back in the old days," he said, "Koloa Road and Route 50 didn't exist. Only one road traveled to the west side. Lauoho," he said, running his finger on the map along the snake-curved road I knew well.

"You're kidding. Lauoho? That means she rode right by the property where my cottage is now?"

"Yeah, that was the only way she could go," he said. I shivered in eerie delight. Hawaiians have a name for the goose-bumply reaction to strange and beautiful events that seem to have been divined by unseen forces.

Chicken skin, they call it.

WHEN HE HEARS ME honk the horn, he usually comes
running out of the brush and races to the pasture gate as if he
were Secretariat, snorting and stamping and showing off. But
today he doesn't appear, nor his girlfriend, Zealy, a mare from
New Zealand. I open the old metal refrigerator lying on its side
that we use as a feed locker, and scoop out pellets of compressed
alfalfa. And although I keep whistling, still no Bo.

I start the long hike back through the brush, along narrow
horse trails, up a rock pile, and through a scrub forest. Fresh
droppings. Evidence that they've been down this way recently.
Air plants fill the field with tall stems shooting up to waist
height with thousands of lanternlike translucent pods that
dance in the bright morning light.

Silent beehives lean at angles, remnants of a long ago plantation house. Wild cane and grass grows higher and higher, until
it closes over my head. I seem to shrink smaller and smaller, as
if going back to my childhood wanderings in Minnesota, where
parents allowed their children to roam out of sight without fear.
My friends and I would go miles into what we called "the Secret
Woods," far from adult supervision and into a fantasy of adventures and dangers, of deep glens haunted by witches and winged
horses named Pegasus.

With slight apprehension, I enter the horses' private realm
as if finding myself inside the zoo cage with the animals. Nests
of beaten-down brush form their private rooms of tall grass. A
rustling of leaves and thud of hooves announce their approach.
Suddenly, Bo towers before me, head thrown back and nostrils
flaring. The sun burnishes his dark brown coat to a shiny copper. He lumbers over at a slow walk, lowering his head shyly and
preening. He noses behind my back for a carrot. I let him take

it in his mouth, but don't let go, so he'll bite off a big chunk. I give the other half to Zealy, close on his heels. Bo nuzzles my hand, and I pat his neck then reach up to give him a hug, which he tolerates for a few seconds.

As I head back to the front pasture, Bo follows me, his nose too close, bumping me on the shoulder. Then both he and Zealy simultaneously remember that I usually leave grain in their feed pans. They prick their ears up, look forward, then rush off in an almost silent run, weaving through the trees. It takes me longer. I find the two of them with their heads down in the feed. I easily slip a halter over Bo's neck and wait for Val to show up.

I was surprised that horses were such a ubiquitous part of the Hawaiian landscape, and have been for a long time. After English and American colonists arrived with bulls and cows in the early 1800s, so many cattle escaped that they bred into dangerous herds stampeding over several islands. Finally King Kamehameha III imported Spanish *vaqueros* from Mexico to teach Hawaiians how to rope and ride. The Hawaiians coined the word *paniolo,* from the Spanish word *español,* for these island cowboys. Riding, roping, and rodeos remain an important part of rural Hawaiian life. Declare any day a holiday, and Hawaiians hold rodeos and parades that may have few participants or spectators, but always attract *paniolos* astride their horses, festooned with leis.

Mark Twain and Isabella Bird both noted in their Hawaiian journals how much the Hawaiians loved to ride. Nineteenth-century ladies dressed up in long Victorian gowns, donned leis of crimson ohia flowers, and galloped in packs down the streets of Honolulu. Bird wrote, "The women seemed perfectly at home in their gay, brass-embossed, high peaked saddles flying along astride, bare-footed, with their orange and scarlet riding dresses streaming on each side beyond their horses' tails, a bright kaleidoscopic flash of bright eyes, white teeth, shining hair, garlands of flowers and many colored dresses."

Isabella herself concocted an island riding outfit that must have startled the natives. She donned Turkish-style bloomer pants, New Zealand boots, Mexican spurs, and a flannel riding coat.

I HAD FOUND Bo by chance. I often spent Saturdays or Sundays in the office, but one late Friday afternoon, hungry for a change of routine, I impulsively booked a weekend trail ride at Silver Falls Ranch on the north shore.

That day I joined a group of six, all tourists I presumed, and followed a guide on a rather tame, flat trail. We stopped at a waterfall tumbling into a dark green pool, and some of us plunged in for a swim. One of the other riders, a woman named Val Pilari, accompanied her ten-year-old granddaughter on the ride. As water cascaded over our heads, I learned that Val, too, was a resident, and lived near Poipu Beach on the south shore. She already owned one horse, but wanted another so she could ride with her grandchildren or husband. It all seemed natural and plausible when she asked if I'd be interested in going halves on a horse. Sure, I said offhandedly. Although I had some riding experience, owning a horse in Philadelphia had cost too much to contemplate. I had fantasized about trying to re-create Isabella Bird's horseback adventures. Unexpectedly, I was presented with the means to realize that dream.

When Val telephoned a few weeks later to report that she had found a horse, I was skeptical of entering such a partnership with someone I had met only once. Yet I instinctively sensed honesty in Val. She had owned horses all her life, for which I would be immeasurably grateful when she schooled me on the particulars of feed and the treatment for rain rot, a fungus that appeared on Bo's hindquarters during the rainy season.

We drove together to the Anini Beach polo grounds on the north shore where weekly games are held, a vestige of the old plantation elite's pastimes. A grizzled, not particularly trustworthy-appearing polo wrangler wanted to unload a six-year-old island-bred mix of quarter horse and thoroughbred. The horse, named Bo, hadn't taken to the fast pace of polo. An excellent recommendation in my mind.

The man easily roped and saddled a dark brown horse so skinny his ribs showed. Val elected to watch while I mounted and trotted around the polo field, gratified when the gelding responded to my commands to turn, slow, and halt. I reined in, reporting that Bo appeared well trained.

We paid, the wrangler threw in an old, broken-in saddle and some sorry-looking tack, worn and stiff with disuse, and we had our horse. Later, when Bo showed himself difficult to handle, Val would say, "That guy drugged Bo the day you tried him."

For an unbelievably low price, Val rented a five-acre fenced pasture near Poipu. Tall grass grew so deep that the horses could eat themselves fat, eliminating the need for daily feeding. Best of all, riding on Kauai meant saddling up and riding cross-country in whatever direction we pleased. We spurned the Western saddles used by most riders in Hawaii in favor of English, and were among the few who wore safety helmets. I, the greenhorn, followed Val, her long blond ponytail bobbing ahead of me with insouciant confidence, as she led us on cane-haul roads up into the hills, canters around the Waita Reservoir, and along spots of deserted coastline. My hands scrabbled desperately to cling to Bo's mane as we galloped the dirt road that circled a long-dead volcano cone like a racetrack.

One day, as we broke from the cool shade of feathery ironwood trees, the horses' hooves clattered on hard lava rock. As always, I thrilled at the deserted beauty of Mahaulepu Beach's two miles of uninhabited shore stretching below us, while fighting terror at how close we pranced near a cliff edge over unforgiving waves and rocks forty feet below. Bo contentedly followed Val on Zealy and we turned onto a narrow trail that disappeared into a forest of ironwood pine. Down, down we lurched until we reached a small stream. "Wait, wait, not so fast. I have trouble holding him downhill," I called in panic.

Bo had quickly fattened up and now snorted full of life, stubborn and resistant. I could barely hold him back from a run. We reached the stream delta as it emptied into the sunstruck ocean, wading into the water, the horses wet up to their girths. Zealy splashed, kicking up sparkles of water. It's against the law to ride on the beach in Hawaii, but nobody saw us in the early morning or at twilight. Bo ventured only a few feet into the swirling waves. I turned him toward land, into a slow canter along the hard sand at water's edge. His legs stretched out further and further as we flew, seemingly afloat a few feet above the ground. We followed a path along cane fields and out to a small cove where a half dozen Hawaiian fishermen camped for the weekend. We cantered up dunes, then out to a headland peninsula, surrounded by the warmth of the sea breezes and the sunny azure of the Pacific.

I had become determined to know the island, and Bo allowed me to trek further into its depths. I'd never cover it entirely, nor lose the fear of getting lost. The jungle greens run together as endless camouflage, and you often can't tell whether you're up or down, much less east, west, north, or south. In the islands there are only two useful directions, *makai*—toward the ocean, and *mauka*—toward the mountains. Although the island was only thirty miles in diameter, hikers and hunters often became disoriented, sometimes wandering without food or water for three days or more before stumbling on other hikers or search parties. Some people never get found. They step closer to a cliff's edge for the view, not realizing until too late that the greenery underfoot grew over air, not terra firma.

I had an urge to replicate Isabella Bird's three-day trek on horseback from Koloa to the homestead of Mrs. Eliza Sinclair in the hills above Hanapepe on the west side. In the early 1800s, the Sinclairs had emigrated from Scotland to New Zealand, where they amassed a shipping fortune. When her sea captain husband died, Eliza loaded up her large family onto a sailing vessel and set out in search of a Utopia. She bought the small island of Niihau, seventeen miles northwest of Kauai, but later moved the family over to the more populated Kauai. Her descendents, the Robinson family, still owned one-third of the Garden Island. About twenty Robinsons remained on the island, holding shares of an estimated one hundred thousand acres, worth more than half a billion dollars. Patriarch Warren Robinson appeared on the cover of *Fortune* magazine in an article that described the family as one of the five hundred wealthiest in America but cash poor, crippled by inheritance and property taxes. Another cousin, Bruce Robinson, told the magazine that he was so poor that he ate in a restaurant only three times a year and subsisted on meat hunted in the mountains.

Isabella Bird had set out from the Sinclair mountain homestead for Hanapepe Falls, a perilous journey that required crossing and recrossing a boulder-strewn stream until she reached the sheer drop of water over green walls into a mist-shrouded pool. Now everybody calls them Jurassic Park Falls, because they formed a backdrop for a dramatic shot by director Steven Spielberg for his movie of that name. Because the Robinsons employ armed workers to protect against trespassing, about the only way to see the falls now is from a tourist helicopter ride.

One Sinclair descendent, the eccentric Keith Robinson, tended what he called his "Outlaw Preserve" in the inaccessible hills. Forget it, everybody told me; you'll never get in. He hates the National Tropical Botanical Garden and everybody in it. Unless by some miracle I could sweeten up the Robinsons, I would have to give up on re-creating Isabella's ride to the falls.

Yet I couldn't shake the desire to live Isabella's experience. As she pierced the fern-shrouded Kauai forest and climbed higher on that trail one hundred years ago, she reached a high meadow. All around them soared knife-edge peaks covered in velvet green. She reveled in a day as brilliant and as cool as an English June, writing: "The sweet, joyous trade wind could not be brewed elsewhere than on the Pacific. The scenery was glorious, and mountains, trees, frolicsome water, and scarlet birds, all rioted as if in conscious happiness. Existence was luxury and reckless riding a mere outcome of the animal spirits of horses and riders, and the thud of the shoeless feet as the horses galloped over the soft grass was sweeter than music. If happiness is atmosphere, we were happy."

AFTER A RIDE, I would hose down Bo, rinse my own arms, streaked with sweat, horse smell, and red dust, and, alone at my car, I might wiggle into a swimsuit and drive down to Poipu Beach, only five minutes away, to fall into the ocean. Although my stiff and bruised limbs protested at the initial plunge into cold salt water, I did it just because I could.

Now I regularly kept my saddle in the trunk and snorkel gear in the backseat.

When I moved to Hawaii, I was conscious that I followed in a long tradition of lady writers retreating to pastoral countryside to write, to observe nature, to face solitude, to lick our wounds.

There was Annie Dillard and her astonishing *Pilgrim at Tinker Creek*. Who could forget her account of watching an insect suck the innards out of a frog, or her other quiet observations of the natural world? She wrote it at twenty-five and promptly thereafter won the Pulitzer Prize.

But while admiring her, I was more interested in middle-aged women like myself, who faced adversity. Their country retreats became do-or-die missions. They were determined to write truth, find peace, and live fully. I needed to know how they survived and triumphed over all the slings and arrows that the world had flung and still got up and lived with joy.

When digging my first garden in Philadelphia, a friend gave me a copy of May Sarton's *Plant Dreaming Deep*. Like so many other women, I was enchanted by the sensitive poet's account of moving, in her late forties, to her first house, a dilapidated eighteenth-century New Hampshire farmhouse which she renovated into a cozy nest. She dug out the surrounding land to build gardens. The book turned Sarton into a cult object, an early icon of feminine independence, particularly among young female undergraduates.

With some eagerness I plowed through some of Sarton's later journals, written at age seventy, eighty, and eighty-two, to find clues about how a woman alone faced old age. She continued to create, particularly the poems that constitute her best work. She wrote frankly of struggling to garden at age eighty, missing it when she couldn't plunge her hands into dirt. I picked up her journal about how she eventually left New Hampshire to occupy a rented house on the coast of Maine. In it she confessed continuing doubts from which I'd like to be free. "Thinking so much these days about what it is to be a woman. I wonder whether an ingrained sense of guilt is not one feminine characteristic," she wrote. "A man who has no children may feel personally deprived but he does not feel guilty, I suspect. A woman who has no children is always a little on the defensive."

I learned from a later journal that her Nelson, New Hampshire, house had not been terribly isolated, and in fact fronted on the town green. The first biography of May Sarton, by noted literary biographer Margot Peters, further destroyed my enchantment. Peters revealed Sarton as often hysterical and self-delusional, prone to martini-fueled rages. Even her romance of life alone at the Nelson house was semi-fake, mere snatches between hectic, frenzied activity and multiple visits from various lesbian girlfriends. Worse, she desperately stalked some targets of her frantic, unrequited lust.

Of course, many of our most famous solitaires were not as sequestered as they let on. A modern examination of Thoreau's letters and notes show that he frequently forsook the quiet of Walden Pond to run off for dinner with friends in Cambridge, a distance of fourteen miles. I abandoned May Sarton as a role model, repelled by her looniness, and turned to Sue Hubbell's classic, *A Country Year: Living the Questions.* Her story is irresistible. When a thirty-year marriage ends, she is alone and broke, making a living by keeping bees and selling the honey. Hubbell writes more knowledgably about her natural surroundings than Sarton ever could, and she emanates a rock-solid common sense. Perhaps more important for any memoirist, she abhorred the confessional, writing more as an astute reporter.

My own observations of the natural world began early. Shortly after my birth, my parents moved west from a small house in Minneapolis to the more countrified suburb of Hopkins. They expanded a big house to fit what eventually became a family of five children, in a charmed setting called Sherwood Forest. While my parents joined the other adults for entertainments, we children formed our own pack to climb trees, build forts, and wade for tadpoles and frogs in ponds and streams.

When I was four a new girl named Laurie Shepherd moved close by, and the two of us became best friends. We prided ourselves on running barefoot and bare-chested, pretending to be boys or Indians or Huck Finn. In truth, Laurie was more of a free spirit than I. She took our games more seriously, and even then I sensed she pushed the boundaries more than I dared. By junior high, we drifted apart; then at age thirteen, my family moved to Connecticut. I never saw Laurie again. I heard that she was building her own log cabin in the deep woods of northern Minnesota and was writing a book about it.

For decades, I avoided finding that book, *A Dreamer's Log Cabin: A Woman's Walden,* most likely out of jealousy. When I finally hunted it down, it brought tears to my eyes to read her remembrances of playing Robin Hood and Peter Pan in Sherwood Forest. I learned that after graduating from the University of Minnesota, she taught art in the small-town public school of Wabasha in southern Minnesota. She never let go of an ambition to live in a log cabin. To save for land and logs, Laurie quit teaching, sold her house, and worked almost around the clock as an insurance agent, bus driver, dishwasher, janitor, Army reservist, chimney sweep, and piano tuner. At age twenty-eight, she lived in a tent with her Siberian Husky and two cats and began constructing her dream house.

Laurie peeled bark from felled trees, bathed in the river, and fashioned a boom to lift her logs into place at the same time that I was married, living in a Manhattan apartment, and commuting to *The Record* newspaper in Bergen County, New Jersey. My foes were not large logs, but a newsroom full of aggressive reporters competing for good assignments.

Often when people speak of searing childhood memories, they refer to mean poverty or abuse. Our adventures in the woods branded Laurie and me not only with a desire and need to forge strong friendships, but to run free in wild places. She still lives in her cabin, now with a husband and two children. And two decades behind her, I was soon going to inhabit a secluded cottage surrounded by empty Hawaiian valleys.

CHAPTER NINE

My Plantation Cottage

*I*LIKE THIS HOUSE," Mike Faye said as he walked from room to room on one of his late afternoon inspection visits at the cottage. "There's an almost Japanese quality to it, an openness. Out the kitchen windows you can see Mount Haupu." He gestured at the far-off mountain. "And on the other side," he pointed to the back door, "you see the valley."

The main room could be easily fixed up with a new coat of paint and a few patches of trim to replace termite damage. But sagging kitchen cabinets needed to be torn out, repaired, and reattached. Faye said he could rehab the cabinet doors with raised molding and paint them in white lacquer to give them an English-country look. We'd add a microwave, cover the counters in gray-granite Formica, and install stainless steel double sinks. I stopped worrying about James's warnings of burglaries. "He was just trying to scare you," Scott Sloan, assistant director in charge of the grounds crew, told me. "He liked having the house empty."

A stickler for historical detail, Faye insisted we install traditional Canec for the bathroom ceiling: a spongy, fibrous board made from sugarcane fibers. We argued over light switches for two weeks. Old-style plantation cottages like mine had single-wall construction, which meant just that: a single wall of heavy lumber served as both exterior and interior wall, allowing no hidden spaces for electrical wiring. Traditionally, builders enclosed wires in ugly squared tubing with raised boxes for switches, all in dark brown. I hated them. Faye stubbornly countered, "It's historical." He finally gave in, and found me modern, paddle-style toggle switches. In white.

I brought in a second telephone line for a fax. Connected cable TV. Installed a dishwasher. Wired the closets, as storing clothes in humid Hawaii could lead to disaster. The Kleins told me that their wool jackets broke out in green mold after a couple of months. At Ace Hardware I found electric heat tubes for the closet baseboards to keep the closets dry. I salvaged a chest and two coffee tables from the old cottage furnishings. Everything else, I told John Rapozo, the Garden foreman assigned to oversee renovations, I never want to see again.

The plastic lavender tub had to go. We worked out a plan for an open Japanese-style shower on one side of the ten-by-twelve-foot bathroom. Faye presented me with an antique showerhead the size of a plate that looked like it had come from a 1930s Malaysian rubber plantation. He designed a long vanity and mirror to stretch along the entire opposite wall. His carpenter built the cabinet of fir, then stained it a deep, glossy cherry so it looked like fine library furniture. Dr. Klein approved the plan without a murmur over costs. "Lucinda, I want you to be happy here," he said. "I want you to feel that every issue has been resolved, so you can put it to rest and just concentrate on your work." Wow.

Mike Faye had researched the plantation cottage style, and one day I got him to tell me about it. In the early 1900s, sugar plantation owners faced more and more criticism over labor conditions for their workers, imported from Japan, China, the Philippines, and Korea. Foreign embassies protested housing conditions, which often consisted of rough campsites or dormitories. As Hawaii was seeking statehood, the planters felt the pressure. They began building what was called "sanitary housing."

"For the first time," said Faye, "families had their own houses and privacy. Lo and behold, it led to a baby boom." When all the baby boys grew up, they went off to become soldiers in World War II, and fought in the famous 100th Infantry Battalion and 442nd Regimental Combat Team of Japanese-American soldiers. They were given the most dangerous assignments, and more than half of them were killed. But those who survived came back to Hawaii as war heroes, got involved in politics, and changed the whole political and economic landscape in Hawaii. Democratic landslide elections overwhelmed the Republican stronghold of Hawaii. The state earned the reputation as so Democratic as to verge on socialism. "And all because of these houses," said Faye with a smile.

He showed me his collection of old pattern books used as construction plans by the all-powerful Hawaiian Sugar Planters' Association for its "sanitary" worker villages. They included common bathhouses, baseball diamonds, incinerators, and small stores. "The lighter your skin, the better your house," Faye explained. "It wasn't right, but that's the way it was." Supervisors, called *lunas,* were mostly *haoles* and claimed the largest houses in the center of the village. Japanese workers received

higher wages and better houses close to the center, while the
Filipinos on the bottom of the caste system got lower wages and
houses on the village outskirts.

Plantation owners imported Japanese temple builders to erect
Buddhist temples. When the carpenters finished those jobs, they
went to work on the managers' grand Victorian chalets, then
later, smaller residences. Each temple builder had his own signature marks, like the crude exterior window frames on my house
that extended slightly over the window tops, like ears. Faye
and his carpenters became connoisseurs of the nameless temple
builders. Someone might tell them that this house or that was
built by the Japanese temple builder in Waimea, but they'll look
at it and say, "No way. Maybe the Hanalei builder."

When Faye's crew crawled under my cottage, they discovered
paint on the underside of the living room floor. He pointed
out a seam in the flooring between the living room and dining
areas where the two rooms had been joined together. After the
war, he said, builders recycled many houses because of a scarcity
of lumber. Faye concluded that the cottage living room must
have originally been used elsewhere, perhaps as a second-story
porch.

It explained why the house had such an open-air feel.

EARLY MORNINGS I adopted the habit of stopping by
the cottage to see how renovations were going. Often Faye's
workers had already arrived, telltale surfboards extending out
the backs of their pickup trucks, as the guys liked to catch some
waves before work. But today I had the place to myself. I stood
on the front porch and surveyed the empty landscape. I was
falling in love with the place.

I heard a vehicle and saw a brown truck hurtle up the drive. Garden superintendent John Rapozo frequently dropped by to check on progress. I always liked to see him, and thought of him as the Man in Black, like country singer Johnny Cash. Rapozo had a craggy, rawhide face and always wore the same uniform of neatly pressed black pants, big black cowboy boots, buckskin hat, and a black T-shirt imprinted with the Garden's breadfruit logo. Now he only picked up the guitar to sing for family gatherings, but in his younger days he and his two brothers, Mannie and Georgie, played regularly at the Coconut Palms Hotel. John said he used to bring the house down when he strummed "Try a Little Tenderness."

From a west-side Portuguese ranching family, he spoke pidgin staccato in a rough, smoker's voice. His dialect was so thick that even his wife sometimes didn't understand him. I missed about every fourth word. *Haoles* often mistake anyone speaking pidgin as a dumb hick. Rapozo was a simple man, but I sensed intelligence and an inner toughness that gave him unquestioned authority. He had worked for the botanical garden since its beginning, first as a contractor, later as foreman. He personally had bulldozed most of the roadbeds.

His favorite activity was to move earth with big machinery.

"Is this house ever going to be finished?" I asked laughingly when he got out of the truck.

"Lucinda. I call them this morning," his finger jabbed the air emphatically. "I told them: By the end of next week. Finished."

I sighed happily. This was vastly different from renovation projects at my Philadelphia house. I had been looking for someone like John all my life. I didn't need a husband. I needed an enforcer.

Faye warned me that the grass walk to the cottage would turn into a sea of mud during the winter rains. John hauled in rock to form a stepping-stone path from the front porch to where I parked the car. One night I returned home to find a fresh layer of cinders and gravel spread over the dirt drive. John, of course, I knew in an instant.

When he learned that my family called me Lucy, he did, too. Sometimes he popped his head into my Garden office to report on construction at the cottage. When I started hearing mysterious chewing sounds at my cottage, John dispatched one of his sons, Chad the exterminator, to investigate. Chad immediately diagnosed the problem as roof rats that climb trees and sneak into attics. "Lady, you've got to realize you're in the middle of a jungle," Chad told me. He returned with traps that caught a cat-sized rat, and stuffed up holes and cracks in the attic walls with copper Brillo pads.

One late afternoon at my office I turned from the computer and saw John standing in the doorway. Everybody followed the no-shoes rule at headquarters, so he stood in his stocking feet, his hands tucked behind his back, hiding something. "Lucy," he called softly. "I've got something for you." He brought out his two hands. Each held a softball-sized green glass ball. My eyes widened. These hollow glass fishing net floats, lost from Japanese ships, were becoming increasingly rare. I coveted one. Nowadays fishing fleets mostly used plastic buoys.

"I found these in the tall grass down on Lawai-Kai," John said. "By the Hawaiian graveyard. Would you like them?"

"Oh, John, would I ever! Are you sure you want to give them up?"

John smiled in satisfaction. When he left, I placed the balls on my desk, positioning them so they would catch the light. The Coke bottle–green globes seemed to hold the ocean, with frozen bubbles of spray. So fragile, but strong enough to be tossed on waves and thrown ashore. Later, Dr. Klein came into my office, papers in hand. "Look what John gave me," I showed him.

Dr. Klein beamed. "You've found a friend!"

CHAPTER TEN

Sow a Seed, Reap a Life's Work

WEEKS PASSED WHEN it seemed like I never left the office. Like a hamster in a wheel, I churned out reports, brochures, grant proposals, campaign materials, and thank-you letters to donors. Lost was an earlier vow to go down to the Garden grounds every day, if only for ten minutes. I felt guilty that I wasn't riding Bo enough. But one morning I impulsively shut off the computer and walked out the door, hurrying down the lanai along the front of the office before anyone could stop me with a phone call or question. Only Henry, the rooster who stalked the office entrance looking for handouts, saw me.

Shifting the car into low gear to drive down the steep grade and sharp curves into the Lawai Valley, I swooped past a grove of young *Pritchardia,* native Hawaiian palms, then curved around a bend to fly past the water lily pond. A gray gallinule, or Hawaiian coot, darted in and out of the pink flowers and lily pads.

The road followed the Lawai Stream under overhanging red rock cliffs to an old plantation railroad bridge that obscured the view of any oncoming cars. I honked my horn to warn approaching vehicles, then splashed through six inches of water. The Garden hadn't yet solved the problem of a stream running across its sole access road. I parked at Pump Six, the former irrigation station that housed the Garden's carpentry shop, offices for the grounds foremen, and whatever else could be crammed under its termite-ravaged rafters. Behind its red barn, three tents of green cloth formed the nursery.

As I entered the shade, I knew that this was what I had missed—a connection to plants, the feel of the humid, languid air that conspired with hot tropical sun, daily rain showers, and rich soil to produce the vivid tropical flora of Hawaii. Dr. Klein called the nursery "the Emergency Room," site of the Garden's most significant plant-rescue work. Rows of waist-high tables held hundreds of seed flats and pots, all color-coded: yellow tags for common plants. Blue for rare. Red for federally listed endangered species. Most of the tags were red.

"Hi, Simon," I called to the shy black-and-white cat that snoozed between two pots on a far table. He roused himself to quickly escape under the table. Rats used to sneak in at night and gorge themselves on all the rare seeds before they sprouted, until Simon arrived. Now we honored him as an important staff member.

The nursery manager, a tall woman with carrot-colored hair named Kerin Lilleeng-Rosenberger, rose to greet me from a rain-stained wooden desk in the back. Her steady, frank eyes could shoot sparks if provoked. I felt a kinship with her and we smiled easily. We were both loners of a sort, and outsiders at the Garden. Kerin worked by herself, without benefit of mentor or instructor, perennially battling the rest of the staff. The Garden's glamorous plant hunters Steve Perlman and Ken Wood returned from field trips around Hawaii or other Pacific isles and dumped bags of seeds on her desk, booty from their

explorations. "Always the seeds are given to me with no instructions," she'd rail. "Here's a bag of seeds, Kerin, go at it," they'd
say. Sometimes she'd plead, "Give me at least a hint. Did they
grow in mesic forest or rain forest?"

We walked to the front of the nursery to inspect two high
wooden planters. Each container cradled a low-growing shrub,
with crooked branches and tiny, parsimonious leaves. Like most
native Hawaiian plant species, it didn't look like much. Yet this
was one of the Garden's big success stories. Perlman and Wood
had discovered the last two known specimens of this scraggly
bush on the small, degraded Hawaiian island of Kahoolawe, used
over the last fifty years by the U.S. military as a practice bombing
target. By chance, the two collectors climbed over to a stone column that did not look as if it had ever been botanized. Perlman
lowered Wood by rope down to a small ledge, where he found
two skeletal plants. When they brought a sample back to the
botanical garden for identification, it initially mystified the staff
botanists. They pronounced it to belong to a new genus never
before seen in Hawaii, and named it *Kanaloa kahoolawensis*. Ken
and Steve collected a few seeds and brought them to Kerin.

"The most difficult problems for me are these real rare plants,"
she said. "They won't grow from cuttings or air-layering. Basi-
cally they kill themselves. It's like hybrid fruits — they become
so hybrid that they are asexual or sterile and can't reproduce."
But she succeeded in growing *Kanaloa kahoolawensis,* and she
was the only one who ever had. Seeds had also been sent to
Lyon Arboretum on Oahu to be cloned and grown in test tubes.
Yet despite Lyon's state-of-the-art techniques that worked well
on other species, those seedlings died. The roots just spiraled
round and round, cramped in glass tubes.

Kerin studied seeds to divine their requirements. In the case of the Kahoolawe plant, she immediately recognized a legume (bean) seed and knew from experience that it needed scarification, a nick in the shell to allow the germ within to escape. She then figured out that the plant had adapted to long periods of drought by sending out unusually deep roots. She was surprised by its speedy growth. It germinated in a day and a half in a tiny seed flat. By the end of the week it needed a one-gallon pot, and after that, progressively deeper containers.

By successfully growing two of the seedlings into bushes, she doubled the world's population, from two to four. Even so, they only survived here in captivity as museum pieces.

"Are the Hawaiian native species going to be saved at all?" I asked.

"Only in zoos, like the botanical garden. Not in the wild," she said. "The odds are against them. Totally. Goats, sheep, rats, deer, maile and mokihana hunters who plunder the forests for lei making, all are destroying the rarities. I'm like a Band-Aid. It's unrealistic to think we're going to bring them back to a preserve and they'll be able to repopulate. But I accept the zoos."

Near the garden entrance, dozens of *Brighamia* plants, now the Garden's unofficial mascot, flourished. Some towered above us, germinated by Kerin from tiny seeds, half the size of a sesame seed. I told her: "When I was up at Kilauea Lighthouse last weekend I saw that they have whole beds of *Brighamias*. Hundreds. Are they all yours?"

"They all started here. From the first, mother plant, I grew three or four hundred. I used to grow whole flats of *Brighamia* and give them away, and gave demonstrations on how to transplant them." Again, Kerin had succeeded because she tried to analyze conditions from the seed's point of view. "I used to ask: Where are the seeds going?" she explained. "The *Brighamia* plants were growing on cliff crevices, so naturally the seeds were falling down the cliffs into the ocean. Where else could they go? But once we brought them back here for cultivation, they started flowering and producing." Kerin disputes Steve Perlman's theory that *Brighamia* solely depends on the endangered sphinx moth for pollination. Here at the botanical garden, the *Brighamia* are engaging in all sorts of sex, pressing an unknown number of pollinators into action—birds, bees, and perhaps other moths.

THE GARDEN OFFERED a respite for Kerin, an antidote to a brain-numbing bartending job at Brennecke's upstairs bar on Poipu Beach. It wasn't the first time I questioned whether we were saving the plants, or they were saving us. In her off-hours, she had started volunteering at the Garden, first growing plants for a monthly giveaway program. She puzzled that she was asked to grow exclusively nonnatives such as ti or plumeria. When she arrived, the National Tropical Botanical Garden did not possess many native Hawaiian plants. Everything was imported from tropical regions around the Pacific, India, or Africa. Incredibly, the Garden had only six *Pritchardia,* the native Hawaiian palms. Kerin set out to change that. As her interest grew, she attended horticulture classes at Kauai Community College. The more she learned, the more curious she became. Yet she couldn't find a single text for growing native plants. She resolved to grow all one thousand native Hawaiian species.

After the Garden hired her as a part-time nursery manager she formulated her own classifications, dividing seeds into three types: pulpy, dry, or hard, which need to be stripped manually. Obviously, in nature, no humans perform this work, but a rat might do the job of gnawing away the hard seed coat, or it may be nicked by pebbles when rolling down a stream bed, or eaten by a bird or animal, digested, and excreted. Initially, Kerin divided hard seeds into test groups, soaking them for one, twelve, thirty-six, or seventy-two hours. After six years of experimentation, she discovered that a twenty-four-hour bath was ideal for most: the duration of a good, hard rain. In her experiments with *mokihana,* a native vine that grows in high, wet mountain areas, she found that the seeds needed to be soaked for five days and fermented for another three months. "Nobody thinks about soaking *for five days,*" she says. "If I weren't a patient person I wouldn't have succeeded." She plants seeds from each species in as many as twelve different soil mixes before she hits the right formula of soil, temperature, and water.

Eventually, Kerin deduced methods to grow 870 of the 1,000 native Hawaiian plant species — all except those so rare she couldn't obtain seeds. "I grew them from the heart," she says. "I really, really wanted them to grow." After five years of hard work, Kerin inventoried the Garden's new native plant section and found that only a quarter of what she had grown had survived. To her distress and volcanic rage, she discovered flats of her seedlings parked under bushes, never planted and dead. The groundsmen became used to her furies and shrugged them off. But she acknowledges that the biggest problem was not the ground crew's lack of diligence. It was the hot, windless Lawai Valley. The Garden had no nurseries at higher elevations that could harbor mountain plants that needed cool breezes and nighttime conditions near freezing. No wet rain forests could be replicated at the Garden, either.

Only one person on Kauai, or for that matter, in all of Hawaii, knew how to transplant endangered species seedlings into the landscape and keep them alive: the hermit Keith Robinson. Keith acted as a one-man plant-rescue operation who tended his Outlaw Plant Preserve, a hidden garden of the rarest Hawaiian plants. According to rumors, it was a marvel, eleven miles from civilization, an evocation of how the island terrain looked one thousand years ago, filled with native palms, flowering hibiscus, and other trees and shrubs that have all but vanished elsewhere. He reportedly does all the work by hand, including carrying water in buckets from a stream.

In defiance of federal and state authorities, Robinson hikes into state forests and other government-protected land, snatches seeds, and digs up plants. In the privacy of his preserve he fusses over them until they bloom into prize specimens. Unlike Susan Orlean's now famous orchid thief John Laroche, who stole orchids for no apparent reason other than the obsession to possess, Robinson was the Robin Hood of the endangered species world. He stole to save them. Every once in a while Robinson emerges, on a radio show or at a public hearing, to rant against government interference, the "eco-Nazis," the Endangered Species Act, the federal government, and especially the National Tropical Botanical Garden. In 1993, curiosity overcame Garden botanist Ken Wood, who trespassed onto Robinson land. Robinson men armed with rifles surprised Wood, marched him down to the Waimea Police Station, and filed a trespassing complaint.

Robinson himself carried a pistol or machete, and was convinced that a recent U.S. Fish and Wildlife Service proposal to protect endangered species on Kauai was a plot to seize his preserve. He swore to shoot anyone who tried.

I had seen a disturbing copy of Robinson's latest missive sent to Hawaii's U.S. congressmen. He wrote that in order to foil the government's planned "takeover," he would render his land useless by turning it into an enormous weed patch. He threatened to seed his family's entire watershed "with highly aggressive nonnative wetland vines, to replace this dangerous native ecosystem with a more benign nonnative one that will not attract all sorts of spying, trespassing, meddling, environmentalist bullying, and government seizure attempts."

Stay away from my preserve, he warned, or he would let loose all the alien species that were already trampling Kauai: banana poka, Japanese honeysuckle, Australian acacia, blackberry, cat's claw, kudzu, and the most dreaded of all, *Miconia*.

Although he sounded odd, even disturbing, I was intrigued and wanted to see what he had accomplished.

CHAPTER ELEVEN

Local Style

WAIST-DEEP IN the chill ocean, I pulled on my rubber fins, rubbed spit in my mask, rinsed it, strapped it on, and sank below the surface. Fish swam close, even in knee-high shallows. I paddled alongside a school of pale yellow- and black-striped convict tangs. A Picasso triggerfish with baby blue nose and geometric markings bounced lazily along the rocky floor. In this silent realm, the fish seemed oblivious to anything but the possibility of food or danger. My slow stroke offered neither, so they were unconcerned. Once I was submerged, the initial cold shock mellowed to a comfortable coolness.

Further out, craniums of coral anchored on the ocean floor. Most mornings I jogged around the beach roads at first light, then cooled off with a swim. The underwater rock formations at Poipu Beach had become as familiar as the island's terrestrial geography. In deeper water, big black and orange jacks darted in synchronization next to unicorn fish with their single horns and expressions of startled stupidity. Deeper still, a shower of bubbles sparkled around me, signaling the wave break above. A sudden shiver trilled down my spine, an uncontrollable reaction when the thought of a shark splashed into consciousness. None had surfaced near Poipu Beach in recent memory, but every year there were one or two shark attacks around the Hawaiian Islands. A surfer might lose a foot, or a swimmer, an arm. I sprinted for shore.

The hurricane had ruined the beach's grassy expanse, turning the park into patches of weeds and red dirt. Nearby, the boarded-up wreckage of the Waiohai Resort remained an eyesore.

According to the morning radio surf report, south shore waves rose a mere two to three feet. Although it was only 7 a.m., already four or five surfers bobbed on boards a hundred yards offshore, waiting for a decent swell. One sprung to standing position and skimmed left ahead of a curl.

An outdoor shower at the edge of the sand beach consisted of a simple concrete post with four showerheads. Mothers doused their bare babies here next to locals with warrior tattoos. Cold water only, but sufficient for Hawaii's preternatural, nearly continual perfect weather. I brought a small bottle of shampoo to lather up. Sometimes I went for days without an indoor, hot-water shower. Rinsing the salt from my rubber mask, I hung it on the faucet, then tucked the fins into the narrow crevice behind the shower pipe to drain, local style. A surfer walked over to join me. I had seen him other mornings, startled by the intensity of his good looks. Strong, perfect white teeth. A mop of auburn, curly hair. Rivulets of water streamed through graying chest hair. He flashed a high-voltage smile that reduced me to a blush, which I tried to conceal.

"Morning," he said with a grin, sticking his head under the water. There was something intimate about showering with a stranger, even if we were outdoors and wearing swimsuits.

"Fine way to start a day. Fine way," he said. I primly agreed and turned off the water.

"That's a real antique you got there," he said, eyeing my black snorkel mask, bought for a Caribbean trip fifteen years ago.

"I know," I said. "But I have a small face, and it's the only one I can find that doesn't leak."

"You just keep on using it."

The islands attracted lots of these guys, who had come for the surfing and now drifted from job to job, woman to woman. Would an erotic plot twist be worth it? Kauai was the smallest of small towns. Kansas in the middle of the ocean. People noticed where your car had been parked and knew if you drove to Lihue, or stopped at Koloa Landing to snorkel the deep water. At the botanical garden, grounds workers learned about plans to renovate my little plantation cottage almost before I made them. The coconut wireless, they called it. How long would it take to get around that the Garden fund-raiser was having a fling with a surfer?

I could see in his eyes what he registered in an instant: mutual sexual attraction. An animal behaviorist would see it as a scenting, an atavistic response to a receptive mating partner.

BACK IN THE CAR, I drove through the back streets of Old Koloa Town with its little wooden houses, remnants of a plantation camp. Jumbles of potted orchids and fountain-like red and green ti filled the cottage gardens with gaudy color. Japanese stone lanterns stood in many of the tiny yards. Other gardens pressed tires, buckets, even an old bathtub, into use as planters. Gardens on Kauai fell into two categories: the Polynesian Adventure landscapes at the big hotels, or these mixed-up plantation cottage gardens. I had come to prefer the hodge-podges that festooned the small cottages.

Down the road I passed the Koloa Fire Station, which like all volunteer brigades on the island maintained cribs of small boxes for lost shearlings. At breeding times the night birds become disoriented by the electric lights on the island and land on lawns. People pick them up and deposit them in the fire station boxes, so forest rangers can return the birds to a beach, to head back into the wind.

After passing the New England–white steeple of the Union Church, I entered Koloa Town proper — three blocks of ramshackle, one-story wooden buildings on dusty streets. After one unsatisfactory experiment in high-rise resorts that allowed a six-story hotel, now the Marriott, to be built in Lihue back in the 1960s, the people of Kauai insisted that no building could rise higher than a coconut tree. Thus, the Koloa tree tunnel of eucalyptus trees and the lines of Norfolk pines trimmed by the hurricane into tall bottle brushes gave the lowland coastal landscape its only high points.

Spreading monkeypod trees shaded a dozen Koloa Town tourist boutiques, two surf shops, Fathom Five Divers, Kauai Fish Market, a handful of restaurants, and two grocery stores. At the corner under a purple jacaranda tree stood an almost naked man, bare gut hanging over baggy shorts. He wore "rubba slippas," as the locals call their ubiquitous flip-flops. People walking around nearly unclothed had startled me at first. Now I joined them, wrapping only a sarong over my wet suit to go into the grocery store.

To pick up some milk for breakfast, I parked in front of the Big Save, the catch-all grocery that devoted an entire aisle to fishing gear and suntan lotion. I nodded to the clerk at the cash register, gestured to another acquaintance. We locals hardly noticed the tourists. It was as if we put on special sunglasses that screened them out and made their rental convertibles disappear.

That initial, alarming encounter with local food at Sueoka's market on my first weekend turned out to have been a good introduction to island food, with its mixture of six great culinary traditions: Japanese, Chinese, Korean, Portuguese, Polynesian, and Filipino. Most meals, either in highbrow restaurants or at private parties, featured samples from several cuisines. Luckily, dishes bore no resemblance to what I tasted as a teenager in West Hartford Center's South Seas Village, with its pupu platter and deep-fried chicken in sweet-sour glop studded with pineapple and maraschino cherries.

Even so, I mournfully passed the produce sections of the large grocery stores those first months. Fresh fruits and vegetables were mostly shipped in from the mainland and were extraordinarily expensive and often poor quality: peaches like sawdust; red bell peppers with astronomical prices; pallid tomatoes. While the islands may be the extinction capital of the world for the plant and animal kingdoms, it's a fruit fly's paradise. Scientists have identified more than one thousand species of fruit flies proliferating in Hawaii, ready to attack fresh produce before it can be harvested. Only truck farmers fussing over small quantities of fruits and vegetables can keep the flies at bay.

Though the produce section disappointed, I exulted over the fish counter with its ahi, mahimahi, and occasional *opakapaka*, all flakily fresh. I tried them all. Next door, the Kauai Fish Market's glass cases offered an even more dazzling array, including its daily lunch plate specials with choice of fish, rice, macaroni salad, and greens. Per capita fish consumption in Hawaii is twice that of mainlanders; the consumption of tuna ranks second only to Japan. Hawaii's unique contribution to raw fish cuisine is *poke,* small chunks of rough-cut raw fish mixed with Hawaiian salt, chopped seaweed, and roasted, ground *kukui* nut. Fish stores offer a half dozen or so styles, perhaps tuna, marlin, or swordfish with seasonings that might include scallion, *shoyu* (soy sauce), onion, sesame oil, and chili peppers.

At Garden headquarters, Clarissa and Evelyn in the finance department brought in more strange and exotic foods: dried plums dusted with a hot Japanese spice; pickled green mango slices; squishy mountain apples with their creamlike white flesh; *manapua,* white buns stuffed with pork; and the Hawaiian snack *Musubi*—a mini-meal that can be bought at convenience stores for a dollar. Of Japanese origin, its rectangular bar of sticky rice is wrapped in nori seaweed and contains a slice of SPAM or egg.

SPAM continues to hold an unfathomable but revered place in Hawaii's diet. A condensation of the words "spiced ham," so named in a 1937 contest sponsored by the Hormel Company, it reigns as a holdover from pre-refrigerator days when canned meat was prized as a sign of wealth. Grocery stores sell out of SPAM. People hoard cans during wartimes. Locals mix it with Chinese fish cake, make SPAM wontons and SPAM tempura, or fry it with rice or eggs. All this means that Hawaii's population eats three times more SPAM than any other state of the union—and suffers a high rate of obesity, diabetes, and heart disease to go along with it.

Not until I discovered the Monday Koloa Farmers' Market

did I start to realize the full culinary possibilities in Hawaii. At precisely noon, the official and strictly enforced starting time, the market grand master drops a rope barrier and lets the crowds in. "Walking only," he calls to little avail, as shoppers rush to several dozen vendors hawking fresh-picked, foot-long beans, bouquets of local Manoa lettuce, yams, purple potatoes, radishes, Maui onions, bay leaf, pineapples (yellow and sweet or the pale white low-acid variety), grapefruit, cucumbers, even corn on the cob and beefy tomatoes.

I marveled at the dozens of foreign fruits such as bitter melons, which resemble pale green cucumbers with warts, giant papayas, and avocados the size of cantaloupe. One vendor whacked ice-cold coconuts in half with a machete and offered them to customers. Some locals prized the spoon meat, a thin, gelatinous layer of slippery flesh that lines immature coconuts. A bag of tangerines was so cheap that one could squeeze them for juice—nectar of gods!

On my first trip to the market, I purchased a nosegay of deep purple orchid sprays circled with maidenhair fern, then grabbed bunches of tall red heliconia stalks and periwinkle blue agapanthus blooms. A pickup truck displayed barrels of white calla lilies. I bought a dozen. The vendor presented me two for free. A full armload of tropical flowers for practically nothing!

On the mainland I had despised anthuriums for their glossy red elephant ears and dangling pistils. Here, I grew to love the lime-green varieties, or those of bubble-gum pink. Even the deep-red ones soon appealed to me, as their loud colors seemed at home in the tropics. Most of all, I adored the large, transparent blooms shaded from palest whisper pink to greenish white. Called *obake,* Japanese for *ghosts,* they grow so thin you can see light through them. Some extend to a foot long, and more. I became a connoisseur, searching out the largest and most transparent.

As I edged closer to local life, I experienced for the first time what it was like to be a minority, as Caucasians accounted for a mere 11 percent of the population in Hawaii. Most of the residents had a mixed ancestry of Chinese, Japanese, Korean, and maybe a dash of native Hawaiian or Portuguese. The state attorney general announced that she couldn't comply with a federal order to track hate crimes because there was no standing majority. I had heard tales, mostly from the mean streets of Honolulu, that locals shunned white people. But on Kauai I never experienced any such discrimination except for the hazing at the office, which I attributed to general suspicion of outsiders and fear of competition. The people of Kauai prided themselves on what they called "the Aloha spirit," of welcoming. One guidebook said that Kauai locals were so accommodating that they stood by the side of the road, waiting to yield.

When Alexis de Tocqueville visited frontier America in 1835, he observed that the national characteristic was the propensity to form associations "of a thousand kinds, religious, moral, serious, futile, general or restricted, enormous or diminutive." This trait endured on small-town Kauai in a way not often still evident in the continental United States. On any given weekend, Boy Scouts and soccer leagues, canoe clubs, high school bands, and an orchid society organized car washes, shaved-ice stands, hot dog sales, walkathons, and countless other activities.

MIKE FAYE AND HIS CREW had finally finished their work on the cottage, allowing me to move in. A huge container filled with my household goods and furniture from Philadelphia arrived. I had brought Sam the stray cat over from the Kleins' *ohana*, and, in record time, he took command of the large yard, wormed his way into the house, and now slept every night on my bed. As I dressed for work one morning, I heard the clanky sound of an approaching car chugging up the long bamboo-tunneled drive. James the caretaker. Twice a week he showed up early in the morning to mow the lawn or tend the bromeliads and orchids. James and I had come to an accommodation—I didn't ask him to change a thing, and he maintained a wary distance. "You not going to work today?" he called from outside.

"Yes, I'm going. I go in later," I answered through the bathroom window. If I hadn't left by 8 a.m., James regarded me as appallingly late. Garden groundsmen observe plantation hours, reporting to work at seven.

Getting dressed here meant throwing on a pair of khaki pants, a white linen shirt, and a pair of sandals. My hair dried itself. Makeup now consisted of a few swipes of color. I went out to the front porch. James put down his rake and sputtered with anger.

"The pigs are back," he said indignantly. "Ten of them— momma, poppa, and eight little piggies. They're rooting around, ruining the grass. Digging up my plants," he snorted. "Making a mess."

I only half-believed him. Oh, I had heard about the wild pigs that roamed the interior mountains of Kauai. Hunters stalked the tusked boar as big sport. Some carry only a knife and a sewing kit—the knife to slit the pig's throat and a sewing kit to sew up their dogs if they got gored. But surely the wild pigs didn't dare come so close to civilization.

Just after sunset that night I drove to the end of the cottage drive. Under the big mango tree stood what looked like a large German shepherd. Then a pack of smaller animals appeared, some coal black, others slate gray. The pigs. I counted seven little ones, as well as the big he-boar. He looked more wolf than barnyard pig, standing on tall legs, staring at me from tiny eyes that glittered devil-red in the headlights. I steered the car over the lip of the driveway and onto the lawn, stepped on the gas pedal, and charged, honking the horn. The pigs scurried around in a panicked circle, then disappeared down the ravine.

The next morning I found signs of their rooting in the newly seeded grass, not ten feet from my parked car—practically on the doorstep! Over the next weeks, I saw the pigs from time to time as they grew older and bolder. Their manes ran stiffly down their spines just like a razor. Pigs are mean, a new friend Diego the Texan warned. "They can kill you. Then they'll eat you, too," he said. "They're meat eaters." Some people like the pigs, which reputedly make good pets. One Garden employee confided that he and his ex-wife used to sleep with their pet pig, all two hundred pounds. The pig had her own pillow.

I had grown oblivious to the countless roosters, hens, and broods of chicks that wandered in and out of the yard. But I'd be damned if I would share the place with pigs. James also grew more and more infuriated. Finally, I gave him the okay to invite his friends in to hunt. I didn't see the pigs anymore, although once or twice I heard a far-off gun crack.

CHAPTER TWELVE

Alien Species

*P*IGS WEREN'T THE only pests on Kauai. For the past week, Kauai's radio stations broadcast public announcements seeking volunteers for "Operation Sweep." About fifty of us mustered in the Anahola Valley. Our mission: to repel a vicious invader, the ivy gourd plant. This innocent-appearing vine had crept across Oahu and the Big Island, consumed hundreds of acres, smothered utility poles, and buried whole valleys. It stole sunlight and ground space from other plants, until all that remained was a thick carpet of pale green ivy. Ivy gourd could grow a foot a day. And now it threatened Kauai.

Many volunteers showed up outfitted in heavy footgear, protective hats, and T-shirts with yellow letters stenciled across the backs: Pest Action Control Team. Thirteen young sailors from the frigate USS *Crommelin* had volunteered a day of shore leave to pull weeds while their ship was docked in Nawiliwili Harbor. "There would have been more of us," explained the ship's recreational officer, "but last night they went ashore and some didn't feel too good this morning."

The idea of weeding the jungle seemed impossible. But the crowd reverberated with hope that they could take back the island from the eight thousand or so invading alien plant species that were ruining it. Jimmy Nakatani, Hawaii's chairman of agriculture, flew in from Honolulu for the sweep to see if, for once, his soldiers could make a dent. "There's a good chance we can wipe out ivy gourd," he boomed over a portable sound system. "In the case of *Miconia*," he explained, "we waited too long to do something. In this case, we decided to do it. *Just do it*." The megalomaniac *Miconia*, an invasive tree from South America introduced to Hawaii in 1969 as an ornamental species, was Public Enemy Number One. So far nothing could stop its explosive growth, not biological warfare with imported insects or fungi, nor weeding, nor pesticides.

A short man with a canvas duck-hunting hat pulled low over thick glasses milled around the fringes of the crowd, throwing off energy even in repose. He introduced himself as Guy Nagai, the Agriculture Department's noxious weed specialist. He had been patrolling Kauai's backwoods when he discovered a wall of ivy gourd behind a hollow of houses — the first sighting of it on the island. "Today's objective is not complete eradication," Nagai said as he took the mike. "We're looking for annihilation of the plant at its one-acre core."

Most enterprises in Hawaii begin with an appeal to the gods, so we gathered in a circle, locked hands, and bowed our heads. A burly volunteer dressed in a sleeveless T-shirt gave a long, lyrical blessing: "Thank you, Lord, for helping us to do this work for the good of the community and to get rid of this noxious weed that we don't need. Thank you for the people who came from land and sea. Let them work in safety as they go into uncharted territory in the valley."

My team headed down a road walled with giant, spiky agave

and morning glory, another pest vine that long ago had spread over Kauai. Our division leader, a volunteer named Ed, stopped and pulled back a green leaf curtain. "This is what we're looking for," he said, tugging on an inch-thick vine dangling from a host tree. He pointed to another gnarled vine, as thick as a man's forearm. "And this is what we call the mother of all mother vines."

"We're at ground zero," Ed announced when we reached a settlement of three wood houses, built in a vaguely hip, California style. Our man Nagai had discovered that a woman from Thailand had occupied the third house. She had apparently bought some shoots at an outdoor farmers' market and planted them in her garden. Thai grow ivy gourd for its sweet, young leaves, which when steamed taste like a tender spinach. The woman moved back to Thailand three years ago, but her garden continued to flourish. The ivy vines produced thousands of little gourds, which spilled open, releasing untold millions of seeds into the immediate vicinity and beyond.

We broke open boxes of sawtooth machetes, quart bottles of pesticide spray, and cases of burlap gunnysacks. Our team spread out along the base of the hill and started pulling. So delicate, so harmless seemed the tendril-like shoots. Larger vines with thick, woody stalks put up more resistance. We felt as if we were trying to uproot small trees bare-handed. In a few minutes I had filled my gunnysack. It was dirty work. The troops revolted. Too many vines, too few gunny sacks. We resorted to a new tactic, which was just to cut at the root and spray the stump.

By lunchtime, we quit. But our commanders were happy. Nagai estimated that we had killed 70 percent of the plants in the one-acre core. "We did a lot of damage," he announced happily. Agriculture and Fish and Wildlife personnel would later arrive for serious spraying. Nagai planned to rappel down cliffs at the far end of the valley to clean out the ivy there. In another three months, he predicted, all known ivy gourd on Kauai would be dead. He and his troops would continue their monitoring, quickly zapping any new growth.

STATE BIOLOGISTS HAVE no real hope of ever eradicating most alien species. Since European and American colonists arrived in the early 1800s, importations of foreign plants, animals, and insects have been both deliberate and accidental. A woman who wanted berries for pie, for instance, probably transplanted blackberry brambles in innocence. Barnyard goats and pigs burrowed into the hills, but without larger predators they quickly bred out of control, now responsible for much of the devastation of island vegetation. Stowaway ants on colonists' ships crawled ashore and have been decimating the local insect kingdom ever since. Due largely to alien invasions, 70 percent of the Hawaiian bird species are now extinct; 10 percent of the native flora is gone. Most of the flora's habitat was the islands' dry, or mesic, forestland, plowed under over the last century for pineapple and cane. Less than 10 percent of that fragile habitat remains.

All over the world, the extinction rate has accelerated. The great biologist E. O. Wilson conservatively estimates that every year, 27,000 plant or animal species — three per hour — are extinguished, never to be seen again. Scientists predict that by the year 2050, two-thirds of the planet's plant species could disappear entirely.

Some argue that nothing can really be done to stop the onslaught of imported plants. After all, they argue, people have been transporting slips, seeds, and roots from one corner of the earth to another since Marco Polo. These people point out that Hitler's Third Reich tried to enforce a native-plants-only policy.

In truth, plant introductions have immeasurably enriched our landscapes and diets. The yellow iris and rugosa roses that flourish in New England, as well as the cherry trees in Washington, D.C., are all introductions. Only three native American fruits are still in commercial production—blueberries, cranberries, and Concord grapes. Our wide array of citrus, peaches, melon, plums, and other vegetables and fruits—even the apple—come from elsewhere, thanks to Johnny Appleseed, exploring botanists, and nurserymen. So the problem isn't just imported species; it's the unknown Pandora's box factor. Which of the imports will be useful to man and which will explode into monster plants?

For almost as long as imported species have been causing problems people have been trying to undo the damage. One of the most famously misguided experiments in Hawaii was the turn-of-the-century introduction of the mongoose onto the larger islands, to hunt the rats that ate through acres of sugarcane. Only after the mongooses had bred themselves out of control did the farmers observe that mongooses hunt in daylight, rats at night, and never the twain shall meet.

Rats still flourish to this day in Hawaii. The Garden's botanists have found that even on remote cliffs and atolls, the rodents eat the seeds from some of the rarest plants. Mongooses overran Oahu and Maui long ago, raiding so many birds' nests that the seabird and wetland bird populations have almost completely disappeared. Only Kauai and Lanai remain mongoose-free. Inhabitants are determined to keep it that way. A few days ago, I picked up a flyer in my driveway printed in old Wild West lettering, with a black silhouette of a mongoose:

WANTED:
Mongoose Sighting Reports

I called up the state wildlife biologist, who told me that a tourist had reported spotting a mongoose at the banana plantation right around the corner from my cottage. Usually such a report spurs state officials to saturate the area with traps. But the biologist expressed skepticism. Foresters suspected that the last purported mongoose found on Kauai twenty-five years ago was merely a hoax — somebody probably had imported a dead carcass. The recent tourist may have actually seen a cat, he speculated.

I worried. My cat, Sam, was just the right shade of brindled brown and gray. Sam could have easily been over at the banana farm, sneaking around like a mongoose. I had a vision of Sam trussed up as an alien species.

While the specter of mongooses causes alarm, residents fear brown tree snakes even more. These snakes ate the entire native bird population of Guam. Honolulu Airport personnel have discovered frozen brown tree snakes in the wheel wells of planes arriving from Guam. So far no live snakes. Authorities, however, are pessimistic. The state biologist confided, "The snakes are here. If we've found one dead one, it means there are dozens alive that we just haven't found."

Last week, Agriculture Department officials convened a

brown tree snake SWAT team training session, attended by fifteen eager Kauai citizens. Instructors hid plastic snakes in trees to train volunteers to hunt and trap them at night.

There's something sweet about the idea of trying to keep serpents off the Garden Isle. But I fear that locals have as much chance as Adam had in Eden.

IN A CHAPTER entitled "Evils of an Exotic Civilization," Isabella Bird regretfully noted that small-mindedness and the inability to band together for a common good plagued the Hawaiian populace. The island peoples were so divided into nationalist and ethnic origins that they exhibited "an absence of larger interests shared in common," she wrote. "Except sugar and dollars, one rarely hears any subject spoken about with general interest. . . . Those intellectual movements of the West which might provoke discussion and conversation are not cordially entered into, partly owing to the difference in theological beliefs, and partly from an indolence born of the climate, and the lack of mental stimulus."

That observation, made in 1873, seemed still valid today when it came to plant rescue in the face of impending disaster. Perhaps more than any other place on the planet, the Hawaiian botanists had a mandate for staging a concerted, organized effort to study and preserve the native plants before they disappeared. Yet many botanists here wasted much of their energy arguing. The Garden's botanists were mad at the Nature Conservancy for grabbing credit for discovering species; other botanists were annoyed at the Hawaii Department of Land and Natural Resources for proposing regulations governing propagation of endangered species. Rearranging deck chairs on the

Titanic, I called it. Botanists couldn't even agree on counting the species, much less saving them.

Nowhere was this more evident than in the feud between Harold St. John, Hawaii's botanical titan of the twentieth century, and upstart Warren Wagner. St. John was a little guy, short and wiry with a crew cut, who marched into the field on plant collection expeditions wearing his World War I–era buttoned spats over high boots. A cutthroat tennis player, his motto was "If I can't win, I won't play." He stayed on the courts until age ninety-eight. St. John spent most of his long life in Hawaii, roosting at Honolulu's Bishop Museum, dominating the islands' botanical studies.

Some taxonomists are lumpers, lumping together different variations of one plant into one species. Others are splitters, who consider each and every distinction, no matter how minute, to constitute a separate species. St. John became the biggest splitter of all time, dividing what he had earlier classified as one species into two or three, or in some cases, two dozen or more.

St. John epitomized botanists of his era, thrilled with the dramatic speciation in Hawaii, the formation of multiple species from a single ancestor. Nowadays, botanists are trained to look for hybrids—crossing of species resulting in what appear to be new species but are really just variations. As St. John grew older, he continued to split and subdivide, claiming more and more new discoveries.

Starting in the 1960s, biologists' interests shifted away from the pure revelatory amazement at the diverse speciation on islands to a concern for determining the why and how of evolution. What factors drive a species to diverge, mutate, and adapt? What are the underlying mechanisms that allow for this divergence? When Warren Wagner arrived in Hawaii he embodied this new approach. Another small, intense man, Wagner had straight, dark, lank hair and a big walrus mustache that lent him a slight chipmunk appearance. Bright, aggressive, with a newly minted Ph.D. and full of the know-it-all obnoxiousness of youth, he eagerly flaunted his newfangled thinking. Wagner was more balanced, and sometimes lumped and sometimes split. He examined all available specimens, identified general characteristics, but allowed for some variation.

Honolulu's Bishop Museum hired Wagner in 1982 to produce a new, comprehensive Hawaiian flora. It was to be the most complete list of flowering species ever compiled. The first and, up until Wagner, the only flora of the Hawaiian Islands was published in 1888 by William Hillebrand, a German doctor who spent twenty years in Hawaii studying the vegetation. Wagner was charged with creating the definitive record of Hawaiian plants for the twentieth century and well beyond. It would consume him and nearly sixty collaborators for a decade.

Warren concluded early on that St. John was just an old coot, and so deliberately left him out of the flora project. Wagner and St. John had a daily opportunity to sort out their disagreements but did not. During Wagner's tenure at the Bishop Museum, he, St. John, and the rest of the botany staff lunched together every day, seated at a picnic table outside the herbarium. They got along cordially but didn't talk about Wagner's book.

As Wagner neared completion of his project he had identified 2,270 plant species growing in Hawaii, including 988 native Hawaiian species. St. John apparently grew more and more furious. He seethed quietly, like a spider in waiting. And then he struck. Just after Wagner sent the final galleys of his book to the printer with his last revisions, St. John let loose a flurry of publications in tiny, obscure botanical journals. He claimed to identify a total of 800 more Hawaiian native species, nearly doubling the number reported by Wagner.

St. John succeeded in casting doubts on the accuracy of Wagner's new flora before it was even reviewed. The old man died a few months later, just a few months shy of one hundred years. He left a tangled, spiteful legacy of disputed classifications that has taken Wagner and other Hawaii botanists more than a decade to sort out. How silly. This was just the sort of petty malice that wasted time. Why couldn't they have joined forces and sorted out the classifications together? Perhaps it was the island effect of confined spaces; it seemed to drive people to stake out a small patch of turf and defend it to the end.

CHAPTER THIRTEEN

The Rosetta Stone of Evolution

W HEN WARREN WAGNER was still a graduate student at Washington University in St. Louis, he received some valuable advice from G. Ledyard Stebbins, the landmark geneticist and evolutionary biologist who was among the first to apply modern evolutionary theory to plants. By all means, study the Hawaiian endemics, Stebbins said, but if you really want to study evolution, study the new weeds. They're the future of the archipelago.

After completing the Hawaii flora, Wagner became a leading voice in the new field of plant evolutionary genetics on oceanic islands. He's still studying the weeds, now as chairman of the botany department at the Smithsonian Institution in Washington, D.C. Every few years or so he flies to Nuku Hiva, then sails to the small outer Marquesas Islands, made famous by Paul Gauguin and Herman Melville. For three to six weeks, he treks up mountains and through rain forests to collect plant samples for DNA extractions. Wagner's work shows an ancestral genetic link between the Marquesas Islands and the waif plants that settled in Hawaii, 2,800 miles to the northeast.

Some scientists call Hawaii the Rosetta stone of evolution: the perfect place to decode the formation of new species, that elusive process that Charles Darwin called "the mystery of mysteries."

Geography dictated evolutionary fate. As most of the Hawaiian Islands lie within the earth's tropical zone between the latitudes of the Tropic of Cancer and Tropic of Capricorn, sun rays hit them directly, at times perpendicularly, creating a hot zone. The higher temperatures warm the ocean and increase evaporation, which allows trade winds to vacuum up enormous amounts of water, then disgorge it in seasonal monsoons that made the islands habitable.

Because the Hawaiian Islands are *the* most isolated in their distance from continents, very few plants or animals could travel the vast distances over open water to reach the archipelago. Once on the islands, the colonists met an onslaught of varied climates and ecologies, all packed into a tiny area smaller than Rhode Island. It was adapt or fail to survive. This superheated, supercharged evolutionary crucible caused the few colonists to evolve new traits in a shorter time compared to elsewhere. It produced Hawaiian plant and animal species so diverse, so multiformed and adaptive as to represent one of the natural wonders of the world.

The central questions for evolutionary scientists are, When did adaptation occur, and why? Many of the Hawaiian species exhibit affinities with continental species, yet how were they transported such great distances? Where did each of the immigrant lines come from? Did they evolve here, or exist unchanged from their original form, perhaps from now-disappeared land masses?

These puzzles have consumed scientists for centuries and drove Darwin to formulate his theory of natural selection. Now, however, new techniques using computer programs and DNA analysis are beginning to provide real answers.

What Darwin suspected and could only postulate based on careful observations, Wagner now proves.

As I dug deeper into scientific papers and tomes, I found that the story has been revealed in odd places—in the giant chromosomes and many-shaped penises of the Hawaiian fruit fly, in a remote Arctic violet, and in a common California weed.

WHEN HAWAII AND ALASKA were admitted to the union in 1959, my fourth grade class at Oak Knoll Elementary School in Hopkins, Minnesota, celebrated by constructing relief maps of the mountainous terrains of the forty-ninth and fiftieth states. Sculpting the continental Alaskan landmass out of a crumbly mixture of salt, flour, cream-of-tartar, and water was easy compared to trying to make the Hawaiian archipelago. We created a Pacific Ocean by painting a box lid blue, then formed islands from little blobs of homemade Play-Doh. We learned that a long, undersea fissure in the earth's crust created escape hatches for molten lava lurking at the center of the earth. Each leak erupted into its own volcano that grew and grew until it parted the sea waters above. When cooled, the lava spire became an island. The explanation could almost have come from the Book of Genesis: Let the dry land appear, and it was so.

The story has changed dramatically.

That very year, Princeton Geology professor Harry Hess informally presented his hypothesis that the seafloor was in constant motion, slowly spreading apart. Three years later, in his 1962 paper "History of Ocean Basins," one of the most important contributions in the development of plate tectonics, Hess outlined the basics: molten rock (magma) oozes up from the earth's interior along mid-oceanic ridges, forming new seafloor that spreads away from the active ridge crest and, eventually, sinks into deep oceanic trenches. The earth's hard crust floats over a slippery core, propelling continents to move in massive plates—similar to the way a cracked shell slides over a hard-boiled egg. Subsequent testing of the ocean floor showed Hess was right in his estimate that ocean sediment had accumulated only for three hundred million years or so, a very short time compared to what it would have been if the sea bottom had rested undisturbed since the oceans first formed.

Hess's work soon led to an explanation for the Hawaiian Islands. Canadian geophysicist J. Tuzo Wilson postulated in 1963 that the islands formed successively over a fixed hot spot, then slowly moved, conveyer-belt style, to the north and west. The eight current high Hawaiian islands occupy the southeast end of a much longer submerged archipelago that extends 3,616 miles north and west, culminating in Meiji Seamount (an underwater mountain) up near the Bering Strait. Those ancient underwater islands resulted from initial volcanic activity about seventy-five to eighty million years ago. Thus, over a compacted span, islands formed some of the highest mountains in the world, then eroded or broke off in great slumps into the ocean until they dwindled to mere atolls or slips of sand barely a few yards high. And then many of them disappeared under the ocean's surface.

The southernmost volcano, Kilauea on the Big Island, has flowed more or less continuously since missionaries first sighted its red-hot spouts and belches in 1823. Farther south, the underwater seamount of Loihi is currently forming, although scientists project it won't poke above water for another million years or so.

Tectonic movement is slow: three and a half inches per year.

The end result of these scientific advances is that we know that many of the Hawaiian Islands were quickly created and then disappeared, all in neat and tidy order, which now can be almost precisely dated.

Back at Oak Knoll Elementary, we also learned that Hawaii was called the melting pot. The islands attracted peoples from around the Pacific Rim and North and South America, and they lived together peaceably.

As I investigated island biology further, I found that the melting pot metaphor also serves well to explain the truly exceptional fauna and flora of Hawaii.

ALTHOUGH DARWIN BECAME the world's most famous naturalist, it didn't always look like he, or his theories, would amount to much. Captain Robert FitzRoy hired the twenty-two-year-old genteel Darwin as company for a two-year surveying voyage to Tierra del Fuego and the East Indies. Loneliness and isolation had been known to drive sea captains insane, and Captain FitzRoy wanted diversion. The voyage of the HMS *Beagle* stretched into a fifty-seven-month journey through the Pacific islands and around the South American continent. It turned Darwin into an acute observer. Although dazzled by the Galapagos Islands fauna, it was the birds that inspired his eureka moment.

He noticed that the Galapagos finches all resembled the common finch on mainland Ecuador but varied slightly from island to island. Seed-eating finches cracked open nuts with gross, heavy beaks. Others developed straight, narrow, chisel-like bills to pry insects from trees. Still other species' beaks grew thin and curved, all the better to sip nectar from flowers. Perhaps, Darwin theorized, they had somehow descended from the same parental lineage. "The most curious fact is the perfect gradation in the size of the beaks," he wrote in his journal. "There are no less than six species with insensibly graduated beaks. . . . Seeing this gradation and diversity of structure in one small, intimately related group of birds, one might really fancy that from an original paucity of birds in this archipelago, one species had been taken and modified for different ends."

Fascinated by the way that plants and animals moved around the globe, Darwin sensed that long-distance dispersal might be key to how and why species evolved, or what he called "radiated," into different forms. He reasoned that Galapagos animals must have traveled the six hundred miles from South America over water, as no evidence of a land bridge existed. After his return to England, he mounted experiments for several years, to test whether plants and animals were capable of long-distance travel. He put seeds into saltwater tanks in the basement of his house in Downe, happily reporting later, "I found that out of 87 kinds, 64 germinated after an immersion of 28 days and a few survived an immersion of 137 days." He hung a pair of chopped-off duck's feet in an aquarium and with satisfaction observed that freshwater snails clung to them, evidence that the mollusks could have traveled as stowaways. He shot partridge after a heavy rainfall, then counted the seeds in the mud stuck to the birds' feet.

He finally published his five-hundred-page tome, *On the Origin of Species,* in 1859, twenty-three years after the return of the *Beagle*. Buttressing his theories was an impressive array of evidence, including a growing fossil record, new estimates of the geological age of the earth's strata, and his own experiments. He postulated that species evolved slowly by a process he called "natural selection." Traits that contributed to successful survival tended to be reproduced through the next generations in greater proportion. Eventually a trait mutated, or evolved, into a different species or even split into several directions of mutation, in response to new surroundings.

Darwin noted even then that endemism was a byproduct of evolution — the creation of species that exist in only one place and nowhere else.

What would have happened if Darwin had visited Hawaii and seen its honeycreepers, regarded as perhaps the most spectacular example of adaptive radiation in the world, even greater than that of the Galapagos finches? All thirty-three known Hawaiian honeycreeper species and another fourteen known from fossil records share similar bodies. But the honeycreeper bills vary in astounding directions, from a short chisel to a long, curved scimitar. Tongues also grew, some like Pinocchio's nose, in astonishing lengths and directions. Would the differences be so startling that Darwin would have missed their commonality?

He based his studies on morphology — the examination of form and structure. He put forth the idea of drawing evolutionary trees — grouping species that exhibit the same characteristics and branching into ever-more refined, distinct features. In the old days, botanists such as Harold St. John manually sketched family trees to diagram familial relationships; these sketches were called "cladograms." The new evolutionists like Warren Wagner use such structural study only as a starting point. Sophisticated computer programs now spew out faster and more complex cladograms.

But only DNA molecular analysis provides rock-solid evidence of genetic links. New techniques have led to the discovery of an almost unlimited amount of data, locked up in DNA molecules that can be extracted from fossils millions of years later.

By measuring one lineage of Hawaiian honeycreepers, such data suggests evolution produced about a 2 percent divergence every million years. Assuming a constant molecular clock, that puts arrival of the original honeycreeper ancestor in Hawaii at about 3.5 million years ago.

Rapid evolution is not only possible, but frequent. Change after arrival on the islands appears inevitable. Five species of endemic banana moths in Hawaii have evolved in the approximately one thousand years since humans introduced the banana to the islands. In Lake Lanao in the Philippines, four endemic genera of cyprinid fish evolved in ten thousand years or less. And new plant species have been discovered in the newly formed lava islands just over a century after the 1883 eruption of Krakatoa in Indonesia.

While scientists have studied birds, animals, and plants to decipher the secrets of evolutionary magic, evolutionary biologists regard the Hawaiian fruit fly—*Drosophila*—as supreme, the Mount Everest of DNA analysis for island biology. More than seventy-two scientists joined together in 1962 to form the Drosophila Genome Project to study this amazing insect over the next decades.

In part this is because there are so damn many species—more than one thousand, and still counting—of these tiny flies, which have evolved into so many different ecologies. Before you wonder how even enthralled scientists observe differences between flies no bigger than a speck, it's helpful to know that there are two distinguishing physical attributes. Even closely related fruit fly species are distinguished by the shape of the male penis, so distinctive an identifying mark that it has been likened to a fingerprint in individual humans. Complex courtship behaviors also offer clues. Some species of males court females in the hopes of being chosen. Other *Drosophila* males aggressively jump on females from the get-go, in a more wham, bam, thank you, ma'am, style. Fruit fly DNA analysis is easy, compared to other organisms. The fruit fly develops giant chromosomes in its salivary glands and other parts of its larvae. Different-colored bands on each chromosome can be read like road maps into its genetic history.

These genetic maps show that the thousand-plus fruit fly species all descended from a single colonist, or at most two. Using DNA trapped by amber fossils, scientists found evidence that two distinct Hawaiian fruit fly lineages began to split 30 million years ago. Kauai, the oldest surviving high Hawaiian island with the kind of rain forest habitat favored by fruit flies, is only about 5.1 million years old. Thus, the fascinating implication: The original fruit fly colonization occurred on older, more northern islands in the chain that have since disappeared. As one island degraded and lost its wet mountain habitat, the flies moved south to greener pastures.

JUST AS DNA TESTING has been used to settle human paternity cases, it has turned up some surprising relatives in the plant world as well. The genus *Viola,* for instance, is a moderate-sized and largely herbaceous group of about 550 species worldwide. Wagner identified seven Hawaiian species (and three subspecies) in his 1990 *Manual of the Flowering Plants of Hawaii.* For years, botanists thought that the original violet colonist in Hawaii must have come from South America, as they shared a similar appearance. Wrong, according to chromosome data. DNA showed the Hawaiian violets to be closely related to those in Alaska and along the Bering Strait: *Viola langsdorfii.* They don't look alike. The Arctic violets grow classic pansy-like flowers and circular leaves that we would all recognize as similar to common violet houseplants, while the Hawaiian violets sometimes grow into shrubs as tall as twelve feet.

The evolutionists only briefly puzzled over how a violet from the Arctic region could get to Hawaii. Obvious. By air. More than fifty species of migrating birds breed in the Arctic but winter in Hawaii. Conducting their own Darwin-like experiments, modern-day scientists trapped birds to examine their feathers, finding plentiful evidence of seed stowaways.

Not all new arrivals in Hawaii built dynasties. Wagner showed that 10 of the original 291 original plant colonists radiated into multiple new adaptations, so many that they account for about half of Hawaii's plant diversity of about one thousand native species. Of native birds, only the Hawaiian honeycreepers diverged into radiations. The 19 other native Hawaiian bird lineages exist in only one form.

Once established in their new tropical habitats, many of the newly evolved species lost their competitive edge. Plants discarded the ability to emit toxins, or the armament to deter herbivores with oils, resins, stinging hairs, or coarse textures. It's as if they expended all their energy into fitting into the new surroundings, and then kicked back, luxuriating in paradise. Under rapid, though irreversible, adaptation, some Hawaiian plant and animal species became excessively specialized to their niche environments, some no larger than a single valley. They lost whatever immunities and resistances they once had, becoming vulnerable to any import of disease or parasite. While this loss of competitive ability is exhibited in endemic island species around the world, nowhere are the native plants so poorly equipped for competition than in Hawaii. There is no easy explanation, but it means that almost any continental species of plant seems capable of moving in and annihilating the native inhabitants. Grazing by human-imported cattle and goats and rooting by pigs aids the death marches of these alien species, as weeds thrive on newly disturbed soil. Moreover, the native Hawaiian species show poor ability to replace themselves after disturbance.

This pernicious habit of alien invaders to move into newly plowed ground provides a particularly dismal outlook for conservation efforts. We can work like hell to weed the aliens by pulling up roots, but it only disturbs the soil and thus welcomes more intruders. And many of the invaders are spread by birds that eat their seeds and then widely excrete them like crop dusters. "Not only are weeds well-entrenched in many areas of the Hawaiian islands, but efforts to remove them would very likely only renew and widen the areas of disturbance and encourage more weedy growth than before," noted Sherwin Carlquist in his 1974 landmark book, *Island Biology*.

But all this genetic theory is difficult. When I came to the case of the Hawaiian silversword, I had a better sense of how the miracle of evolution can turn a lowly weed into a majestic tower of a plant.

Tourists come from continents away to trek up the cinder-covered dry slopes of the dead volcano of Haleakala on Maui. Many travel an hour and a half up the winding mountain road in the dark to watch dawn creep up over the crater's 10,023-foot-high summit. Others come to see the great silversword, *Argyroxiphium sandwichense*. As it nears death, it produces a spire of upward-turned, silvery bayonet-type spears. From its center rises one stem, up to six feet tall and covered by hundreds of purplish rosette flowers. And while its royal appearance is truly remarkable, its story is what draws the crowds.

Most likely birds carried sticky, resin-coated seeds from a now-extinct tarweed that was growing in coastal California. The avian carriers flew across the ocean, unknowingly delivering seeds and depositing them into the evolutionary cauldron of Hawaii, where they underwent a rapid transformation into the dramatic Hawaiian silverswords, greenswords, and some twenty-eight other island species in what is called "the silversword alliance." Originally in the sunflower family, in Hawaii tarweeds grew tall. And low. Leaf anatomy developed into varied shapes.

One species grows on Kauai's rainy Mount Waialeale. Another Kauai silversword cousin grows into a ten-foot-tall one-stem tree. Dryland species on Hawaii and Maui sprout hairs, thick leaves, and different internal tissues to cope with drought. Some of the dry land relatives form matlike clumps in lava fields. One wetland silversword species evolved into a vine. Other silverswords adapted to wet, poorly drained bogs. Or Alpine desert. Midlevel forest. Species moved back and forth between such niche climates at least five, and likely more, times over the last few million years, suggesting that a change of ecologies was fundamental to its diversification.

While the silversword exemplifies the drama of evolution, its near extinction illustrates both human destruction and human rescue.

Climbers to the Haleakala Volcano summit used to prove they had reached the summit by plucking a silversword flower and taking it home. Although the volcano was declared a National Park in 1916, park rangers didn't crack down on this vandalism until the 1930s. The first official count of silversword, in 1935, estimated that the total population had dwindled to four thousand individual plants.

Thanks to intensive replanting projects, the population swelled to 64,800 silverswords by 1991. Using Steve Perlman's paintbrush breeding techniques, Hawaiian Silversword Foundation volunteers and state foresters pollinated a cliff-dwelling variety, then collected seeds and grew thousands of seedlings in the University of Hawaii's Center for Conservation Research.

My own experience with trying to weed Kauai of the ivy gourd left me feeling that no matter how massive our efforts, they would probably only succeed in small pockets. Yet the silversword projects demonstrate how dedicated individuals and institutions can snatch a few species from extinction. Sherwin Carlquist, the author of Hawaii's evolutionary history, offered a fair-minded and plausible challenge: If there are reasonable, simple, practical measures to conserve the earth's most fragile inhabitants, why not take them?

PART THREE

Light After Darkness

CHAPTER FOURTEEN

Hearts in the Snow

*T*HAT JANUARY AFTERNOON the *pueo* swooped in circles, staking her territory around Garden head-quarters. Small and gray, this Hawaiian owl flies in daylight. I watched through the window in Dr. Klein's office as a group of us met to review the year's final budget numbers. As always, Dr. Klein commanded the head of the conference table, surrounded by easels holding architectural drawings of his expansionist plans for all of the Garden properties. Many donors liked to wait until December to review their tax bills before deciding how much to give away in charitable deductions. We sweated in the final days of the year as we opened envelopes that contained checks from board members of $5,000, $20,000, $50,000, and more.

Two or three times a day, Doug Kinney, the Garden's chairman of the board, telephoned from his Florida golf retreat, always growling, asking for the latest figures. A businessman, he wanted to report that the Garden had ended the year in the black. "How much do we need?" Doug demanded. If we hadn't received an expected gift, he called the reluctant trustee to remind him or her to step up to the plate.

"And so we balanced the budget," Dr. Klein announced to

the gathered staff. "But I submit," he said, his pasty complexion turning the telltale pink that signaled high pique, "that balancing the budget is not the mission of the Garden. Education and research and conservation are the mission of the Garden." *Right on, Dr. Klein!*

My attention faded from the staff meeting. As always during times of sorrow, my work sustained me, giving me a focus. The last two months blurred together in a river of grief as I recovered from my father's death. At age eighty he was still working two days a week, though he had grown frail from a series of small strokes. We had expected it when the massive, killing attack came. Still, I had not anticipated the penetrating sadness, the sudden engulfment in memories that brought sharp pain and the realization that he was gone forever.

Dr. Klein's secretary interrupted the staff meeting to ask, "Lucinda, are you taking a call from June in Minneapolis?"

"Oooh. That call I'll take," I told the group and got up from my chair to go to my office, happy to escape for a few minutes. I knew that my mother expected a visit from my nephew, Will. But my sister-in-law was on the phone to report that Will had been waiting at the Connecticut airport for three hours and Mom hadn't arrived to pick him up.

It was already 9 p.m. in Connecticut. I called Chuck, the young lawyer who lived across the street from my parents' house. "The house is dark," he reported. "I'll go over. Weird. I didn't see her get the Sunday paper yesterday. There was an ice storm here, and I don't think she's been out of the house for three days."

I put down the phone and went back into Dr. Klein's office. Forty-five minutes later came the second telephone call. "I better take that," I told Bill and the others at the meeting, laughing. "My mother seems to have gone off somewhere, so there's a family alert."

"Lucy, your mother is dead," Chuck said.

RITUAL TELLS US what to do. Call relatives. Plan another funeral. Go home to Connecticut again. I closed the door of my office and started telephoning. When I heard a knock on the door, I opened it to see Janet Klein. Bill had become so worried about me that he had called her in.

Later that night, Bill and Janet arrived at my cottage door, expressions of concern on their faces. I had turned down their dinner invitation, as I needed to pack for another emergency red-eye flight to Connecticut.

They carried twin Styrofoam takeout containers from their favorite Italian restaurant. "We couldn't decide whether you'd like spumoni or chocolate mousse, so we brought you both," Bill explained. Food, particularly chocolate, at a time of grief and crisis is never a mistake. I made tea and we sat in the living room as Sam the cat entertained us by walking from lap to lap in an oddly companionable evening. Instead of talking about the looming funeral, they decided to distract me with Garden and island gossip.

As they said good-bye, Sam slinked through Bill's ankles in a last bid for more attention. "That is one friendly cat," he said.

"Yes, he is," I said. "At least I'm pretty sure he's a he. Sometimes I'm not sure."

Bill picked up a willing Sam and laid him on his back and pointed out the genitalia. "And there's something about his head that looks male," said the professor.

"Good night," called Janet. "I'll pick you up around one o'clock to drive you to the airport."

HIGH PILES OF SNOW lined the streets. White buried all of Connecticut. My brother Breck unlocked the house and with apprehension we went into the foyer, icy cold because the heat had been turned way down. In the blue and white kitchen, we began to follow a trail of objects. Her eyeglasses lay upside down in the usual place on the counter next to the phone. When Dad was alive, he grabbed them away from her and washed them in a daily devotion. But now fingerprints smeared the lenses and dust settled in the corners. We walked with heavy steps down the hall into the bedroom. The flowered bed covers in the king-size bed lay at the foot in a tangle, as if turned back in a rush. Mom was constitutionally incapable of leaving a bed unmade during the day, so she hadn't been up very long. A small bowl on the bedside table cradled a half-eaten cracker.

We went back to the hall and looked into the small bathroom where she had died on the floor. The room reeked. Breck turned up the heat and went to get my bag from the car. After the overnight flight from Hawaii, I needed sleep. Most of the relatives would arrive tonight or tomorrow. But first I got down on my knees and scrubbed the bathroom floor.

The morning after the funeral service, a dozen relatives gathered to scatter the ashes in the quiet memorial garden next to the Universalist Church. No sun penetrated the flat, gray sky—just the kind of winter day that Mom hated. Eighteen inches of snow shrouded small trees and shrubbery in ghostly forms. Breck and our brother-in-law, Max, wielded shovels to break through a crust of ice to find a suitable place for the ashes.

They shoveled away snow from under a scrawny, leafless Japanese maple, the same spot where only two months before we had sprinkled Dad's remains. Dad loved Japanese maples so much that he used to drive around town in autumn to jot down locations of the trees with the brightest reds, then return in spring to pick up seeds to grow in coffee cans. When Breck and Max reached bare earth with their shovels, they revealed the pure white grains of Dad's ashes, stark against black dirt. Then Breck turned the shovel around to use it as a sculptor's tool. With a couple of decisive strokes, he carved the hole in the snow into the shape of a heart.

"Though we walk through the valley of the shadow of death," intoned the minister. Each in turn, we dipped a hand into a cardboard box of nearly weightless ash. I scooped up a tablespoon or two of gritty powder and cast it back and forth, to form a layer of fine gray over the particles of white.

BACK ON KAUAI, the early winter darkness caught me by surprise. I hadn't anticipated that the sun would set early, even if the weather didn't change much. For once home before dark, I took Sam for a walk down the long yard. The setting sun washed the plateau a varnished orange. Palms cast long black shadows, tinged with coolness, like a New England fall.

I strode up the small hill next to the cottage. Sam nibbled grass while I stopped in the green shadows to listen to the shama, a Hawaiian mockingbird, its cascading song lilting from branch to branch. Of course, the inevitable had happened. I had taken Sam for a checkup, and the moment the vet saw the brown, gray, and black fur, he said, "Oh, it's a girl." Turns out that mutiple coloring is a sex-linked female trait.

"Good thing you went into botany and not zoology," I ribbed Dr. Klein.

Now, as I reached the line of macadamia trees at the center of the yard, I turned back to call: "Sam, Sam, the jungle cat." Her head bobbed up, ears alert, one paw cocked like a bird dog. Then she came trotting low to the ground.

Hawaii, with its year-round breeding temperatures, fostered bounties of fleas, so for curative measures I bathed Sam. First I'd fill a bucket with tepid water, dip her, lather her up, then rinse her in the bucket again before holding her under the shower faucet for a final rinse. I can't say she ever liked it, but she loved her fresh-smelling coat. Steve Perlman said he shampooed his cat every weekend and the cat loved it so much that he'd jump into the outdoor sink.

I continued to walk farther down the long lawn until I stood under the giant mango tree where the tip of the plateau opened to a view over two valleys to the sea. As I headed back to the cottage, my faraway brass student lamps cast comforting orbs of golden light through the windows like beacons.

Night descended so thickly, so completely, that once inside, I rarely left again until morning. I would have given anything to be able to call a friend and talk. But because of the six-hour time difference between Hawaii and the East Coast, all my friends and family had long gone to bed by the time I left the office. I climbed the steps to the front porch and opened the cottage door. I smiled at the transformation that had been wrought. The cottage had changed from a place where no one would want to live to a comforting retreat, a lady's colonial plantation camp, full of light and air. The outdoors seemed to spill inside.

Bits and pieces of my previous life melded with the new surroundings. The blue and white Chinese rug created a frame for the white canvas-covered sofa and chaise. I had upholstered two chairs in a faint white and blue plaid and covered pillows in blue and white toile print. Here on Kauai I picked up more blue and white pillows, quilted silk with Hawaiian themes of coconut palms and pineapples, swimming sea turtles and leaping dolphins. Deep red and blue antique Oriental carpets glowed like stained glass against the painted slate-colored floors. A dark wood Chinese armoire and two coffee tables with a Far Eastern motif salvaged from the cottage's original furnishings helped create a South Seas theme.

The massive purging of possessions I had undergone in Philadelphia had simplified life. No fancy dishes or fussy furniture. I had brought only a few remnants of elegance to contrast with my primitive surroundings. Crystal and silver perfume bottles and embroidered sheets added some glamour. I propped on top of the armoire a gold-framed oil painting of a Connecticut autumn scene that I had bought cheap at auction and didn't care if the tropical climate ruined it. Some doubts crept in about the degree to which this scheme bespoke of New England. Those misgivings vanished when I visited the Mission Houses Museum in Honolulu. As I walked through the wood-frame house that had been shipped in pieces from Boston around Cape Horn in 1820, I recognized New England dark furniture. Straight backs and hard seats emanated moral rectitude against tropical indolence. I had laughed when I saw the toile curtains.

I could have left all my possessions behind. But like the first Connecticut missionaries who settled in Hawaii, I drew comfort from the power of a few familiar belongings. That's why we call them belongings, because they give us a sense of belonging to something when we've left behind one life and have no compass to guide us through the next. I liked dining at my Queen Anne dining room table from my great aunt Elizabeth who had lived in the Connecticut countryside. I often touched the wood jewelry box my father had carved for me.

As darkness fell, the banks of windows turned into black mirrors, entombing the cottage. I hustled into flannel pajamas, socks, and a robe. Although winter brings sunny mornings and usually a perfect eighty degrees by 11 a.m., nights grow chilly up here in the hills, with temperatures falling occasionally into the fifties. Like most houses in the islands, the cottage had neither heat nor air-conditioning, so I closed all the windows to keep warm. I slept with both blanket and comforter.

Evenings I crawled home exhausted. Too many foreign realms overwhelmed me: the strange flora of this hothouse climate; the mellifluous Hawaiian names in the almost consonant-less language; a new house; new routine. With so many conversations required in the office and so much work to be done, my days were very long. The sudden deaths of both parents left me in a state of gray funk. Every night I meant to write at least five thank-you notes to people who had made gifts to a scholarship for medical students in honor of Mom and Dad. Yet grief wearied me so heavily that I couldn't write a one. I hadn't enough energy to make dinner. That night I popped an envelope of popcorn in the microwave, poured a glass of milk, then carried the paper envelope to the couch and ate popcorn lying down while watching the old movie *South Pacific*—filmed entirely on Kauai.

With familiarity, I watched as World War II Navy nurse Nellie Forbush wavered over the decision to marry the handsome island plantation owner Emile, so different from anyone she knew in Little Rock, Arkansas. She learns that Emile had killed a man in France before he fled to the South Pacific.

"What are you running away from, Emile?" she asks.
"Who is not running away from something?" he answers.

Nellie returns to the Navy base, where the handsome young lieutenant Joe Cable from Philadelphia agrees with her that life here is too strange, too different. He sings the nostalgic song: "Far, far away, Philadelphia, PA." I remembered my own forsaken Philadelphia. Armageddon had arrived at the *Inquirer.* Another downsizing buyout was offered, and more than twenty-five writers and editors, including several of the top brass, took it. Corporate headquarters demanded another increase in profits. I couldn't go back even if I wanted to. Nor had I any reason to return to Connecticut anymore. Now I really was marooned.

Sam snuggled close to me on the couch, waking briefly and stretching out her front legs in a request for petting. I complied. With regular meals, Sam's dusty gray coat had deepened into a deep gloss. I stroked her black-bottomed feet, one palomino-colored paw, and tiger-striped face. Dr. Klein had hooted: "That cat moved in on you so fast you didn't know what hit you." Turning serious, Dr. Klein added bluntly, "I'm worried that your social life revolves around your cat." Privately I felt that I could do worse. He and Janet constantly invited me along on their island activities. We drove up to Waimea Canyon—the gorge that ran from the high peak to ocean, its sides banded in shades of red mineral—or into Kokee State Park, Dr. Klein lecturing on tropical botany. They roped me into a benefit dinner at Wilcox Memorial Hospital and concerts and plays at the

Kauai Community College auditorium. On new-moon nights we drove out to the Navy base for the astronomy club stargazing events. Sometimes I hiked with Rick Hanna and his friends up into the misty rain forest on the Pihea Trail or through the fog drifts over the spongy Alakai Swamp, an incongruous marsh over the island's high-elevation aquifer.

Mostly, though, I hadn't the zest to start building a new life. As *South Pacific* concluded with its happy-ending sunset, I turned on a Beethoven CD and lay back on my chaise. Albert Schweitzer once said, "There are two means of refuge from the miseries of life: music and cats." How true, although Dr. Schweitzer obviously never had a garden. Sam climbed up and over me to her pillow roost, and settled against the back of my head. We closed our eyes.

THE ALARM RANG in the dead of night to wake me in time to watch the Leonid meteor showers. I climbed to the top of the ridge on my cottage property, then sat on a low beach chair, wrapped in a terry cloth robe and sipping coffee. The cocks crow all night, not just at dawn. I can hear the deep lowing of cattle grazing on nearby farms. I live alone on five acres of darkness, on a small island in the middle of the Pacific. People ask me if I am afraid, but I'm not. The police blotter column in *The Garden Island* newspaper provided more entertainment than cause for alarm, with its accounts of loose horses, cockfights, and often comical altercations. Crime seemed far away. I struck a match, surprised at the enormous sound in the deep silence. I pulled a smoky drag on a cigarette. I hadn't smoked for a couple of years, but in times of upset it provided a quick fix. It made me feel close to Dad. We used to joke that his blood consisted of a brew of cigarette smoke, scotch, and black coffee. He liked the stars, too.

Sam ran up the lawn to join me and climbed on my lap, assuming her favorite petting posture, forepaws hooked over my knees, back presented for stroking. The night skies offered some of the best stargazing on the planet. Far from lights of any major city, or even neighbors, galaxies swirled in brilliant profusion. The Southern Cross sank low in the sky. A moving point of light, like a plane, evaporated. Comet? Perhaps, but too slow. Then a streak of light fell vertically from the Big Dipper, like a drip. Definitely comet.

I missed Mom and Dad, longed to see their faces, hear their voices, know them beyond the identities I had assigned them as parents. Bill Klein said he had experienced the same phenomenon after the death of his father. "It's as if your parents have to die before you really understand who they are," he said. Memories tumbled together. Mom met Dad during World War II at the University of Minnesota Hospital, my father a psychiatric intern, my mother a student nurse.

My mother was a first-generation American, her mother and father German immigrants who arrived separately, met in Chicago, and married, probably unwisely in my grandfather's case. His three daughters suffered his rages and would remark that he never should have had children.

My parents rarely spoke about their childhoods. Once my mother told me about the shame she felt about having to live at home while attending the University of Minnesota Nursing School. The poor students ate their homemade lunches on a bench where they hoped no one would notice them or their brown bags, a searing brand of poverty. My aunt showed us the location of one of the many cheap apartments she and my mother had lived in as children in south Minneapolis. Certainly Mom would not disclose that secret. But she had class. An expert seamstress, she used *Vogue* patterns to conjure up a wardrobe. While Mom was getting dressed in her mustard tweed suit to chauffeur us to doctor or dentist appointments, she permitted us to forage through her blue earring box. All the wiles of womanhood were contained in that box along with tiny turquoise knob earrings and a heavy set of faux pearls and rhinestones. Later, when I inherited the box after her death, I realized it was only a plastic case lined with rayon velvet. I kept it, all the same.

Dad had almost as humble beginnings. His father kept a dry goods store along the main street in Sterling, Kansas, a town whose locations were used for the film *Picnic,* a tale of escape from small-town restraints. Dad told how days would go by during the Depression without his father selling even a single handkerchief. Dad won a Summerfield scholarship to the University of Kansas, then advanced to Yale Medical School. His brother, Richard, ended up at Harvard Law. According to family legend, when Uncle Dick graduated from law school he announced he would travel west until no one had ever heard of the name *Fleeson,* a reference to my interfering great-aunt Doris. The joke was that he settled in Bellingham, Washington, as far west and north as one could go.

Aunt Doris Fleeson was the family celebrity, a famed journalist and World War II correspondent for the *Woman's Home Companion* — the only publication she could find to hire a woman — and a longtime national political columnist. She was president of the Washington Press Club, the precursor to the

National Press Club. Whenever in Washington, I'd visit her picture hanging outside the second-floor ladies' room of the Press Club. That was fitting, as she had forced the U.S. Capitol Press Galleries to install women's bathrooms, unheard of when she first started covering Congress. Tart-tongued and bossy, she had tried to push Uncle Dick into running for Congress. My father just ignored her, so sadly I never met her.

My parents' ascendancy to professional rank and middle-class comfort represented more accomplishments, over more serious obstacles, than any of their children would achieve. Careers, five children, fifty-two years of marriage.

In the 1950s, Mom and Dad enthusiastically settled into postwar prosperity in the small suburb of Hopkins, Minnesota. Dad was a neighborhood hero called to the scene when a kid broke his leg. At the school fair he manned the popcorn machine and escorted me on the cakewalk. In probably my father's boldest moment, he bought a sleek racing sloop and dashed about Lake Minnetonka. In his second boldest move, he left the University of Minnesota to help build a new medical school at the University of Connecticut. I had just turned thirteen.

We desperately missed the *Paradise Lost* of Minnesota. My father wore gardening shorts to their first Connecticut neighborhood cocktail party, a glaringly gauche move as the other men dressed in suit and ties. Worse, when invited to take a yacht club sailboat out for a spin on Long Island Sound, he turned the boat turtle, damaged the rigging, and slunk home embarrassed, never to be invited again. Not many got close to him. He never talked about his disappointments, although we all knew about them, as he would withdraw into near silence, sometimes for months. More and more he descended to his basement workshop, where he carved beautiful chess sets of cut and polished stone. The projects went on for decades, until he started keeping a scotch bottle down there, and my mother made him promise not to use power tools in the evening hours anymore. My mother dealt with Connecticut by becoming the executive director of a social agency—but like my father, at night her drinking hours grew longer, the brooding darker. I quit my own nightly martinis several years ago when I recognized that I was following the same pattern. I escaped that genetic Molotov cocktail, but narrowly.

All of us seemed to slink around in those years, as things started going wrong. One brother abandoned his wife and three small babies, leaving my parents to help with their raising. We lost another brother to mental illness. Great balls of sadness descended, and the family solution was to pour alcohol over it all. Galactically dysfunctional, one brother called us. I remembered what Zorba the Greek said when asked if he was married: "Oh, yes. Wife. Children. Home. Everything. The full catastrophe."

For me, the move to Connecticut occurred just as I entered teen years, a time that magnified the need for social acceptance. It took years to recover from my disastrous first day at school, arriving at the bus stop decked out in new wool plaid vest, corduroy skirt, and uncool white ankle socks. I quickly learned that junior high girls wore light cotton summer clothes well into chilly October, until the day when the group, en masse, made the seasonal wardrobe change. And *never* ankle socks. Only penny loafers, barefoot.

Sartorial blunders aside, we were lonely.

Neither of my parents adopted pretensions or materialism.

They valued education, common sense, fairness, fulfilling responsibilities, returning library books on time, hard work, and Democratic politics. My parents had aged without my paying attention. Just three years ago, we had all convened at an Arizona dude ranch to celebrate Mom and Dad's fiftieth wedding anniversary. He smoked a cigarette astride a horse, looking like a prototypical Marlboro man. We all smoked. You could have more than two drinks at the Fleeson house and smoke all you wanted.

After Dad's funeral, Mom insisted on driving me to the airport for my 6:30 a.m. flight to Hawaii. All of the relatives had already left. Snow crunched loudly under the tires in the freezing night air as we passed snow-covered fields and dark farmhouses. "That was a nice send-off," she said. "We did him proud." The Universalist Church minister really revved up for the service. Two of Dad's medical school colleagues delivered inspired eulogies. During that rushed week, I slept on the living room couch because relatives crowded into Mom and Dad's small retirement house. Late one night, I shivered in my nightgown outside the closed bathroom door, waiting my turn. The door opened, and my sister Libby came out, also in her nightgown. Mom, in a long nightdress, opened her bedroom door. In the dark, Libby and I wrapped our arms around Mom. We each pressed a cheek against her cheeks. "My girls," she murmured. "My sweet girls."

I had told her, "Now, Mom. Come out to Hawaii in March, after the Garden's board meeting,"

"I'd rather come in February when the weather's bad here," she repeated.

We've already been over that. "I just can't do it then. I'll be running around getting ready for the board meeting. March is better," I said with a finality meant to close the discussion.

She and I usually reverted to patterns established in my rebellious teenager years. Mothers generally fall into two categories: those who abandon or those who smother. Oddly she was both. I resisted her intrusiveness, her supervision, and her constant inquisitiveness, countering by withdrawing into quiet secrecy. Her only career advice was so retro, so unliberated: Study nursing so I could marry a doctor. I felt an unspoken dialogue underneath most of my exchanges with Mom. *You missed all the important things in life,* she'd reproach me with her eyes. *Had I?* I would answer. Poor Mom. She wanted us all to be conventional, settled, with happy family lives. Instead, she had two daughters who were non-producers, her name for childless women.

"Romeo and Juliet" one of their friends had called them, in explanation of why their deaths came so closely together. We never knew exactly why Mom died, as we elected no autopsy—she was dead anyway, we figured. "Don't you know? She died of a broken heart," said my brother. Some cruelly implied that she was better off this way. I resented the easy assumption that she simply gave up and died rather than face life alone. I wanted to shout: "Where do you think we are? India? We don't throw the wife on the husband's funeral pyre!"

And yet, guiltily, I realized that without parents I could do whatever I wanted. My own father had quoted Freud to me: "No man is free until his father is dead." Adulthood had finally arrived, and I had no excuses. I had protested their vision of conventionality for me but now realized that I had adopted and internalized those constraints as my own. I could peel off cultural expectations, parental approval, and outdated identity struggles, yet I still needed to discover what remained at the core. The task of man is consciousness, Jung said. Looking up into the vast night sky, I felt immeasurably small, as if I were at the bottom of an immense glassed snowflake dome, shaken until every particle whirls.

CHAPTER FIFTEEN

A Walk on Mahaulepu—
Deconstructing Extinction

WHENEVER IN NEED of a restoration of the spirit, I drove to Mahaulepu, the stretch of deserted white sand I deemed the best beach on earth. My purpose was often simply to be on the beach, to see it, feel the warmth of the sand or let the infinity of the waves wash over me while I made my amateur naturalist's observations.

As sundown approached, I lurched from side to side along the rutted road trying to miss the deepest potholes. More than once I'd gotten stuck in a big mud hole. But willing young locals who'd been diving for *tako*—octopus—came along and cheerfully pushed me out. On either side of the dirt track, tall silver tassels of sour grass, *Digitaria insularis,* rippled elegantly in the breeze across gentle hills. Both it and a shorter, more purple finger grass, *Chloris radiata,* are native to the Pacific tropics, which means they are growing, more or less, in a place close to their origin.

That couldn't be said of most of what I saw. As I neared the beach, light blue and violet morning glory blooms gaily lined the roadside. It's become a pest plant. A ring-neck pheasant burst into the air with a soft thudding. Before such introductions were tightly controlled, modern hunters imported pheasants and other game birds to the islands. At the end of an even more deeply rutted, muddy road lay a small cove, gloriously empty at the end of the day.

Walking along the shoreline, I stopped at a small tidal pool to watch tiny fish zip away from my intruder's eyes. The endless stretch of turquoise Pacific, the meeting ground of sand and surf and the glow of the sun, put me in a state of serene coexistence with the island elements. The sea reminded me of its infinite power to break mountains into grains of sand, to wash away entire islands, to rise and fall in waves for vast, endless eons. I saw our human world as subject to its rhythms and pace, as it undulates and roars without acknowledgment of our presence.

After every big storm I searched for the petroglyphs, although I never expected to find them. Even Nelson Abreu, the Grove Farm security guard who locks and unlocks the Mahaulepu gate in mornings and evenings, had never seen them. One lucky morning after a storm, a sandstone ledge at water's edge had surfaced, revealing the carved outline of a turtle about the size of my hand. Nearby, a primitive one-armed man with a spear was scratched in the soft stone. Later that day I rushed back with my friend Fran to share the sighting. By then the tide had started to surge in, settling sand over the rock ledge, and we could not find the carvings.

At the end of the beach, the brown muddy water of Waiopili Stream empties into the ocean. I bent aside dusty milo trees to head upstream, then veered toward a sheer limestone bluff. In the corner, a triangular cave entrance beckoned. I often crouched down to hop through a low tunnel, damp and clammy. The dark entrance widened almost immediately, leading to a dappled-sunlit open sinkhole.

David A. Burney, a scrawny paleontologist from Fordham University, had begun drilling thirty-foot-deep samples into this unusual limestone cave system. When he first popped up on Kauai, Dr. Klein immediately befriended him. Bill encouraged Burney to put together an ambitious project proposal and lent him living quarters in a Garden cottage. The sinkhole began to yield an extraordinary diversity of plant and animal remains, remarkably preserved.

Long gone are the King Tut glory days of archeology when diggers exhumed treasure chambers of ancient rulers. Nowadays, archeologists detect the presence of humans from microscopic particles of charcoal. They reconstruct diet and agricultural economies from the tiniest of fossilized seeds and whole plant ecologies from spores or, in the case of Dave Burney, duck turds.

Not much carbon dating of fossils or other remains had been carried out in Hawaii, and on Kauai in particular. There was too little money and not enough interest until now. As a result, for years more than six hundred archeological samples sat unanalyzed at the Bishop Museum. But Burney brought impressive credentials to the task and won grants from the National Oceanic and Atmospheric Administration, the National Science Foundation, the Smithsonian Institution, and the National Geographic Society. He had used carbon dating and other paleoecological techniques in Madagascar caves to pinpoint the period when extinct lemurs and a dwarf hippopotamus flourished. He dated human arrival on Puerto Rico and studied the relationship between humans and cheetahs in Africa. In 1988, he performed carbon-dating experiments on a cache of duck coprolites — fossilized turds — deposited in a Maui lava tube by an extinct waterfowl. By analyzing pollen grains and spores, Burney determined that the duck ate a diet of almost exclusively fern fronds.

He was drawn to the Kauai sinkhole, the largest intact limestone cave system in the Hawaiian Islands, because it was so easily accessible yet almost entirely undisturbed. Old maps showed that a large pond had flooded the entrance prior to the twentieth century. Because the present floor is still damp in spots, and because it lies only a few feet above sea level, Burney theorizes that a lake or marsh likely occupied the site. All these factors meant that sand and silty clay slowly accumulated on the sinkhole floor, undisturbed. Each layer trapped and preserved mollusk shells, pollen spores, tree seeds, and animal bones, as well as tools and other human detritus. Determine a date for each layer and decode history.

Burney argues that no other single date is more important in evaluating possible causes for extinctions than the arrival of humans. Although he exudes an air of a mad scientist, Burney looks more like an Amish farmer, with a knobby nose and a long, scraggly white beard. His cheery optimism attracted more than three hundred volunteers on Kauai, who willingly got covered in brown mud head to toe.

Investigators and his trained volunteers removed sediment by trowel, teaspoon, or hand, then wet-screened the material in fine mesh boxes. They set out bones and shells to air-dry, while sealing perishable wood, seeds, and wooden artifacts into plastic containers for storage in refrigerators.

Back in mainland labs, experts analyzed samples from each

sediment layer for the sudden presence and volume of micro-scopic charcoal particles—evidence of fire, and an effective method to elucidate human arrival.

Some of the foremost experts on bird, mammal, and mollusk fossils, as well as Warren Wagner of the Smithsonian, compared the Mahaulepu fossils with the vast holdings in their museums and herbariums. The result is a ten-thousand-year natural history of Kauai, all in one place.

About four hundred thousand years ago, chalky sand dunes solidified into rock. Acidic groundwater carved the Mahaulepu cave, occasionally depositing mollusks and other sea creatures on its floor. The walls weakened. The roof collapsed about seven thousand years ago, nearly blocking the cave entrance and seal-ing it against incoming tides. Silt and sand slowly settled, trap-ping shells from at least fourteen different endemic land snails, a giant land crab, and more than forty bird species—about half now extinct on Kauai.

A bone fragment from the ignoble Pacific rat denotes the first presence of arriving Polynesians. Burney found the fragment of a pelvic bone of *Rattus exulans* ten feet down, in layers of sediment dating from A.D. 1039 to 1241. No doubt the rodent had stowed away on Polynesian canoes. While modernists tend to blame white Europeans for all the extinctions in Hawaii, the wreckage actually began as soon as any humans, white or brown, stepped foot on the fragile island ecosphere. The bones of many birds now extirpated from Kauai can still be found in the sinkhole's layers from the Polynesian era—the Laysan duck and the Hawaiian hawk, for instance—but they and endemic snails became more scarce. Burney's crew found bones of large flightless ducks—evidence that the turtle-jawed moa-nalo once waddled over the island. Probably related to the mallard, it had grown as big as a turkey, equipped with a tortoise-like beak to mow down grasses like a turtle.

By the time the Renaissance occurred in Europe (A.D. 1430–1665) artifactual evidence indicates that Polynesians lived near the sinkhole, tossing their postprandial bones and other refuse into it. Historians have long presumed that the new Hawaiians hunted and roasted the fat, flightless ducks, thereby quickly contributing to the extinction of the moa-nalos. But although Burney found lots of chicken, dog, and pig bones from feasts, flightless duck skeletons had already become scarce by this time.

Pollen, seed, and plant fossils show that the early Hawaiians found a profusion of native trees and other plants growing along the dry coast—rare Kauai species that now survive only in small numbers, atop mountains or in high-elevation rain forests. Burney documented a wealth of native *loulu* (*Pritchardia*), including a species that no longer grows on Kauai. Interestingly, he also found screw pines, or *hala* trees, extensively used by native Hawaiians for weaving and long presumed to have been imported by the earlier Polynesians. Not so, says Burney. They predate humans.

Burney detected the arrival of Captain Cook on Kauai by the sudden presence of iron—nails, sharp tools, and other bits—previously unknown to the stone-age islanders. Even before Cook, the Hawaiians had cleared much of the coastal lands on Kauai for complex agricultural systems. They dammed lowlands to grow taro, and constructed seawater fish ponds. But while the Polynesians had contributed to the loss of the native island ecology, it was nothing compared to the rapid and chaotic transformation after contact with Europeans.

Many previously well-represented plant species disappeared entirely. Others became increasingly rare. The remaining native terrestrial snail species declined after European arrival, then disappeared entirely once a carnivorous American snail arrived—*Euglandina rosea*. During the nineteenth century, the sinkhole's abundant bones of cows, horses, and other European livestock supported historical accounts and photographs that feral livestock ranged along the coast, eating any vegetation in sight. Burney's pollen data confirmed the open and disturbed character of the landscape at this time and the introduction of trees and other European plants. A thick layer of sand from the denuded landscape blew into the sinkhole and settled. By the twentieth century, plantation owners drained the pond outside the cave, plowed the nearby fields, and quarried the hills. All led to the highest sedimentation rates recorded at the site—more than one hundred times the previous rate.

Ironically, I seek spiritual restoration at Mahaulepu, although the site is yielding a record of the sad loss of Hawaii's biology. While Warren Wagner studies the genesis of the island's plant life, Dave Burney deconstructs its demise. Yet Burney has big plans for the Mahaulepu sinkhole. On the mainland, sometimes landscapes can be restored by a process known as ecological recovery—simply let the system alone, keep people out of it, and the native landscape will eventually recover. "That never works in Hawaii," says Burney. "No management is the worst. Exotics gain the upper hand."

Burney wants to stage what is called a "rehabilitation," an attempt to restore the elements of the sinkhole's original ecology without trying a complete restoration or recreation of the original system. Already he has compiled a wish list of trees and plants that would have been at home here. Steve Perlman and Ken Wood have been collecting seeds from elsewhere on Kauai and throughout Polynesia to grow in the Garden's nursery. In the following months and years I'd return to the sinkhole, astonished by the lost world being reconstructed.

CHAPTER SIXTEEN

Mango Madness

*A*S I SETTLED MORE into Kauai, I became involved in the lives of new friends. So when the coconut wireless telegraphed the news that John Rapozo had throat cancer, I worried, even more when I heard that his doctor wanted to removed his vocal chords. The image of Big John without a voice struck me as impossibly unfair. His rough island pidgin, the authoritative commands leveled at other men, the sentences that grew quicker and tumbled together when he was excited—they were as much a part of John Rapozo as his calloused fingers.

I telephoned his home that night. "John, what's going on?"

"The doctor said he's going to cut. He said if he don't cut, it's going to be all over for me."

As I walked into Garden headquarters the next morning, Dr. Klein was bent over his secretary's desk, arranging flights to Honolulu. He had gone into his memory banks of all the hundreds of people he had charmed over the years. He remembered a prominent cancer research scientist at the University of Pennsylvania. Magically, John Rapozo had an appointment tomorrow with the best cancer doctor in Honolulu. Dr. Klein quietly paid for John's airfares.

After a week of tests in Honolulu, John announced that there would be no surgery. He now spoke in a scratchy whisper, as radiation treatment had begun. "The doctor, he laid down the law," he said. "No more smoking. And he said I've got to lose weight and eat right. I'll never sing again. But I'll talk."

As often happens in crisis, our friendship deepened during the hard coming months.

THE TRADE WINDS had arrived from the northeast Pacific, exhaling their soft, welcoming breezes, blowing out the recent humidity, and tempering the hot tropical sun with puffs of clouds. The trades transform summer from unbearable to paradise, and bring a lightness and sparkle to the air, particularly on Kauai.

One Saturday morning, I walked into the clear morning air to join James outside the cottage. He seemed to have realized that I would not change his routine or duties, so he had relaxed and started showing me the treasures in my yard. James plucked a couple of low leaves from the lollipop-shaped "Autograph Tree." Using a blunt pencil, he scratched my name on a shiny leaf. A half hour later, the letters developed bright and clear, like a print in a photo lab. The macadamia trees had started to drop dark brown, globe-shaped nuts. When their thick husks split, they revealed hard marbles. My trusty *Wise Encyclopedia of Cookery,* source for solving all cooking conundrums, warned that the hard shell would crack an ordinary nutcracker. When I told James this, he laughed. "You got to find a rock with a little dent in it, put it in, smash it. Don't eat too many, you get trots." The lychee trees now bore cherry-sized pink balls with a hard rind covered with spikes. Their cloudy white flesh resembles a

peeled grape. The mango trees grew thousands of elongated ob-
long fruit of dark jade that blushed yellow, bronze, and reddish.
James sniffed dismissively at them. "Water mangos. Watery inside," he said. On Kauai the prized mangos are Haydens. The
gardening staff carefully monitor the Hayden trees in Allerton
Garden. When the mangos turn into a red ripeness, the fruit
mysteriously disappears.

But plenty of people liked my mangos. My friend Jeanie
came over with her own bags and took away dozens. She sent
some of them back, in the form of Mango Betty, made just like
the apple version, although tangier. Rick Hanna picked a year's
supply to freeze for mango smoothies. Not content to reach the
lower branches, he used a picker on an extension pole to go after
perfect specimens at the top. We peeled them with potato peel-
ers at my kitchen sink, then sliced and bagged chunks until our
hands were almost raw.

Sometimes locals came and asked for permission to cut some
of the bamboo shoots that lined the hill drive. I had pestered
James several times to dig up some shoots so I could see how to
eat them myself. He disapproved: "Shoots are bamboo *keikis* (babies). Dig up all the *keikis* and pretty soon, no more bamboo."

All the same, today he went to the tool shed and came out
with a machete. We walked up and down the bamboo tunnel,
searching for young stalks. James kneeled by a thick, pointed
spear that looked as tough as a rhinoceros horn. He whacked it
off near the ground and handed me a two-foot shoot. Not satisfied, he sheared off a more tender, one-foot spear. I boiled and
boiled it, until it turned a translucent pink and tasted awful.
Later, John Rapozo counseled that I should have frequently
changed the cooking water.

I continued to ask James questions about the Allertons, feints and advances which he usually resisted. Despite a growing obsession with unraveling the Allerton story, I could find few clues about them or their lives. Robert and John Allerton lived guardedly. I began tracking down Garden scientists, employees, friends, and others who knew the Allertons in their later years but found that the two Allertons left little evidence of their interior lives. Their only record was a material one, of their elegant possessions, many now in museums. Scholars in the tiny, growing field of gay and lesbian history say homosexuals who lived through eras of prejudice or banishment typically destroyed incriminating diaries or other records. Gay history must be written by inference and analogy, pieced together from slim hints and clues.

I tried James again. To my surprise, he returned the next day bearing a stack of scrapbooks.

James began working as a gardener for the Allertons in the mid-1950s. After two years, the Allertons called him to work in the house. "They wanted me to start immediately, serving lunch to guests that day," James remembered. "I told them I had to go home and get my fancy clothes. John said, 'No, no,' and took me into his room and gave me shirt and shoes. They were so big on me, I look like a clown. Then they show me, 'Do this, do that, take the dishes this way.' They had these tiny little coffee cups—what you call them, demitasse? I had never seen them before in my life. So I serve them, so nervous the spoons rattle on the plates." James's wife, Sarah, started doing laundry for the Allertons, and then Robert said she had better come inside, too. In those days, the house was often full of houseguests, mostly men, creating undercurrents of jealousy.

"James, what did you all think about all that?" I asked.

"Whatever they do, they do," he said. James had tremendous admiration for Robert and John Allerton.

Anyone of import who could get the right introduction wangled a visit to Lawai-Kai. Jackie Kennedy alighted from a helicopter on the beach, just in time for a tour and cocktails. Robert showed her his collection of ballet books. James met John Wayne and other stars who filmed movies at Lawai-Kai. When Richard Nixon stopped by, John asked James to take pictures of him talking with the president, and James showed me his photo albums to prove it.

"I've seen poor and I've seen rich, and I like poor better," was James's conclusion. "The rich, all they talk about is money, money, money. I seen. I served them all. They would be invited for nice meal, nice time, and then they would want something, ask them for something. That's how it works."

James drove off, done reminiscing for the day. I walked down to the giant mango tree. Rick had left his fruit-picking basket, and I extended it to its longest length. Above my head dangled a prize specimen. If I stood on my toes, I just might reach it. With a jiggle of the pole, the mango plopped into the basket. It was a moment of sweet happiness. I couldn't explain it, but even though I had few close friends yet, and grieved the deaths of my parents, I felt more alive, more healthy, and less lonely here than I did in Philadelphia. The insomnia that racked my nights in Philadelphia had disappeared, and I slept soundly through the night. Even my allergies had improved.

Isabella Bird had also sampled mangos. "The mango is an exotic fruit," she wrote, "and people think a great deal of it. . . . I think it tastes strongly of turpentine at first, but this is a heresy.

The only way of eating it in comfort is to have a tub of water beside you. It should be eaten in private by any one who wishes to retain the admiration of his friends."

Now I spent much of my time outside the office in a bathing suit and flip-flops. Even the elastic strap of a swimsuit sometimes felt too restrictive, so alone on weekends at the cottage I'd wear only a *pareo,* a beach scarf, as a sarong. The scented breezes and easy lifestyle made me want to shed my old skin along with my clothes.

I was totally alone. I took off the swimsuit I wore for gardening and ate the mango naked. Why not? No one could see me. Juice ran down my arms, but I didn't care. I tentatively started a forgotten ballet step. Then it came back to me in a surge of remembrance, and I danced a waltz, spinning around the yard in leaps and pirouettes.

CHAPTER SEVENTEEN

Last Tango in Paradise

O N MY MORNING JOGS, I kept running into the oversexed Poseidon with whom I had shared the outdoor shower at Poipu Beach in my early days on Kauai. In my mind I called him "The Surfer." His name was Cal. One Sunday morning after a swim I confided to him that I wasn't quite sure about my snorkeling technique. "I float on the surface and look down, but I haven't figured out how to dive," I confessed. "I'm afraid that water will go down the tube."

"That's not so hard to learn. You want me to show you?"

"Yeah. That would be great."

"When do you want to go?"

"How about right now?

"Okay. I'll get my gear from the car."

I watched as he returned carrying a surfboard under one arm and a net bag of masks and snorkel tubes in the other hand. Barefoot, he wore only a faded pair of surfing jams. He carefully laid the board on the sand and dug one hand down the front of his swim trunks, pulling out a small plastic bag of bread crumbs. "Fish food," he explained.

He waded into the water, floating the surfboard. "Hold onto the board while you gain confidence," he instructed. Underwater, through my mask, I watched as he dove with powerful strokes, his hair floating around him in a nimbus, like an angel's. He released handfuls of food, drawing toward him mobs of fish. Small fish twisted and scattered in zigs and zags. Bigger ones raced to his hands, grabbing crumbs in dazzling antics.

Diving together, gesticulating underwater to a companion, and allowing myself to be pulled into deeper water reminded me of slow dancing. Our heads broke the surface at the same time and we reached for the board, breathing hard. One of his hands grazed mine as he grabbed hold, and the touch was warm, flush from the cold water that brought the blood to the surface.

"That was great," I said. "Can you show me how to blow the water out of the tube when I come up?"

"That's more advanced," he said judiciously. "You're getting tired. Do baby steps. You've had enough for today."

I nodded meekly. We got out of the water and toweled off, our bare skin close and salt-kissed. "Thanks a million," I said as I walked away. I had become accustomed to the order of my life and didn't entirely welcome the reentry of sexual anticipation. It generated fear as well as excitement, as it was both certain to be fulfilled if I wanted it to be, yet uncertain enough to be unpredictable, the kind of taut lust that gathers force and speed until it becomes unstoppable. I remembered the febrile blood rise that could spill into a headlong, risky, full-speed-ahead torrent. Let loose, it could fly me to the moon or break me on the rocks below. Perhaps the only thing more dangerous would be to say no. I was aging. Sometimes I worried that I had forgotten how to do it anymore.

I turned and called out, "Come for lunch sometime."

• • •

THE NEXT WEEK he telephoned. "I'd like to take you up on your offer for lunch," he said.

"What do you like to eat?" I asked, immediately imagining luscious tropical fruits, a composed salad.

"Sandwiches," he said simply.

He arrived on Saturday, a half hour early. I was outside, unloading my saddle from the car trunk, sweaty and disheveled after a morning ride.

"You're early," I yelped. "I'm filthy. You're going to have to wait while I take a shower." I shooed him to a chair and handed him a stack of magazines. "I'll be quick," I promised as I backed away, struck again by the power of his physicality.

Back in the kitchen, my hair damp and curled from bathroom steam, I hurriedly gathered sandwich ingredients and laid them on the counter. "Chicken all right?" I said in the overbright voice of the nervous as he came into the room.

He didn't answer. From behind, his body circled mine, a bare tanned arm catching me by the waist and pulling me backward against him.

"Why don't I give you a back rub?" he whispered.

I laughed at the clichéd pretense. "I don't think that's such a good idea," I said, intent on the lettuce.

In reply, he spun me around in one sure motion, laughing as he bent his head. Our mouths touched, our breasts cleaved, but I kept my feet a teenager's chaste distance away. With easy nonchalance, he reached up my skirt, cupped a cheek, and pressed me to him, from chest to knee. We spun and strained, I nearly gasping when he released me.

"Just a little back rub. It will relax you," he said levelly.

"Oh, no, no," I protested like a high school girl in the back of a car. He had unzipped my skirt and slipped it down to the floor. His hands roamed under my T-shirt as if I were already naked. Silently, he turned me against him and started walking us to the back of the house. In the small bedroom he pulled off my shirt with one hand, then turned to the bed and picked up two pillows, stacking one on top of the other. He released his own surfing jams with a pull of a string and kicked them off. Oh god, I heard myself say over and over, where did he learn this? I erupted so quickly, with such overheated response that I saw him smile in amusement. Then, over my shoulder, in the oval wall mirror, I glimpsed a reflection of him on his knees, his slim body so hard and muscled that he could have passed for twenty. Oh, man, he breathed, his only loss of control.

Like a deflowered virgin, I was pinned to the bed, stunned, in pain and bewilderment, face pressed to cool, ironed sheet. Had it been so long that my body had lost its shape, or was he Superman? I had heard about this from older women friends, a trick of nature foisted on the menopausal.

While I lay motionless, he rose and grabbed his shorts. I heard water running in the bathroom. Lunch, I gasped. I'll get lunch. I threw on a loose dress that was hanging on a hook behind the bedroom door, and went into the kitchen to finish the sandwiches. I set a pretty tray with mats and napkins, and brought it out to the small outdoor table off the back porch. "You know I was a journalist," I gushed, in a flood of girlish confidences about my work. I wanted him to know my full story. He didn't volunteer much, and I sensed my résumé recitation was an error. I stopped talking in midsentence. Even to my ears, asking him intently about surfing seemed like condescension, but I tried. He answered shortly, indulging the uninitiated.

"How about some mango ice cream?" I asked. "Mango is supposed to have aphrodisiacal powers," I teased. "Although you don't need it." He laughed, his eyes smiling into mine.

CAL VISITED EVERY week or two, or three, never with any regularity or habit, and we coupled in the same animal, often wordless, swiftness. We exchanged the least amount of information or preliminaries. We both knew we had entered into a game, an unstated pact that kept ourselves unknown to each other, as if we realized this was an odd, suspended time and should remain mysterious, almost anonymous. Sometimes it was stand-up sex on the rug before we even got further into the house. Or we would start on the couch with some opening pleasantries, then he would rise as if time was wasting and unbutton my shirt. It was usually serious lust, although once I rolled off the couch by mistake and laughed so hard it broke the spell. No one noticed any change in me, and given the nature of our limited activities, I would not be introducing him to friends. Yet a shiver ran through me when we arranged an assignation, and I'd spend the day in flushed anticipation. I experienced a quickening of senses, a reawakening of the sense of play, forgotten in all my earnest pursuits. I remembered watching a pair of squirrels as they chased each other in the sunlight, sometimes one catching the other, dissolving in a mass of gray fur as they wrestled together, turning somersaults.

I learned that Cal had built a decent business as a jack-of-all-trades handyman, in constant demand by the condo community. "Oh, work," he shrugged. It was all done for the surfing, his one true obsession that had brought him here from the West

Coast twenty-five years ago and kept him doing anything to remain.

Sam the cat retreated outside during our liaisons and stayed away until long after Cal left. At bedtime on those days, I would have to go out in search of her in the starlight. Often it was so dark around my cottage that I did not see her approach, but would feel her weaving around my ankles in greeting until I picked her up and slung her over my shoulders. Those nights she kneaded the quilt and sniffed in disapproval at the smell of a stranger before settling into her habitual roosting spot between my calves. She then turned her back on me, closing her eyes. She liked being the only object of my affections and did not care to share our bed.

Every once in a while, perhaps in some memory of heat, Sam refused to sleep. She paced the floor in the bedroom and yowled, no matter how long I ignored her. In defeat, I would get up. Before I could fully open the front door, she squeezed through the narrow opening with rocket speed and disappeared into the night. Across the road lived a big, gray tomcat that bothered all the females in the neighborhood. One morning Sam slinked home, a golf ball–sized swelling on her back. It was infected, probably a fight wound or a love bite, diagnosed my vet, Dr. Nishimoto. He cut the pus out. See what happens when you go out and tangle with boys, I cooed. But it was too late.

Back in my thirties when I was looking for a second husband, I once followed a suggestion in a meditation book: Before you go to sleep, ask your God for a companion who is compatible in mind, body, and soul.

When I met one, it just about killed me.

The guru had forgotten to mention a fourth ingredient—unmarried.

After that romance ended, I used to lull myself to sleep by remembering our cocooned arms. After far too long, I willed myself to forget.

In a traditional narrative, my affair with Cal would be considered as the moment when the heroine Embraces Life. Yet I knew it only constituted a pleasant diversion, no more, no less, a welcomed shot of life that did me more good than a year of spa treatments. I had known the soul-soaring fecundity of true love but didn't miss the havoc it usually brought. For now at least, the dalliance with Cal made me feel like I had gone to Las Vegas, won the jackpot, and left town before I lost it all.

With amusement, I discovered that Isabella Bird had had a fling herself. A larger-than-life, sexy, and entirely inappropriate one. After Hawaii, she sailed for California with born-again exuberance to continue a planned journey throughout the West. No longer the proper Victorian clergyman's daughter, she had unleashed a new Isabella, free to kick up her heels. She described herself as a reckless lady "with the up-to-anything and free-legged air."

In Colorado she hired a guide, a cultured English gentleman turned frontiersman known throughout the region as Mountain Jim. A surviving photo of Jim shows a middle-aged, handsome man with shoulder-length golden curls and a swashbuckling air; he wore a patch to cover an eye lost in a bear fight. He lived a ruinous life devoted to whiskey and rowdiness.

Isabella and Mountain Jim set off alone together to conquer the 14,259-foot Longs Peak. Snow, frozen temperatures, and altitude sickness nearly turned them back, until Jim tied a rope around Isabella's waist, pulling and dragging her to the top. Fascinated by his erudite conversation and desperado looks, she felt inflamed with attraction for him, fanned no doubt by the melodramatic mountain landscape.

But once back in her Estes Park cabin, she announced that she needed to see more of the Colorado Territory and fled for several weeks. On her return, Jim declared his love. Unfortunately, he also unburdened himself with a lengthy, alarming confession of the depths to which he had descended.

Although they were an improbable match, Jim stirred Isabella in every sense, probably for the only time in her life. In a letter to her sister, Henrietta, she confessed in pre-Freudian innocence that she dreamed that he had fired his gun at her!

"There's a man I could have married," she wrote to Hennie, although adding that he was a man "no sane woman would marry."

She and Mountain Jim parted tearfully. A year later, back in England, she received word that he was dead, shot in the head by an acquaintance.

I STILL HADN'T COMPLETELY shrugged off my 1950s imprinting that decreed the traditional family as ideal. I wasn't the first woman to be deeply torn between social convention and desire for independence. But that these doubts still lingered at middle age, surprised and even embarrassed me.

Why was there no steady man in my life? I could not readily explain. Various answers to The Question had occurred to me.

Perhaps a deep-seated lack of self-esteem controls my choices, sabotaging the chance for love. I don't try hard enough. When I could be squeezing into a sensational dress, whipping myself into an enthusiastic countenance to go out and scintillate prospects, I often prefer to stay home with a book. I am too introverted. Maybe too extroverted. Too bossy. Too strident, too opinionated, too confident. Too cranky. Way, way too picky. Perhaps the wounds and scars from previous tries left me hiding in a shell of self-protective defenses. Or had I been *too* lucky in love, experiencing it so profoundly that I couldn't accept less? I had adapted to a solitary state that kept me at a middle distance from others, close but not too close, guarding my privacy and requiring fewer compromises. Fate and destiny set me on a different path.

All of the above.

None of the above.

Who cares? Single life is vastly underrated.

The decade of my thirties had been fruitlessly spent searching for a second husband to father children, and it was clearly the most miserable of my life. I used to wake in the morning in a panic, as an emptiness stretched ahead. Somehow, somewhere, that feeling disappeared — poof! Now I felt that I should get down on my knees and thank the lord that I had not married any of those husband candidates. I endorsed an old proverb: It takes a mighty fine husband to be better than no husband at all. Some women secretly choose not to marry, unable to disclose the choice even to themselves. Once released from the hungry need for a partner, I found myself relieved. Without really knowing it I entered another realm, with few guides or signposts. The world of living alone and liking it.

How did I envision old age? There weren't lots of models for us single girls. Some women took themselves out of the game, wore dowdy clothes, let their bodies go soft, and retreated into a sort of virgin status. Others engaged in serial affairs, or looked for rescue by Prince Charming as they approached sixty, feeling their lives still incomplete. I knew only a few women who got it right: those who had men in their lives, or not, had love affairs, or not, and went on with the business of living.

PART FOUR

Living Well Is the Best Revenge

CHAPTER EIGHTEEN

The Pansy Craze

A LTHOUGH I HAD heard that the Allertons sometimes staged movie nights in the upstairs theater
at the guesthouse, most of their film collection and home movies had been swept away by the hurricane. But when sorting
through a file cabinet of Allerton documents, I reached into the
very back of a bottom drawer and found a bulky stack of three
large manila envelopes, each folded around something circular.
I opened them. Inside were old 16 mm film reels. God bless Rick
Hanna, the pack rat; he'd saved everything he found. The tapes
were so brittle, black, and twisted that they looked unsalvage-
able. I brought them next door into the frigid air-conditioning
of the Garden library, where Rick sorted slides on a light table,
using a magnifying loop. "Look what I found," I said, and held
up the envelopes.

He moved over, and I unrolled a foot or two of the first one.
"Adventures in New Caledonia," was the handwritten title—
obviously home movies from one of the Allerton trips. I put
it away and turned to the envelope labeled "Slave." The film
seemed in better condition, too. Peering through the photo
loop, I could see that it was a professional film that the Allertons
had purchased. I made out the words *The Sultan and the Slave.*

"Let's have a movie night!" I suggested.

It took a few phone calls to locate a vintage projector. To lend an authentic note of Allertonia to the atmosphere, I made curried duck baked in coconut shells from a John Allerton favorite recipe that their housekeeper Sarah, James's wife, gave me. Rick set up the rented projector, threading the film leader into it. The title image jumped up and down with the strain of disuse, but held. The story started with an image of the "Sultan" in brocade Arabian robe, a turban, and a fake goatee. "Slave" was naked, except for an itty-bitty triangle of shimmery cloth that covered an obviously generous endowment. All in campy pantomime, the handsome, young American actors enacted a story of the Slave stealing jewels and gold from his patron. Aside from lingering glances over alabaster bodies, no overt sex occurred.

Rick and I nearly rolled on the floor in convulsions at the costumes and the corny, theatrical gestures of a silent gay B movie. It ended with a scene of remorse. Slave returned the stolen treasure and willingly locked himself in golden chains. A parable for John Allerton, perhaps?

"Gee, I hope their parties were better," Rick finally said, as the last frame faded to black. "This was so tame I could show it to my mother."

Sarah and James remembered the costume parties with fondness. The excitement started in the morning when John instructed Sarah to open the costume closets for airing and then selected the menu, most often his favorite roast lamb or a curry in a coconut. By the 1950s, Hollywood had discovered Kauai as a perfect jungle setting, a small island with epic locations. Sometimes the Allertons invited movie stars for dinner.

Once, while serving dinner, James accidentally knocked off a bangled headpiece worn by the actor Joseph Cotten, who shot him a furious look while suppressing a laugh.

Guests were ushered upstairs into the guesthouse costume gallery to make their choices. Undoubtedly they *ooohed* and *ahhed* as they unfurled the silks and satins, twirling them in the sunlight to glimmer like giant butterflies: lavender and pink silk kimonos from Japan; gold-threaded cloaks from Indonesia; monks' robes from China; iridescent blue saris and scarlet pantaloons from India. Triangular corner cabinets held scores of hats and headdresses, everything from an opera top hat made of beaver to a Punjabi turban. Dozens of pointy shoes and glittery sandals lined the lower shelves, while shallow drawers held ropes of pearls, stagy rhinestone earrings, a hundred bracelet bangles, shiny buckles, and sparkly brooches.

Robert had begun the costume parties back at Allerton Park, his estate in central Illinois, where he scripted a transformation for arriving trainloads of weekend guests. He wanted them to leave behind their everyday life and proper city dress to assume a different persona when entering the garden. For Robert, the garden was an alchemist's stone that allowed him and his guests to discard societal conventions and become whoever, whatever, their fantasies could conjure. It was the place to converge foreign cultures and to mix up time and place, as in a dream, for a bright kaleidoscope of fancy. And for those who spent their whole lives in elaborate disguise, the costumes were a way to be themselves.

On Kauai, after guests had donned their finery, they were invited to pick up a lacquer box that held a picnic supper. As the sun descended in operatic splendor, torches lit the pathways and the plank bridge that spanned the Lawai Stream. Guests could wander as they wished, to find a ledge of trembling orchids or a glen of scented grasses.

To me, the whole Allerton story seemed a little too pat. Rich gentlemen stumble on paradise and move lock, stock, and barrel to a remote island. I had a hunch that something must have been going on in Chicago that would precipitate such a break. People seldom travel to such extremes unless they are escaping something. So on a visit to relatives outside of Chicago, I drove downtown to the University of Chicago's Joseph Regenstein Library. A historian of gay culture had pointed me to the archives of sociologist Ernest W. Burgess. Predating Alfred Kinsey's work at Indiana University by a decade, Burgess led the earliest extensive studies of American homosexual life. He assigned dozens of his students to take notes at nightclubs, interview gay men and a few women, and write term papers on the subject.

To my astonishment, I found that Burgess and his students recorded in detail a growing gay underworld culture, which peaked in the late 1920s and early 1930s in what came to be known as Chicago's Pansy Craze. Gay cabarets, drag shows, and nightclubs openly proliferated throughout the Near North and South Side neighborhoods, a Chicago version of what was also happening in New York City. Annual Halloween balls drew hundreds of men in drag and women in tuxedos. The nighttime entertainments did not just attract the "queers," as they were then called. High society and the middle class flocked to the cabarets for the prurient thrill of dancing with one of the "homos," or just to gawk.

There's no record that either of the Allertons went slumming at the drag shows along with others of their wealthy class. It's hard to conceive that they would not, though perhaps they preferred their own, private entertainments. Years later when John Allerton was alone and elderly on Kauai, he described to a young botanist over late-night cocktails how he and Robert had consorted with their own kind among the Illinois elite at carefully arranged and clandestine male-only dinner parties. A neighbor had outfitted his Chicago mansion dining room with a hydraulic lift to raise the dining table from the kitchen already laid with food, to keep the servants away. That was important, because all the guests were naked.

The Pansy Craze and the accompanying voyeuristic tolerance by the straight world didn't last long. By the Roaring Twenties, Chicago had descended deeply into its reputation as Sin City. Gangsters declared an open season and profited by flouting Prohibition. In 1933, as all of Chicago prepared for the Century of Progress International Exposition, fair organizers, criminals, and social reformers geared up for what turned out to be a last blowout. City leaders legalized beer again. Dozens more cabarets opened on the South Side.

Then the full weight of the Great Depression descended. The tourist trade evaporated. Reformers demanded that newly elected mayor Edward J. Kelly clean up nightlife and campaigned against strippers and female impersonators. By 1935 Kelly had eliminated queer nightlife. Chicago and the rest of the nation then hurtled into a full-scale sex panic over what was named "the Moron Menace." A series of crimes, both petty and heinous, by peeping toms, rapists, child molesters, and murderers surged onto tabloid front pages. Homosexuality was seen as a mental aberration and its practitioners equated with psychopaths and child molesters, all of them declared "sex morons" and "sex fiends." There was some legitimate concern — more than two dozen women and children were attacked over two years. But few by homosexuals. That didn't stop police from stepping up their surveillance of theaters and cruising spots, including the popular stretch of South State Street. Reformers pressed for a law to castrate sex criminals.

In early 1937, Michigan passed the nation's first sexual psychopath law, allowing anyone even suspected of deviance to be sent away for an indeterminate length of time to a psychiatric hospital or penitentiary. Illinois legislators agitated loudly for similar measures. The following year, just as the Illinois legislature prepared to enact a bill to lock up homosexuals, Robert Allerton and John Gregg sailed to Australia for an extended vacation.

REAL LIFE IS MESSY and full of mixed motives. The increasing hostility toward homosexuals may well have provided the needed push for them to escape from the social restrictions of conventional Illinois in favor of the more accepting — and private — Kauai.

But they had also gotten bored. Sifting through another cache of documents, I began to think that these refined men of movie-star appeal must have felt confined in their baronial mansion surrounded by a sea of cornfields. Allerton Park, Robert's Monticello property, was a gift from his famously rich father, Samuel. Perhaps it was a form of banishment as well. As I dug deeper, I sensed an estrangement between the artistic Robert Allerton and his bullish, gauche, and utterly nouveau-riche father. Yet I also laughed over their so-American story of a fortune built on pigs funding a heavenly Hawaiian garden. From stockyard to paradise, all in one generation. And when I finally visited Robert's Allerton Park in Illinois, I saw how its creation had served as a rehearsal for his masterpiece, Lawai-Kai.

Samuel W. Allerton was nicknamed "Farmer Sam," for his habit of expounding on the importance of working the land, an occupation that he actually didn't do much himself. Born in upstate New York, Samuel inherited a lofty lineage as a descendent of a *Mayflower* passenger, but it was of dubious worth — the early Pilgrims blamed Isaac Allerton, a former assistant governor of Plymouth Colony, for its mounting debts and mismanagement of the books, and possibly even embezzlement.

Sam Allerton's genius for making money lay in his ability to use the railroads to transport livestock. When he moved his operations to Chicago in 1860, he located his Allerton Swine Yards strategically at the terminus of the Hudson River Railroad, entry point for most of the hogs coming into the city. According to legend, when the price of pigs dropped to as little as one cent a pound, Sam borrowed eighty thousand dollars, bought every hog in Chicago, and cornered the market for a day and a half. He rail-shipped them to Ohio and Pennsylvania to fatten up before selling them to the Union Army, which was so desperate for provisions it was paying sixty cents a pound. It wasn't pretty — the livestock traveled without water or food, sometimes arriving half-dead.

Sam was a key partner in founding the Pittsburgh stockyards in 1864. He pushed hard for Chicago to create similar stockyards, which opened on Christmas Day 1865 and were ten times bigger than Pittsburgh's. Although their historical role has been overlooked, Samuel Allerton and his family built a livestock empire that enabled them to dominate and influence shipping costs from the Midwest to New York City.

He was so successful that he bought his own Pullman car so he could live in luxury while overseeing his far-flung operations, which soon stretched from New York to Wyoming. He made so much money he had to establish his own bank. Sam Allerton and nine friends founded the First National Bank of Chicago to fuel their enterprises, which became the source of more Allerton wealth.

The *Chicago Tribune* ranked Allerton as the city's third wealthiest man, right behind the retail magnate Marshall Field and meat packer Jonathan Armour. To survive and triumph in Chicago's commodities market required the ruthlessness of a bandit and the ethics of a horse trader. A pirate's glint gleamed in Allerton's dark eyes.

His money allowed him to marry well — to Pamilla Thompson, the daughter of a wealthy Peoria cattle farmer. She bore a daughter, Priscilla, in 1871, and two years later, a son, Robert. The slender, willowy Pamilla contracted scarlet fever and died. Robert, then six, also caught the fever, which left him nearly deaf, motherless, and lonely. Sam quickly married again, to his wife's sister, Agnes. Sensitive and gentle, Agnes shone a light into her isolated nephew's life. She encouraged him to enroll in art lessons at the new Art Institute of Chicago, and successfully lobbied Sam when Robert wanted to go to Europe at age nineteen to pursue painting.

When Robert returned to Chicago after his five-year European adventure studying in Munich, Paris, and London, he declared his painting career a fiasco and set fire to all of his canvases. For the next two years, he did very little. Unlike his ambitious and sometimes uncouth father, Robert would never work a day in his life, distinguishing himself in Chicago society columns as a "club man and philanthropist" who appeared at the opera or gave parties and dinners. At his father's pressing suggestion, Robert agreed to try to make a go of it on the Piatt County farmland that Sam had deeded to him at birth. Robert employed experienced farm managers who actually grew the corn and wheat crops that covered his twelve thousand acres, while he maintained a posh apartment in Chicago and quickly departed for England to find a model for the grand country house he planned to build. As became his habit, he took a young male protégé in tow, Ralph Borie, an architect from Philadelphia. They spent an entire year looking at castles and baronial halls before settling on the Stuart-styled Ham House in Surrey as a suitable design. Robert directed Borie to build a near copy along the banks of the Saginaw River near the tiny Illinois town of Monticello.

Although he named it "The Farms," there was nothing farm-like or modest about the house, with its ninety-foot entrance hall opening into a two-story library and a music room with twenty-two-foot ceilings. He concocted another European grand tour to fill up the house. With another young artistic companion, Russell Hewitt, Robert stormed through Europe, shipping back spoils by the ton. To landscape new gardens to surround his Monticello manor, Allerton again turned to English design, copying its rectilinear angles, walled gardens, and straight allées. His vision soared ambitiously large: He treated the entire 1,500 acres of his estate as a garden. He built a parterre maze of clipped boxwood hedges and laid squared brick beds for spring bulbs and a collection of two hundred peony varie-ties. Robert conceived of "garden rooms" — the Sunken Gar-den, the Lost Garden — as spaces carved from the forest, the surrounding vegetation creating natural walls.

Chicago society eagerly sought invitations to The Farms. The *Chicago Tribune* chronicled Robert's weekend parties attended by the Marshall Fields, the McCormicks, debutantes, and matrons. The newspaper pronounced Robert as the "Most Eligible Bachelor in Chicago." One young woman visited so often that she and Robert became engaged to be married. The engagement was soon broken off. There were limits to his endurance. Gentlemen suitors also came calling, attracted to the uncommonly handsome young millionaire.

As he glided into middle age, Robert sponsored activities for the nearby University of Illinois School of Architecture at Urbana-Champaign. John liked to tell the story of how Robert had been invited to attend a "Dad's Day" football game and dinner at the U of I Zeta Psi fraternity house in the fall of 1922. The childless older man was paired with an orphaned student, handsome John Wyatt Gregg.

Then twenty-two, John was older than most other students. And broke. To earn free room and board, he worked as the steward for the fraternity. His mother, Kate, had died of cancer in 1918. His father, James, a traveling salesmen, had died of pneumonia in one of the killing epidemics that swept the country in 1921. They had raised John in a roomy boarding house two blocks from Lake Michigan in Milwaukee, endowing him with good manners that complemented his natural charm. Tall and slim, with a high brow and clear eyes, he was good-looking, open, and friendly. He sang in the Glee Club and signed up for membership in the Architecture Society. The Ku Klux Klan attracted wide membership in the Midwest in the 1920s, and John Gregg joined the campus chapter, perhaps an early sign of the self-loathing he would later exhibit when he called homosexuals "queers" and "fairies."

After John graduated in 1926, he spent weekends at The Farms as Robert's companion. Robert introduced him as his foster son and took him everywhere—to parties, to the opera, on travels. Some called John Gregg an opportunist. Others, a captive bird in a silken net. Robert arranged for John to work for society architect David Adler, designing big houses, mostly English in inspiration, for the wealthy. John lived in Robert's Astor Street apartment during the week, until Adler's wealthy clientele could no longer afford grand mansions after the 1929 stock market crash, and the architect nearly closed his practice. John moved full-time down to Monticello, becoming Robert's secretary, in-house architect, landscape draftsman to design a garden folly or a flimsy gazebo, shopping companion with an educated eye, and general dogsbody.

With John now free for winter travels, Robert's itineraries grew more elaborate. Something reminded them of a favorite restaurant in Paris? They flew over for a meal. They wanted inspiration for building a new garden room? They booked two weeks to wander the gardens of Italy. The shopping became frenzied. Robert now bought gifts for the Art Institute, bestowing on the museum six Rodin sculptures and a Picasso drawing. He built a wing for the museum, named in honor of his gentle stepmother, the Agnes Allerton Textile Wing (now subsumed into the Decorative Arts galleries), and set out with determination to fill it. Toward the end of his life, Robert was surprised when told by a *Chicago Tribune* reporter that he was the biggest donor in the history of the Chicago Art Institute. Today Robert's extraordinary gifts to the Art Institute are only minimally remembered. A plaque hangs near the main entrance, unnoticed by museum goers streaming past it.

CHAPTER NINETEEN

A Kapu *on the Garden*

Luxury hotels, shopping malls, fast-food chains, and movie theaters glut the western lobe of the figure-eight-shaped island of Maui. Mount Haleakala, the 10,023-foot-high dormant volcano, dominates the eastern half of the island with its cinder-dry moonscape, studded in spots by the giant silversword plant.

Only the more adventurous tourists drive to the tiny town of Hana on Maui's remote eastern tip, following a swerving two-lane road that zigzags through 617 curves, crosses 54 rickety bridges, and threads through jungle terrain that becomes increasingly empty of human habitation. The small settlement of Hana at the end of the road offers little to do but buy an ice cream at the old Hasegawa General Store. The largest remaining population of pure-blood Hawaiians scrape out a meager living here, many on welfare, housed in modern subdivisions that are a world away from the wealthy tourists luxuriating in the nearby five-star Hotel Hana-Maui. Movie stars, moguls, and other millionaires fly into the tiny airport to avoid the drive, then bunker down in mansions tucked in the surrounding hills. A little further out of town, a quiet cemetery holds the unadorned grave of aviator Charles Lindbergh, who ended his days nearby, seeking privacy and peace in a location as far from American society as he could go and still remain on U.S. soil.

If you know where to look, a narrow dirt lane leads to Kahanu Garden, one of the five satellite sites managed by the National Tropical Botanical Garden. The Garden closed it to tours along with its other facilities after Hurricane Iniki. Kahanu doesn't offer much as a botanical garden. Its lonely peninsula is surrounded by jagged lava rocks and crashing waves. A virus-infected palm collection slowly rots away. In one corner, a collection of breadfruit grows in rows.

But all the local residents know about Kahanu and its vast, ancient Hawaiian temple. Elders stay away. The younger Hawaiians creep in after dark, on dares. Locals whisper tales of full-moon animal sacrifices and ghostly sounds of drumbeats emanating from thin air. Former Kauai mayor Maryanne Kusaka swears that when she was a young girl growing up in Hana, she and friends would sneak up to the temple steps and take photographs that, when developed, came out blank.

The great Pi'ilanihale Heiau rises ninety feet from the flatlands, at once dark, brooding, heroic, Mayan in scale, intimidating, and amazing as an engineering feat. It is the largest temple ever built in Hawaii, perhaps in all of Polynesia. The Hawaiian equivalent of Chartres Cathedral. Begun in the fifteenth century, construction spanned two centuries. The structure consists entirely of serrated lava bits and pieces, all fitted together without mortar, like a jigsaw puzzle. When I visited Kahanu early in my tour of Garden properties, I ignored warnings not to walk on the immense platform, the size of two football fields. I carefully picked my way across it, imagining what it would look like filled with platoons of Hawaiian warriors, each a thousand strong. Archeologists say there is no real evidence that Hawaiians made human sacrifices here, but legends stubbornly persist. I believed them.

And so when the *kapu*—Hawaiian for *taboo*—sticks appeared, they were just one more addition to a long history of strange doings at Kahanu Garden.

That early summer day, the garden crew drove up to the gates and discovered two bamboo spears sunk savagely into the ground, blocking their way. Each spear bore an ominous head-sized ball, one covered with red cloth, the other black. Taller than a man, they leered threateningly. A sign in uneven hand lettering proclaimed:

THIS SITE, PI'ILANIHALE HEIAU, IS TEMPORARILY CLOSED

UNTIL PROTOCOLS ARE ESTABLISHED.

SIGNED,

ERIC KANAKOLE, HIGH CHIEF, HIGH PRIEST, KAHANU

"Does this mean that the garden's closed, or just that we can't go through the gate?" asked Adam Rose, the newly hired director of Kahanu Garden as he nervously eyed the spears. Scrawny, bearded, and trained in English horticulture, Rose was only twenty-seven and in his second week on the job. He was hired to open up the site to visitors.

"*Kapu* sticks," pronounced Francis Lono, who along with his son, Arnold Lono, made up the rest of Kahanu's workforce. "Taboo," Francis explained, as the three men puzzled over what they should do. Francis shook his head. "Probably means don't go in," he said. Eric Kanakole had put up *kapu* sticks before. Francis knew all about Eric, his cousin, as many of the residents of Hana were related to one another.

Arnold didn't say a word. Like most of the young men of Hana, Arnold had warrior tattoos circling his biceps, and a long braid spilled down his back, almost to his waist. He merely nodded.

The three men decided to go to work anyway. They simply went around the gate and jumped the fence. But Adam's bewilderment began to intensify. *Black magic*, he thought. *Island voodoo*. What was supposed to be *kapu*—him? Or Dr. Klein's idea of opening Kahanu to public tours?

Later that day, Adam peeked under the cloth of the *kapu* sticks and saw that they were only coconuts wrapped in ordinary T-shirts. But he grew unnerved when he learned that in Hawaiian ancient ritual, red signified blood; black, death. His unease escalated into panic when he discovered more about Eric Kanakole, known more commonly as Ricky Waikiki before he started styling himself as a leader in the Hawaiian activist movement. Eric was a dark figure with tattoos, a long ponytail, and fierce knitted eyebrows. He and other activists harbored deep grievances about what they called a "government seizure" of family land that dated back to the bloodless coup, arranged in 1898 by the Big Five sugar company planters. The wealthy oligarchy ushered in U.S. troops to depose the last of the Hawaiian monarchy and annex the islands as a U.S. territory. They appropriated most of the native lands as well. During a 1970s renaissance of Hawaiian native music, hula, and other traditions, activists began talking about seceding from the United States and reinstituting the monarchy. The movement had no apparent leader nor stated goals, except for demanding some sort of reparations, and appeared to be going nowhere—Hawaii was so Americanized that it was doubtful that the population would ever forgo U.S. citizenship.

All we knew at Garden headquarters was that somehow this century-old discontent was erupting at Kahanu Garden.

We received bulletins from Adam in increasingly frantic phone calls. He pleaded for reinforcements. "The *kapu* sticks could be a precursor to more overt actions, perhaps violence," Adam warned in a squeaky voice. "This guy Eric Kanakole is big and scary! We're sitting on a bombshell that traditionally would have been resolved with physical force."

Dr. Klein promised he would fly over the next Saturday.

No other Garden site would so test Dr. Klein's diplomatic ability. Reviving a closed botanical institution in the middle of nowhere presented difficult, if somewhat graspable, problems. But walking into a blood feud and the wrath of Hawaiian activists demanded another set of solutions. He was a stranger in a strange land.

LITTLE BY LITTLE, we untangled the brewing forces of revenge and anger that erupted in the *kapu* sticks. The story was as old as Cain and Abel. By the mid-1400s, King Pi'ilani had united all the warring tribes of Maui under his rule and began construction of his royal war *heiau,* a temple large enough to hold troops from the entire island. At old age and near death, he summoned his two sons to rule in peace, together as partners. One son, Kiha, did not arrive in time, so the king granted the kingdom to his other son, Lono. Inevitably, the brothers quarreled after a few years and went to war. Ever since, the descendants of Kiha and Lono have been enemies.

The garden's caretaker Francis Lono descended from the Lono line. His cousin, Eric Kanakole, the self-proclaimed high priest of Kahanu, descended from the Kiha side. They might live in modern-day subdivisions in Hana, but the native Hawaiians still knew their bloodlines. They were still fighting fourteenth-century feuds.

The Garden had inherited the temple because no one else really wanted it. It lay abandoned and near ruin, all but disappearing under encroaching jungle. The death of King Kamehameha in 1819 had plunged Hawaii into spiritual turmoil. The king's many wives seized the opportunity to turn their backs on his elaborate *kapu* system that had forbidden women from eating pig and bananas, among other privileges. In one of the weird confluences of history, at almost the very moment that Hawaiians rejected their faith, New England missionaries arrived, preaching Christianity and rapidly converting the natives. All the *heiaus* were abandoned. Sections of walls crumbled at the great Pi'ilanihale structure. Cows from the neighboring Hana Ranch grazed on its platforms.

The Kahanu family of Hana eventually acquired the property, but donated it in 1972 to the newly formed Pacific Tropical Botanical Garden. The Hana Ranch donated another fifty acres adjacent to the temple. The Garden bought another fifty, promising to all that it would restore the *heiau* to full glory.

Regally tall, with mahogany skin and snowy white hair and muttonchops, Francis Lono seemed the perfect man to hire as caretaker. Everybody in Hana knew that Francis descended directly from King Pi'ilani. His father had been the last Hawaiian to live in a traditional grass hut. His royal bloodlines earned him the nickname Blue.

Back in the early 1970s, Blue Lono set to clearing the *heiau*. Reports of it spread all the way to the western end of Maui's gold coast of hotels and condos. Buzzing tour helicopters landed on the temple for champagne picnics, leaving behind corks and trash. The Garden Club of Honolulu donated funds to build a wood pavilion for visitors. Several wealthy Hana residents donated a new pickup truck. Another funded a restroom. In one of its worst public relations blunders, the Garden hierarchy shipped the spanking new truck to Kauai for use at Garden headquarters, and returned a clunker by barge to Maui. Garden leaders ordered a latrine hole dug but never installed the toilet. Although these insults had occurred more than two decades ago, the people of Hana still remembered. Bitterly.

In Dr. Klein's first step as the new NTBG director, he drafted conceptual plans for all of the Garden's sites, including Kahanu. He hired well-known landscape architect Geoffrey Rausch of Pittsburgh for the job, and the two of them devised a plan to catapult the site from the fifteenth to the twenty-first century in one leap.

General Patton–style, Dr. Klein unveiled his plan for Kahanu with a flourish at a Hana community meeting. He ticked off planned amenities: ocean-view cottages, swimming pools, and tennis courts. "If there was one plan guaranteed to unite the community against the Garden, this is it," warned one speaker.

Klein and Rausch deflated like pricked balloons. "We thought of everything but the people we were supposed to be thinking about, which was the community," Rausch admitted. Never to be deterred, Dr. Klein warmed to the challenge. If told that something couldn't be done, he rallied with a war cry: Why not?

Dr. Klein decided to try a Hawaiian approach. This time, Dr. Klein and Rausch planned discreet locations, away from the *heiau,* for a traditional, thatched grass hut meeting pavilion, offices, exhibit space, classroom, and modest apartments for interns and visiting scientists. Dr. Klein waxed large: Kahanu Garden would serve as a gathering spot, bringing together heads of Pacific states for an agriculture conference to study traditional uses of plants for food, clothing, and shelter.

To soften the blow that he was appointing a young *haole,* Adam Rose, to director, Dr. Klein decided to confer the ceremonial title of *kahu,* or spiritual caretaker, on Blue Lono. Dr. Klein gathered guests on the grass at the Maui property and passed coconut shells of fermented *'awa*—a traditional numbing liquor made from ti roots. The ceremony attracted coverage by local newspapers, causing Eric Kanakole, perpetrator of the *kapu* sticks, to seethe. As a descendent of the Pi'ilani family, he exercised his rights to visit the temple, often escorting groups of kids there to explain ancient traditions. Several times Eric had asked Dr. Klein for a job at Kahanu Gardens, maybe as a tour guide. Dr. Klein had not responded.

Then the organizers of an annual hula festival in Hana asked Dr. Klein for permission to use Kahanu Garden as the site for their opening ceremony. Adam Rose warned, *Don't do it!* Hana's Hawaiian traditionalists scorned the hula festival as a *haole* event. One of the Hawaiians wrote a letter of protest to Dr. Klein, asserting that the town's Hawaiian elders would have to give permission to use the temple site.

General Patton fired back: I don't need your permission to do anything. The hula festival was on!

And so, a few weeks later, a hundred guests, mostly *haoles,* gathered at the *heiau* at dawn as drums beat. The Hawaiians of Hana boycotted the event. A martial arts troop of out-of-towners who had come for the hula fest emerged silently from the jungle. Garbed in loose white loin cloths, they solemnly danced to the sunrise.

ADAM ROSE WOULD call it "the Great Standoff."

Early the Saturday after the *kapu* sticks appeared, Dr. Klein flew to the tiny Hana Airport, then paced impatiently for several hours at Adam Rose's cottage, waiting for Eric Kanakole to telephone and name a meeting place. Finally someone called. Everyone was waiting for them down at the *heiau*. Adam worried that the meeting had turned into a group confrontation, out of town and out of sight. Adam's young wife, Lianne, dashed outside and quickly gathered bunches of shiny green ti leaves—the plant used traditionally to ward off evil spirits—and tied them to the four corners of Adam's blue pickup truck.

With the truck festooned like a parade vehicle, Adam and Dr. Klein drove down the dirt road to Kahanu Garden. The gate stood wide open—already an unusual sign. A massive Hawaiian woman, her black hair flowing like Medusa, stood sentry, as if she had reclaimed the property already. "Who are you?" she demanded.

He responded with a booming voice, "I'm Dr. William Klein and I'm trying to find out what's going on."

She said nothing but gave him the stink eye as they drove past. Heavy grass brushed the underside of the truck like cloying fingers. A plume of dust stretched out behind them as they passed a grove of breadfruit trees. Scattered fruit rotted on the ground, some with exposed white flesh that looked like spilled brains. A putrid smell of decay settled over everything. As the pickup rounded a bend, Adam and Dr. Klein could see ahead to a wide plain leading down to the peninsula. A dozen or so men lounged against their trucks, their backs to the *heiau*. They wore T-shirts, blue jeans, and cowboy boots, and most had long braids and tattoos. They looked pissed off.

"Carry on, Adam," Dr. Klein urged. "I'm here to find out what the hell is going on."

From out of nowhere, a pickup pulled out behind them. Then another. And another. Soon Adam led eight or nine big, high-rigged Chevys and GMC models that made Adam's Toyota feel like a Tinkertoy. Adam looked over his shoulder and saw that the trucks, crowded with Hawaiians, had cut off their exit. He swallowed hard and started sweating. Dr. Klein looked ahead, seemingly unperturbed.

Adam stopped with great trepidation. The Hawaiian brigade fanned out in a line behind the Toyota, blocking the road. Adam calculated how fast he could run but looked at Dr. Klein's girth and worried that he couldn't move very fast. The Hawaiians got out of their trucks and started toward them.

Dr. Klein clapped Adam around the shoulders encouragingly and said, "Well, Adam, you may be the first Englishman since Cook to be eaten alive." Then he swung open the truck door and bulled his way out, his chest and belly extending over his belt. He wore one of his green botanical print Aloha shirts and a wide white panama straw hat banded with iridescent pheasant feathers that gave him a slightly goofy look. With his wire-rimmed glasses and fair complexion, Dr. Klein appeared very much the professor. He started toward the group, his face neither grim nor smiling, but seriously peering over his trifocals as if approaching a crowd of rare insects. Then he went face-first right into the bees' nest.

A big Hawaiian guy stuck a whirling video camera under Dr.

Klein's nose and demanded: "Did you or did you not see the sign at the entrance?"

"Yes, I did," Dr. Klein answered matter-of-factly.

"Do you know what it means?"

"No, I don't, and that's what I'm here to find out."

Taki Matsuda, a member of the Kahanu family that had donated the site to the Garden more than twenty years ago, waited at the head of the group. Adam recognized the other men as Eric Kanakole's *hui,* or gang. The high priest himself was nowhere to be seen. Suddenly, everyone shouted and talked at once, waving their arms. "Whose place is this? What's going to happen here? Who's protecting the *heiau*? What are you gonna do about it?"

Dr. Klein calmly repeated, "We're from NTBG. I'm the executive director. I want to make things right. I want to involve you. Look, this is our place now. I understand you have cultural issues. I'm not trying to become involved with Hawaiian issues. I'm here to talk about what we're going to do here. I'm open-minded to any possibility. Let's talk about anything."

After thirty minutes of confusion, they all ran out of steam. Even the video man got tired and switched off his camera. No one seemed to know anything about the *kapu* sticks, what Eric wanted, or even where he was. Adam and Dr. Klein got back into their truck and followed a Hawaiian to a phone booth. The man made a phone call, then reported that Eric had left for Honolulu.

The Great Standoff ended in a draw, although Adam declared it a triumph for Dr. Klein. "We didn't get killed. We didn't get lynched, so he did a good job."

• • •

THE *KAPU* STICKS remained standing all through the summer and into the fall.

At night in their cottage, Adam and Lianne Rose peeked out through closed blinds to watch meetings convened in the Hana Cultural Center and Museum across the street. They could see Francis Lono and other elders seated on the floor of the traditional Hawaiian grass-roofed hut. Adam never learned directly what was said, but he knew that the *kapu* on Kahanu was under discussion.

Meanwhile, Adam implemented his own measures of cultural glasnost. He grew his dark hair down his back and began braiding it, in the style of young Lono and other Hawaiians. "Adapt and survive," he explained.

CHAPTER TWENTY

New Wave Luau

*N*OTHING BUT MILES of cane fields lined Route 50 as it wound through the dry west side. But I had learned to recognize that a line of parked cars along the roadside was a sure sign of a trail to one of Kauai's surfing haunts. As my interest in surf culture grew after meeting Cal, I sometimes stopped at Pakalas, the break also known as "Infinities," to watch him or others ride the long pipeline curl. Some call it the best wave in the world.

I hiked through a shaded forest to the beach. Until the 1980s there was no public access to Pakalas. Surfers had to sneak through two miles of broken-glass fields, risking arrest for trespassing on private property.

"After a good day at Infinities you'll brainstorm for any implausible scheme to raise the cash to purchase a piece of property nearby. Failing that, you'll commit every waking second on Kauai to planning another session here and wonder why anyone would ever want to surf anywhere else," writes Greg Ambrose in his *Surfer's Guide to Hawaii.* He also warns of Pakalas's dangers. In wipeouts, surfers can land on the shallow reef, turning their backs or other body parts into raw hamburger.

Today, monster swells radiating from a recent far-off tropical storm in the South Pacific had arrived, washing up on Kauai in ten- to twelve-foot waves. No Cal, but plenty of other surfing demigods ducked and shot through walls of water with balletic grace powered by brute strength. I could never watch without awe, laughing in remembrance of the Beach Boys song "Little Surfer Girl." Every American female growing up in the 1960s must have harbored a desire to be somebody's Surfer Girl.

My one surf lesson gave me an understanding of the appeal. The instructor—a young dude named Lance—stood in the water, held the back of the board, and gave it a push so that I could experience the surge of catching a wave. Although I stood for only seconds, I felt the ocean momentum and the wish to do it again and again. I emerged from the lesson beat and bloody, my ankles scraped by reef rocks. It's a sport for those who still feel young and immortal.

And Cal and I were riding our own waves.

DR. KLEIN AND I often had meetings in Honolulu, the New York City of the Pacific, and would either fly over for the day or spend the night. Bill introduced me to Alan Wong's, arguably the best restaurant in Hawaii. Neither the location nor ambiance was particularly fancy with its plain dining room in an unfashionable section of Honolulu. Oh, but the food!

As late as the 1970s, the joke used to be that the best food in Hawaii was what you got on the plane coming over. European-trained chefs at the big resorts shipped in all their food—even frozen fish—for classic continental menus. Tourists tasted local cuisine only if they went to one of the commercial luaus or ventured into hole-in-the-wall ethnic restaurants.

Beginning in the late 1980s, Wong, along with a new generation of Hawaiian-born chefs, began to explore local fish markets, exulting in their bounty. They searched out island farmers to grow specialty vegetables and ripe fruit—not the green pineapples or papayas picked for export. The chefs contracted with cattleman to raise island-grown beef and lamb. Lychee and macadamia nuts, coconuts and local fruits such as the soursweet *lilikoi* (passion fruit), mangos and guava soon appeared prominently on menus.

Fossils and electron microscopes aren't the only way to decipher Hawaiian history. Food historians study the ethnic origins of food for what it says anthropologically about the people and evolution of multicultural societies. Sociologists have focused on Hawaii because of its large range of ethnic groups, no majority, and a 50 percent intermarriage rate. Like everything in Hawaii, food underwent a constant melding of outside influences as people arrived, improvised, and adapted.

Nowhere but in Hawaii did Pacific, Asian, and Western food traditions meet in such close proximity. Few other places can date so precisely the arrival of different cuisines. The Polynesians found the islands bereft of carbohydrates, so they packed their voyaging canoes with slips and roots of taro—a sustaining carbohydrate—and dozens of varieties of breadfruit, yams, coconut, and bananas. The first Hawaiian food was eaten raw, or cooked in *imus*—fires burned down to coals to heat rocks, then covered with fragrant leaves, similar to cooking methods found throughout the South Pacific. Chinese laborers started arriving in 1852, most from the culinary-supreme Kwangtung Province with its black bean and oyster sauces. Japanese workers landed in 1868 with soybean products of soy sauce, miso, and tofu, as well as dried seaweed and pickles. Portuguese, primarily from the Madeira Islands and Azores, came in 1878, bringing spicy sausages. Koreans imported pungent pickled cabbage and marinated beef starting in 1903, followed by Filipinos in 1909, with their peas, beans, and adobe style of vinegar- and garlic-flavored dishes. The last great Asian cooking influence flooded Hawaii in the 1970s when Thai and Vietnamese immigrants opened dozens of restaurants.

Alan Wong was illustrative of yet another social upheaval in Hawaii — the emergence of a generation who came of age in the 1970s, determined to reject mainland influences as the only valid culture. They were intent on rediscovering and reviving what it meant to be Hawaiian. It was a trend evidenced in the new wave of Hawaiian music stars such as Israel Kamakawiwo'ole, in the revival of water sports, in a growing insistence on inserting diacritical marks into Hawaiian printed words, and on the menus of restaurants, from gourmet temples to the lowest vendor of plate lunches. Isabella Bird and Mark Twain had both reported on the local people of Hawaii, but, it must be said, were racist in describing the "natives" as curiosities prone to stupidity. Now Hawaiian residents frequently boast of bloodlines from all parts of the world, and their polyglot rules the islands.

ONE NIGHT ALAN let me watch him cook. As I arrived in the kitchen at 5 p.m., one food preparer held open a stiffly starched white double-breasted chef's jacket and eased it over my shoulders. Another tied an ankle-length apron around my waist. At that hour the restaurant held an expectant air of a stage before the curtain rises. Already in place at one of three cooking stations, Alan relaxed liked an athlete stretching before the race. The kitchen's 1,300 square feet is generous by some restaurant standards, but each cook has only three feet of counter workspace, an amount that any amateur cook would deplore. Behind Alan a bank of blazing burners already shot up six- to eight-inch flames, and an aroma of garlic and ginger sizzled into the air.

In his forties, Alan conveyed the ease and confidence of a successful man, the self-awareness of a celebrated artist. His face has a smooth, creaseless blend of Hawaiian, Chinese, and Japanese features and a thick thatch of shiny blue-black hair. His low-riding girth under his white jacket gives him a wrestler's centered power. Alan's facial expressions are hard to read. But when he uses an unusual term, he scans your eyes, as if looking to see if the information arrived. It's a listener's trait, rare in successful men and indicative of a great teacher. When he reverts back to his local pidgin, you get a glimpse of the boy in him. But there is no question that he is the boss.

Alan squatted to open one of the refrigerated cases below the counter containing vats of organic greens and plates already made up with portions of lobster tails and shrimp, ready for searing. He pulled out a long *onaga* fish for his signature dish and started to fillet it with a razor-like blade. As he butchered fish with both hands, Alan signaled Wade, the starch preparer, to spoon mashed potatoes directly into his mouth, then silently circled a finger in the air, indicating a need for more butter.

Finished with filleting, Alan squeezed a teaspoon full of dark sauce from the first of a dozen plastic squeeze bottles aligned on his counter like surgeon's instruments. Methodically, he did the same with each bottle. Each evening, about two hundred different sauces and components make up the night's forty or so entrées and starters. He works on the theory that if the components are good, his staff can compose them, so he tastes the

sauces instead of the finished dishes. Wade returned with another spoonful of mashed potatoes. More salt, Alan mouthed.
Wade returns four times before Alan is satisfied.

Already the heat at the chefs' stations grows intense, smoky
with aromas of grilled meat and fish seared to a flaky crust.
"Oh, it gets very hot," says Lance, one of the entrée chefs. "But
Alan likes it that way. Keeps him on edge." Alan serves as ex-
peditor, calling to the other chefs to hurry an order, or to a
waiter to pick it up while it's hot. "This kitchen is a well-oiled
machine," he says with pride. "When it's performing well, it's
humming. It's a piece of art. This place has *mana*."

Alan grew up in Waipio, a small plantation town on Oahu's
north shore, in the 1950s, when you could pick ripe pineapple
out the back door. The food his mother served was simple but
typically Hawaiian in its ethnic mixtures — rice on the table
every day, as well as Portuguese, Filipino, and Korean dishes.
After a year at the University of Hawaii in Honolulu, the
chronic lack of dorm space forced him to find an apartment.
To pay the rent he went to work as a dishwasher at Don the
Beachcomber Restaurant.

"You're talking about someone from the country. My pidgin
English was atrocious," he told me with a look of red embarrass-
ment briefly flushing his features. Methodically, Alan studied
each job, figuring out what would be required to progress from
dishwasher to busboy, cashier, hotel front-desk clerk, and night
manager. After the last promotion, he wondered, What next?
and enrolled in food-service management at Kapiolani Community College. The classes dazzled him. "When I made my
first loaf of French bread, I never realized I would get turned
on," he says.

Alan won a coveted apprenticeship at the Greenbrier Hotel in West Virginia. Then he secured a prized spot at the foodies' mecca, Lutèce in New York City, working three years for Chef André Soltner. When Alan wanted to go home, he landed a big job at the Mauna Lani Bay Hotel and Bungalows on the Big Island, often ranked by travel guides as the most luxurious hotel in all the islands.

With the same careful methodical research that marked his first restaurant jobs, Alan analyzed Hawaiian cuisine. He and other young Hawaiian chefs developed an haute cuisine of Asian Pacific fusion. Chef Roy Yamaguchi dared to open in Waikiki, the graveyard of restaurants, and was so successful he opened branches on outer islands. Sam Choy was equally prolific. On Kauai, Jean-Marie Josselin opened his Pacific Café with a French twist.

No one drew from the local style as much as Alan Wong. At the Mauna Lani, Alan set up the network of local agriculture producers that he still uses today. Much of the time he had to tell growers what to grow and how to grow it — the perfect vine-ripened tomato still eludes him, but he now features lettuce from a Hilo farmer, lamb from a Big Island ranch, farm-raised shrimp, and vintage estate-grown chocolate from the Kona Coast, the only chocolate grown in America.

He scrutinized the local dishes of his boyhood, taking each dish apart, analyzing each ingredient, then reassembling them in different combinations. One of this evening's special appetizers is "Laulau Lumpia" — kalua pig and salted butterfish on luau leaves with a *lumpia* wrapper (a wonton), fried crisp and drizzled with poi vinaigrette. On the side is a relish of *lomi-lomi* salmon. Voilà! The local plate lunch, dressed up.

When asked to participate in a "New Wave Luau Festival" a few years ago, Alan figured he needed to research the classic luau, not the tourist monstrosity that I had learned to avoid. How did it come about? He learned from a historian that *poke* originally meant *cubed*. In the old days, fishermen didn't go out in big boats, so the original *poke* was made from small reef fish. Hawaiians used very crude instruments made of shells to roughly cut the small fish, then sprinkled them with Hawaiian salt that had been evaporated in fields that imbued it with a red-dirt hue.

The happy result of Alan's research was presented to me tonight: a "*poke*-pine." I bit tentatively into a crispy wonton ball to find cool, red, translucent flesh of sushi-quality yellowfin ahi, set off by a swish of wasabi, the nose-snorting Asian horseradish sauce.

Alan had hated poi when growing up. But after his scholarly study, he decided that the essential ingredient of taro was good but over the years had been transmuted into a lavender library-paste goo. Now his starch chef, Wade, boils taro cubes, puts them through a ricer, and produces a grainy, thick, raspberry-colored taffy, all within a couple of hours.

At 8:30 p.m. Alan looked out onto a sea of diners, tapping a Sabatier knife like a tuning fork on the marble cutting block. "Oh ho, see the storm brewing? All those people? When they all order it's going to be madness," he said happily. Alan called to the chefs and nods in the direction of the crowd, "See you at the finish line, boys."

By 10:15 p.m., the wave had crashed, spent. The bar was finally empty, and the remaining diners lingered over dessert and estate-grown Kona coffee.

Two of the entrée chefs brought me a final appetizer: a liquor glass of roasted tomato pesto soup. Layered like a parfait, pale green, orange, and yellow translucent liquids each contained the essence of ripened tomato, warm as if from sun. A miniature grilled sandwich of foie gras, Kalua pig, and Monterey Jack cheese accompanied the soup. I ate slowly, to savor each bite.

I SOMETIMES LEFT Kauai to go farther than Honolulu on fund-raising missions. For months I had been working on campaign preparations. I wrote a case statement, the official plan that laid out a ten-million-dollar goal with descriptions of proposed building projects, architectural renderings, cost estimates, and lists of donor prospects. Still, the campaign lacked a centerpiece, a spark. Unexpectedly, the sugar company Alexander & Baldwin announced the sale of all its holdings on Kauai, including an old plantation camp of worker houses. We found an abandoned little plantation cottage that still had enough salvageable features that we could fairly easily move and renovate it into a full-fledged visitor center for Allerton Garden. The plan provided the romance we needed to reel in big bucks.

Now we were ready for The Ask. If our target was a big gun on Wall Street, the trick was to find another big gun to bring with us. Better yet if they belonged to the same club or went to the same school or served on the same opera board. I went along to provide details, figures, the timing of the gift, the follow-up, the closing. Doug Kinney, the Garden chairman of the board of trustees, appointed himself as campaign chairman. He warmed to the asking but preferred to make his own deals without consulting anyone. Disastrous. Once he sold board members on a student internship program that wasn't part of the campaign because it was loathed by Bill and the rest of the staff. Fire, load, aim, Bill Klein complained, was Doug's style.

I flew to California to meet up with Doug for our first fundraising trip together. As I drove a rental car down Interstate 280 south of San Francisco on the way to Portola Valley, Doug barked orders to some poor subordinate in the family business on the other end of his cell phone, his silvered Leonine head cocked to one side. A frown lined his long face. His kids nicknamed him "Growlie," and I could see why. He rarely seemed pleased. Doug ordered people around like a nineteenth-century British Army officer. Including me. "Make my plane reservations!" he'd command before hanging up. For a while, I asked my secretary to handle his travel arrangements. Then one day Doug and I were in Honolulu for meetings when he turned to me and said, "What time is my flight tomorrow?" What flight? I answered. Oops. After that, he conscripted Dr. Klein's secretary for such personal services. As a journalist, I'd know exactly how to deal with a Doug, telling him to stuff it. But here I trod on foreign ground, trying to understand the delicacies and quicksands of courting board members and donors. And Doug was both.

Many nonprofit organizations lack a real board leader willing to expend effort and shoe leather to make the necessary personal calls to donors. Doug relentlessly pursued prospects and goals, showing a fierce love for the Garden. Part of his attraction to the institution lay in a powerful connection of family history: He introduced himself as Douglas *McBryde* Kinney in Hawaii, emphasizing his tie to the McBryde sugar family. Doug's great uncle, Alexander McBryde, long ago owned Lawai-Kai before the Allertons bought the property. Another of Doug's great uncles,

Judge Advocate W. A. Kinney, presided over the kangaroo court that prosecuted Queen Liliuokalani for treason after the United States annexed the Hawaiian Islands in 1899 and pushed aside the last of the Hawaiian monarchy. Aside from a family dynasty, I suspected that an even more profound motive drew Doug to the Garden: the possibility of redemption.

Doug had been born with a silver spoon in his mouth, an heir to an electronics company. In his youth, he briefly worked as a bond salesman in New York but after that never found anything to particularly distinguish himself. Now in his mid-sixties, he devoted himself to golf at the exclusive Onwentsia Club in Lake Forest, Illinois, from Easter to Thanksgiving; the Seminole Golf Club in North Palm Beach, Florida, through the winter; and a jaunt to St. Andrews in Scotland every August. He played three hundred rounds of golf a year. "That's my job," he frequently said, and sounded only a little defensive.

When Hurricane Iniki flattened the island, Doug immediately flew to Honolulu and pulled strings to get on the first flight to Kauai. He seized total control. The Garden not only lay damaged but also rudderless, as the previous director had suffered a paralyzing stroke. Performing triage, Doug closed down public operations, laid off most employees, then flew back to his Lake Forest house and ran the skeleton operation by phone. Few ever opposed him or his sometimes wrong-headed ideas. "It takes a lot of energy to fight Doug," one trustee confided to me. "A lot of energy."

Bill Klein had put an end to Doug's fiefdom. Even so, Doug usually telephoned at least once a day, insisting to be put through to whomever he wished to speak to, wherever they were — intrusions that became flash points in the continuing power struggle between the two men. Both had huge shares of confidence and egotism, making their inevitable clashes seem titanic.

Still, Bill and Doug regarded each other with grudging mutual respect. "Dead in the water," Doug often said to describe the moribund Garden before Bill Klein. "We were dead in the water until Bill Klein came. He's doing more things in one year than the previous director did in seventeen. Now we have a real chance to become world-class."

And if Bill valued Doug's devotion and his energy, he counted at least equally on Doug's generous donations. Between fending off Doug's interference and trying to fit Dr. Klein's schemes and dreams into reality, I felt I was in constant battle mode. Trying to coordinate a campaign with them was like trying to take two Great Danes out for a walk.

As we cruised past browning California hills, my attention reverted to the task ahead of us as we turned off the highway at the Stanford University exit and began the climb to Bill and Jean Lane's ranch.

We turned onto a drive marked by a red mailbox, then climbed higher, past horse pastures railed with log fences. A Porsche was parked in a hilltop courtyard in front of a sprawling ranch house that commanded million-dollar views of the valleys below. A heavy carved wooden door looked like it had once adorned a Spanish mission. Jean answered our ring, looking girlish in casual slacks and tailored shirt. A woman servant silently served us soup, tomato salad, and fresh bread while Doug and I listened to Jean. After lunch we moved to the living room with its Western ranch furniture. Doug threw me a softball: "Look, Jean, we want to bring you up to date on the campaign."

I pulled out colored architectural drawings. A scientific research and horticulture building would serve as the heart of the Garden, I explained. A new visitor center complex would be built in phases as a new entrance to Allerton Garden. I unfurled a sketch of the little plantation house we planned to renovate. She sat on the edge of her chair, her eyes darting from one sketch to another. "Gee, both look so good. I just can't decide which one we ought to do," she said. Doug and I avoided looking at each other. We never mentioned figures but the papers were clearly marked with dollar signs. Two million to build the nursery center; half a million for the visitor center.

A WEEK LATER, Bill Lane telephoned with the news that they would donate $500,000 to restore the plantation house, to be named the Bill and Jean Lane Visitor Center. Experienced donors, they asked for a pledge card outlining the terms of their gift and a schedule of payments. I faxed a letter of agreement.

Bill Lane signed it with a big, bold pen, revising the payment schedule so that more money would come sooner.

Over the ensuing months, Dr. Klein presided over noisy, almost party-like sessions to chart renovations of the sugar shack. Spencer Leinweber, a Honolulu architectural expert in historic preservation, flew over to unveil her latest drawings. We hired Mike Faye, who had done such a spectacular job restoring my own cottage. He answered questions about construction. John Rapozo gave his evaluation on excavation. Bill named Scott Sloan, head of the grounds crew, as project supervisor, giving him a new confidence and authority.

Another of Bill's master strokes, I observed. By involving everyone he fostered excitement, dedication, ownership. We were all pinning a lot of hopes on this little building. Sometimes I worried whether it would collapse under the weight of them all. Dr. Klein wanted a new gift shop to help pay for the NTBG's expansion. A museum exhibit to explain our scientific mission. Bookcases mounted on wheels, so they could be pushed out of the way for evening lectures. A small café to sell cold drinks and sandwiches. A series of small gardens surrounding the center to give visitors a taste of the Allerton and Lawai gardens without having to go on a full guided tour. How were all these plans going to be crammed into 1,800 square feet? Faye projected that the building could be picked up, moved, and rehabilitated for about $150,000. I could almost hear the whirl of an adding machine racking up tens of thousands of dollars in additional costs.

"We'll just have to get Lucinda to raise more money," John Rapozo told the group at one meeting.

CHAPTER TWENTY-ONE

Last Harvest

*A*BREEZE CAUGHT MY wide black straw hat, threatening to lift it off. Cars and people already jammed the narrow streets of Koloa Town, gathered for the annual Plantation Days Parade to celebrate the August cane harvest. *Paniolos* on horses pranced up and down the roadway, their mounts decorated with swags of braided greenery. Open convertibles carried rhinestoned teen queens. Hula girls danced and ukulele players strummed atop orchid-strewn floats. A flatbed truck carted an antique sugar locomotive once used to transport workers and cane. In the distance stood the gray metal buildings of the Koloa Sugar Mill, strangely quiet.

Mill operators had announced they would shut down in a few week's time. The last blow had come when Pepsi canceled its contract. All two hundred workers would be out of jobs at harvest's end. Established in 1835, the Koloa mill became the first successful refinery in Hawaii. Over the next hundred years, raising sugar was as good as growing money. By 1955, 1,282 sugar planters tilled the fields in Hawaii. Now only three plantations still operated in all the islands: one on Maui and two on Kauai.

Experimental forays into agriculture to replace cane remained tiny. When riding Bo, I liked to nudge him into a canter through the hedgerows of coffee that had been planted as an alternative, although the idea had yet to prove profitable. Small truck farmers started asparagus beds and papaya. No one really knew what to do with all the former cane fields except build vacation housing. Top real estate agents and time-share salesmen made the only big money on the island.

I spotted the Garden's old Dodge silver sampan, festooned with bird-of-paradise spikes, ginger torches, and elephant ear leaves. Dr. Klein had insisted that the Garden enter the parade, a first for NTBG. As symbols go, it telegraphed that the Garden had emerged from its shell and joined the community. A dozen of us squeezed into the vehicle's rear leather benches. The driver revved up and we moved off with ceremonial speed, falling in line behind the locomotive float. As we approached the center of Koloa, hundreds of people lined the road. A master of ceremonies announced our arrival at the judges' stand on a gravelly microphone system: "And here we have the National Tropical Botanical Garden, folks. That is some car, isn't it? Let's have a round of applause."

Dr. Klein waved excitedly to people, then jumped off the sampan and waded into the throngs, shaking hands and passing out Garden brochures. At the Koloa community ball field, large striped tents held booths hawking Hawaiian crafts, teriyaki chicken, volcano-hot chili, shave ice, saimin, and long rice. Hula troupes and bands would perform all day. A giant plastic balloon of King Kong loomed over it all. But the edge of forced gaiety only partly masked an underlying sadness over the end of an era.

Before Dr. Klein had arrived, entering a parade would have

been out of the question. Garden staff even routinely turned away magazine and newspaper reporters. Now flattering articles about the Garden's renaissance rained in by the dozens. *National Geographic, Preservation Magazine, Sunset Magazine,* and the Royal Horticulture Society's *Garden Magazine* all ran big spreads. The Sunday *New York Times* national page led with a story about the Garden's plant rescue. Tourists filled Allerton Garden tours to capacity. Progress in opening up the Garden could be seen everywhere. Over on Maui, the *kapu* sticks had finally been removed and plans were under way to open the garden. My own job grew easier after I happily watched the departure of the oppressive finance director who resigned to return to the mainland. I liked his friendly new replacement.

As I became more settled and the job became more manageable, my affair with Cal the surfer ran out of steam. The passion had served its purpose but no romance or friendship had developed. Nor would it. Missing between us was a straightforward honesty that in recent years I demanded from all my relationships, whether in work or play. We lacked the essential ability to talk to each other. All of my best romances had begun in conversations that explored each other's minds.

The key to loving island life, my well-traveled new friend Mathea counseled, was to realize that there was no enjoyment difference between attending the opera in London or a potluck with friends on Kauai. Outsiders would ask, Don't you miss culture? The theater, concerts? Although I didn't attend the opera on the mainland, on Kauai I frequented the International Film Festival in June and the Prince Albert Music Festival in November that brought in young prizewinning concert soloists. A pile of us spread blankets under the stars in August for the outdoor Kane Hula Festival, which attracted men's hula troupes from the other Hawaiian Islands to compete in sword-thumping, macho dances.

My routine became stable, even predictable, not like at the newspaper, when I flew out the door in the morning and sometimes didn't know when I'd get back. A long-held flirtation with the idea of adopting a baby from China graduated to a visit to an adoption agency in Honolulu. After decades of using contraceptives, I ruefully acknowledged that with approaching menopause, I probably didn't have a fertile egg left. An adoption could be done in about a year. I had the cash from a small inheritance. I had the schedule, I had the agency. But did I have the will?

A few weeks after the Koloa harvest parade, bills, financial records, and correspondence accumulated in a messy pile on the walnut desk in my cottage study. I picked up the sheaf of adoption agency papers, still blank. Filling them out and retrieving all the necessary documents would take weeks. But that was not what stopped me. Did I need to have a husband, or a child, to feel fulfilled? Or did I just lack the courage to construct a life that wasn't quite what my mother expected or that others defined as the ideal? Was I at heart a conformist? Or did a primal mother-love cry to be answered, no matter what the cost?

A baby would shake up my life to its core, with baby giggles and nighttime snuggles, sand castles and bedtime stories. Yet I remained ambivalent, conflicted.

My generation of women was the first to have easy access to birth control and abortions that gave us so much freedom that more than a few of us forgot to fit children into our grand plans. What brittle irony awaited for women who postponed babies for career or fun, only to find that we couldn't find any potential fathers, or our bodies let us down by turning infertile. These days, modern medicine allowed women my age to produce last-gasp babies of their own. They changed diapers while experiencing hot flashes, perhaps chaperoning field trips with a cane.

I worried about the disappearance of quiet time. The arrival of small children turned a woman's life into a train schedule: up at 6 a.m.; carrying a child out the door in the early light; shuttling to day care; picking up; fixing dinner; playing nonstop games and talking nonstop talk. Solitude, I had learned, was a luxury if it wasn't enforced incarceration. It had become a deepening, gnawing need. It had taken me ten years to get used to living alone, and another five to like it. I didn't mind, even longed for, an entire weekend without talking to anyone.

I now experienced the oddly disconcerting feeling of being in the position to receive what I no longer felt I had to have. I definitely missed what children can bring but was no longer certain that my life lacked its own rich, if different, character. I put the blank application forms into a folder and slipped it into a drawer.

I'd look at them later. Maybe.

ISABELLA BIRD NEVER DIVULGED, in writing at least, any regret over her childless state. But she did give marriage a brief go. After her Pacific and Colorado adventures, Isabella returned to London and found a publisher, John Murray. *Six Months in the Sandwich Islands* appeared in print a year later. A second volume of her Wild West explorations entitled *A Lady's Life in the Rocky Mountains* quickly entered a seventh printing and became her most commercially successful.

Once home in her quiet life in England, however, she relapsed into her former invalid self. A friend made in the Sandwich Islands visited and could barely recognize the carefree and daring explorer of a few months before. Isabella and her sister Henrietta became acquainted with a quiet doctor, Dr. John Bishop. Although ten years her junior, John and Isabella shared an interest in botanical histology—examining tissues under a microscope. The doctor began to court her, ever worshipful, reverential, and as loyal as a lapdog. Hardly the rough-and-tough Mountain Jim, Dr. Bishop was self-effacing and modest, with stringy silver hair plastered against his head, downward-slanted thick eyebrows, and a graying beard. "Very plain," Isabella wrote. She confided to a friend that she was romantic enough to still hold out for a love match. Dr. Bishop's effect on Isabella was a renewed determination to leave the country.

In 1878, she set out again, for Japan. On the return voyage she stopped in the Malay Peninsula, where she chronicled the living habits of the Chinese; the trip led to two more books, *Unbeaten Tracks in Japan* and *The Golden Chersonese.* It was as if the Victorian conventions and strictures that constrained Isabella were so severe that her breakout rebellions needed to be equally acute, requiring her not just to travel but to trek to the ends of the world.

In 1879 her beloved sister Hennie contracted typhoid. Dr. Bishop returned, hovering in the sick house, and when he broke his leg, he gave up his normal practice and moved in with the Bird sisters to supervise and administer care.

Henrietta died. Isabella spun into paroxysms of grief. "She was my world," she wrote. Dr. Bishop resumed his campaign to marry Isabella. This time she consented but barely concealed her doubts. Now aged fifty, she insisted on wearing black to the wedding. She invited no guests. A friend tried to argue Isabella out of dressing for the wedding in deep mourning but got nowhere.

Marriage did little to improve her health. She developed a series of carbuncles close to the spine and was in deep, constant pain — surely an even better excuse than a headache to avoid conjugal relations? Eight months after their nuptials, the doctor contracted blood poisoning when operating on a foreign sailor suffering from a bacterial skin infection. Without antibiotics, it led to four years of crippling, degenerative health. As the doctor became incapacitated, he retained an uncomplaining nobility; at long last, Isabella declared love and devotion for him.

After her husband died on March 6, 1886, Isabella grieved for a year. But then she hatched a plan. What better monument to her good husband than a series of memorial missionary hospitals in the Far East? She went to London to study missionary nursing, then quickly ran off to Ireland for five weeks, ostensibly to study the Irish question, traveling in open carts during midwinter. She revived, discovering again in Ireland what she calls "a sad fact," that delicate and ailing as she almost always was, "a rough, knock-about open-air life" always brought back health and strength. "Oh! To be beyond the pale once more," she wrote, "out of civilization into savagery? I abhor civilization!"

She established a hospital at Islamabad, then that accomplished, she set out for a grand tour through Central Asia and Tibet, riding first on an Arab steed, then on the back of a yak, the half-wild ox of Tibet.

In 1890, she undertook her most perilous and perhaps most remarkable journey, from Baghdad to Tehran, from Isfahan to Erzurum, across snowbound passes and bandit-infested regions never before traveled by a European. She was almost sixty years old. Back in England for only a few months, she then set out again for a three-year trip through China, Japan, and Korea.

In 1900, Isabella turned seventy. She began lessons in advanced photography, conversational French, and cooking. Her only concessions to age were the purchases of a tricycle to replace her usual bicycle, and a small ladder for mounting and dismounting from the powerful black charger she rode through Morocco the following year.

It was her last journey. From October 1903 until her death a year later, she lay confined to bed or couch. Although she unrealistically dreamed of another trip to China, an internal tumor and heart disease finally consumed her. Her last months were spent in bed, surrounded by books and devoted friends.

Nearly to the end, she lived the words she had written decades before:

"I still vote civilization a nuisance, society a humbug and all conventionality a crime."

CHAPTER TWENTY-TWO

In a Heartbeat
Everything Changes

*T*HE HIGH-HEELED silk pumps that matched the beige cocktail dress lay buried in a shoebox on the top shelf in the cottage closet. Torture chambers after months of bare feet and sandals. Holding up suits and dresses against my body, I felt like an archeologist exhuming a past civilization. Dr. Klein had already left for North Palm Beach, Florida, a winter enclave for the wealthy. We needed to attend posh fund-raising parties but also sort out a mess at our Florida garden. Dr. Klein's latest brainstorm had just blown up. With its expanse of lawn overlooking Biscayne Bay, The Kampong's nine-acre estate in Coconut Grove was a Gatsby-like setting. It had only recently been deeded to the National Tropical Botanical Garden and, although it was a nice garden sitting on high-priced real estate, we hadn't really figured out what to do with it. Dr. Klein had hired an event planner who busily rented it out for weddings and parties. Two weeks earlier, the neighbors nearly rioted in protest when a wedding band brayed blasts of loud salsa music late into the night. One neighbor, a Garden trustee as it happened, called the police. "With trustees like that, who the hell needs enemies?" fumed Doug Kinney. He cancelled all future parties.

Bill and I hoped to calm everybody down, and then try to figure out how The Kampong could support itself. But he had another, deeper objective. Doug's intrusiveness into Garden operations had become so irritating that Bill Klein was ready to quit. "Doug's job as chairman of the board is to set policy, not oversee operations," he steamed. "I'm going to tell him that I'm out of here if he doesn't back off." Bill promised that he would get Doug to stop giving me orders, too.

I pulled a heavy suitcase from the back of a closet. I wore a swimsuit for the job. After loading the suitcases into the car for the drive to the airport, I was sweating. I took a last-minute shower before departing.

A UNIFORMED MAJORDOMO at the Seminole Club, an exclusive community for the wealthy in North Palm Beach, informed us that Mr. Kinney was at home. He offered to telephone for us. Bill and I waited in a room of overstuffed chairs and plaid, preppy furnishings. Doug arrived and we went into a room of bridge tables. Expansively, Doug greeted a number of men, retirement age like him. Most of them wore polo shirts with an embroidered head of an Indian on the breast, presumably a Seminole.

Bill pulled a written agenda from the breast pocket of his tweed jacket and started smoothly ticking off accomplishments. When he arrived at the Garden only three years ago, all its Hawaiian sites lay hurricane-damaged or closed. He reopened all four to paying visitors and had begun similar efforts for The Kompong. We raised more money than any time in history.

The annual budget was balanced. Already we had lined up $4.5 million of the $10 million campaign. Annual gifts netted $2.8 million—up $1 million from the year before. Construction had begun on a new, full-fledged visitor center. A new horticulture center would be next. Reconstruction of the Allerton estate house was nearing completion. A Ph.D. scientist was just appointed to a newly created chair of horticulture. A renowned biologist had agreed to a post as visiting scientist. We attracted a bounty of press clippings. Our new publications won awards, including best in the nation from the American Association of Botanical Gardens and Arboreta. . . .

Doug interrupted, "You've had a fabulous year. No question. The Garden is just popping with excitement."

"Doug there's even more going on than you know," Bill countered. And then he moved in, General Patton sending in the right flank. Now that Doug had volunteered his approval, Bill listed instances when Doug had meddled with staff. The Christmas card Doug wrote to Rick Hanna telling him to change computer connections at the Garden, without Bill's knowledge. The instructions to women on the staff to coddle one of the Garden's old-lady donors. His attempt to choose the visiting scientist, ignoring Bill's wishes.

It was all very cordial. Even-voiced pleasantries over egg salad. There were no ultimatums or threats. Doug took it with ease.

I doubted it would change one thing.

After lunch, Bill and I made the ninety-minute drive from Palm Beach to Coconut Grove. In the privacy of the car, I complimented him. "The written agenda was really masterful, Bill, to get Doug to acknowledge the positive accomplishments. How'd you think of that?"

"Experience, my dear. Experience," he said. As we rehashed the lunch, he grew philosophical. "All in all, Doug and I did pretty well together as a team. I know if I had my way, I'd plan everything to death. Doug wants everything done at once. We balance each other."

Something about Bill Klein invited confidences. "One thing I'd like to do is try a less aggressive and competitive approach to work," I told him. "I'm a warrior."

"I am, too," he said.

"Yeah, but there's a spiritual side of you that makes you sort of like a great white chief. I battle too much. Using a machine gun when a fly swatter is all that's necessary. I mean, come on, this is a botanical garden."

I had his full attention. He turned and said urgently, "Don't. The great temptation is to think that because this is a botanical garden, things will be easy and you don't have to fight. Don't believe that for a minute."

THE KAMPONG WAS a beautiful relic of Old Florida, built by plant explorer David Fairchild, often called the father of American botany. In explorations around the globe in the early 1900s, Fairchild collected and introduced to America seventy-five thousand plants. He single-handedly revolutionized the American diet, importing hundreds of new fruits and vegetables that are now commonplace, including soybeans and rice from Japan, cucumbers from Austria, figs from Algeria, sweet potatoes from Barbados, mangos from Indonesia, and a hardy Russian durum wheat able to withstand the harsh winters of our northern great plains. He transformed America's landscape with flowering cherry trees, now synonymous with spring in the nation's capital. He organized the U.S. Department of Agriculture's Office of Foreign Seed and Plant Introduction.

"Press on," was his motto.

In 1926, Fairchild and his wife, Marian, bought the nine-acre Coconut Grove property, which they named The Kampong— Malaysian for *village*. After Fairchild died in 1954, The Kampong was sold to Dr. Catherine Sweeney, a wealthy intellectual deeply interested in botany. In 1986, she bequeathed the property to the Pacific Tropical Botanical Garden in Hawaii. The gift created an opportunity for the institution to successfully petition Congress in 1988 to change its name to the National Tropical Botanical Garden.

Dr. Klein hired a new director for the center, Tom Lodge, an environmentalist and author of a book about the Florida Everglades. Lodge sketched plans to open The Kampong to regular visiting hours and build a tiny visitors' kiosk and badly needed parking.

This evening, strings of white lights twinkled over The Kampong lawn and outlined a large tent on the tennis court, creating a fairyland setting. Weather forecasts warned of a freeze. Guests arrived in wool jackets buttoned up to the neck. A few of the more experienced Florida doyens trailed fur coats. I shivered in a new icy gray Armani silk suit I had bought on sale in Honolulu. One trustee's wife surveyed me from head to toe and sniffed, "I guess you didn't know we dress up here."

When I told Bill Klein about the comment, he guffawed. "Wait until I tell Janet about that. You look mah-velous, just mah-velous."

This was a first for The Kampong, a goodwill dinner for one hundred guests we hoped to cultivate as potential friends and donors. "This is a historic night!" Bill told the guests in his after-dinner speech. He spoke passionately of his new vision for a reawakening at The Kampong, one that would allow it to take its place as an important site in the development of American botany.

After dinner I joined the stream of departing guests, falling into step with Doug Kinney. We walked along the lighted swimming pool. "Bill Klein talked too much," he grunted. "As usual." Doug got into his big black sedan for the trip back to North Palm Beach. Bill and I drove to the Hotel St. Michel, an elegant older hotel in Coral Gables. We were in high spirits, gossiping and comparing notes on the night, which we agreed was a big success.

At the hotel, we walked up the carpeted stairs, parting on the landing to head to our rooms on different floors. "I'll see you in the morning," he called.

"We should leave at nine o'clock so we can get to The Kampong on time," I reminded him.

I telephoned Bill's room at 8:30 the next morning, but received no answer. *Maybe he's having breakfast,* I thought, and went down to the hotel restaurant. I couldn't find him there, either. If he had gone jogging, he needed time to shower and dress. I walked down to the lobby and paused at the small, old-fashioned registration desk. Right then, the desk clerk handed me the phone.

"This is the emergency room nurse at Coral Gables Hospital. William Klein is here and asked me to call you. He fainted when he was jogging, and a rescue squad vehicle brought him in."

I knew Bill had had emergency heart bypass surgery a few years before. But he seemed in good shape, always exercising and watching his diet. I used my cell phone to cancel our morning meeting, then drove to the small community hospital where an ambulance had taken him. The ER physician escorted me into a small area with curtained patient beds. He spoke with professional clarity, "We think he's had a heart attack, but he seems to have stabilized now. There seems to be some occlusion of the veins. He said he had been having tightness in his chest for a few days. I'm not a cardiac specialist, and this hospital doesn't have the facilities to do a catheterization. I recommend that we transfer him to another hospital. Immediately."

Bill lay flat on his back, bare-chested and hooked up to several monitors. He had big, bloody scrapes on his forehead and along his chin, from the fall. He ran a tongue along his teeth. "I've broken a tooth," he said. I didn't see any breakage, but blood stained his teeth.

I took his hand in mind. He was lucid and somber.

"Bill, who was your heart doctor in Miami?" I asked.

He struggled to speak, and whispered a name. I had to bend my ear down to his lips to hear.

"Don't like him," he said softly. "I want the best cardiologist in Miami. Have them go on without me for this afternoon's meeting with the lawyers."

I still held his hand when a nurse walked in. It was a big hand, a strong hand, freckled from the sun. But pale and very cold. I asked the nurse to bring him a blanket.

"I *am* cold," he said, noticing for the first time.

"His blood pressure dropped, lowering his temperature," the nurse explained. She disappeared, then returned with a blue blanket, which she tucked in around him.

"I'll be back," I promised. I dialed Doug Kinney's North Palm Beach number. My voice must have betrayed alarm.

"Where are you?" he demanded.

"Coral Gables Hospital."

"Shit," he exploded.

"Bill may have had a heart attack. They're trying to transfer him to a bigger hospital that can do a catheterization."

When I called Janet, it took several rings before she answered, sleepily; it was only 5 a.m. in Hawaii. She was upset, but we talked about the Miami hospitals. "Tell him that I love him very much and I'll be there as fast as I can."

Tom Lodge, the director of The Kampong, arrived, joined by Mike Shea, the Garden's longtime corporate counsel. Silver-haired and in a dark blue lawyer's suit, he looked very un-Miami-like, lending a reassuring formality to an uncontrollable situation. The hospital located its cardiologist, Dr. Rosale, who came out to the concrete sidewalk to talk to the three of us.

"I don't think he's had a heart attack, but we're afraid he will have one," he said. I wanted to talk to Bill again to let him know we were here. Dr. Rosale warned, "We've given him a lot of drugs to stabilize him, so he might be groggy."

Bill didn't look so good. His skin had turned gray, and he was less alert. I bent down to his ear and whispered Janet's message. He nodded.

"Maybe they shouldn't move me," he said, his voiced strained with pain. A nurse came into our curtained corner and said, "We need to do some more tests. Can you turn on your side?"

"I can do it," Bill said heavily, but the effort was great and he winced.

The nurse asked for health insurance information so I drove back to the hotel to try to find it, then sped back to the hospital. As I walked up the emergency room entrance, Tom Lodge and

Mike Shea stared at me strangely. "There's been a turn for the worse," Tom said tightly. "The doctor came out a little while ago and said his heart had stopped twice."

"Shit, shit, shit," I stammered.

Dr. Rosale walked out of the glass doors. He approached us, shaking his head, his face wearing an odd expression. "I'm sorry," he said. "I'm sorry." I seemed to see the scene played again, in slow motion, its colors blanched into black and white.

"What?" I demanded. "He's dead? He's dead?"

"We've been working on him for half an hour. It's no good. There was too much damage. You should call his wife."

The doctor led me into the emergency room, through shiny, brightly lit hospital corridors to his private office, a darkened room with heavy black furniture. Janet answered on the second ring. "I'm packing and getting ready." She sounded upbeat.

"Janet, it's bad. Bill died a few minutes ago."

The difference between her cheery greeting and the next sounds were something I would like never to hear again. "Did you give him my message?" she asked. We talked a few minutes, then Dr. Rosale gave her a lot of details that she probably neither remembered nor understood, but he did it kindly. He handed the phone back to me.

I heard the quiet click of the door shutting as the doctor left the room.

CALM. CALM. I MUST be calm, I repeated silently. I set up my laptop in the small Kampong office. Janet wouldn't arrive until the next day; meanwhile, arrangements had to be made with a funeral home. Friends and trustees had to be called. A press release had to be written. We called Georgia Tasker, *The*

Miami Herald's garden writer and a Klein fan. She immediately set to work on an obituary that ran on Page One in the next day's paper. Two friends at *The Philadelphia Inquirer* arranged for a prominent obituary there, as Dr. Klein had been a local celebrity. My former editor, now at *The New York Times,* made similar arrangements. Whispered conversations and hunched-over phone calls began that day. Who would replace Dr. Klein? One wife of a Garden trustee wife arrived at the office. She gave me an appraising look and asked, "Lucinda, what are *you* going to do now?" I could see in her eyes what I had yet to fully realize until that moment. I didn't have a future at the Garden. I was a Klein hire and, without him, expendable. The anti-Bill forces would seize power.

I drafted letters and public statements that would go out with Doug Kinney's signature, mourning Dr. Klein's death and explaining interim measures to maintain stability. But I knew that in a matter of a heartbeat everything had changed.

Three days later, I worked at my Kampong desk while Doug Kinney met in a closed-door session with Kampong staff. "Doug requested that you not attend," one trustee stiffly informed me. Several staff members wandered back to the office, indicating that the meeting had ended. I expected Doug to greet me and probably thank me for the crisis management of the last three days. After five minutes, I realized that he was not coming. I walked across the open-air foyer into The Kampong dining room that was used for meetings. Doug was seated, his back to windows shaded by half-closed blinds that cast bars of light and dark over the table. Slanting light washed half of Doug's face in golden sun. The other half lay in shadow.

He did not rise or say hello when he saw me, but appraised

me coolly. "I'd really like to see those letters you drafted," he said.

My face froze. I saw that the uneasy checks and balances of power between Bill and Doug were gone. Doug ruled alone, unfettered. "Sure, I'll get them," I said and turned around to go back to my desk. I returned and handed him the papers. Doug sat silently and read them. I remained standing, as he did not invite me to sit down.

"Fine," he said. Then he rose and walked briskly to the door. I had to run to catch up with him, like a puppy clutching at his pant leg. He looked down. "The person I really feel sorry for is you," he said sadly. "You two were so close."

"Doug, I didn't die," I told him.

PART FIVE

Resolution

CHAPTER TWENTY-THREE

Macbeth

A GREEN ARMY TRUCK rumbled up to Garden headquarters. A ragtag group of reservists dressed in
camouflage tumbled out and unloaded rifles. Two sported long
hair, another a beard. Several had to leave their flak jackets un-
buttoned over middle-aged guts. Dr. Klein had served in the Air
Force, so when Janet inquired about a military funeral service at
the Army office in Lihue, the desk sergeant eagerly volunteered
to provide a twenty-one-gun salute. "We don't get much call for
those," he confided. Looking over this motley group one could
understand why. Their bedraggled battlefield outfits injected a
comic note into the somber proceedings.

Two hundred people gathered on the hillside outside Garden
headquarters for the memorial service. Both friends and foes delivered eulogies. Doug Kinney called Bill "a botanical general. . . ."
He was the best business friend I ever had," Doug said.

Rick Hanna described Dr. Klein as "a possibilitator—he sees
the possibilities and makes them happen."

"Lucky is the man who dies at work," I read from Epictetus.

The reservists fired three rounds of rifle shots.

Tributes ran in newspapers and botanical journals, national
and international. Dozens of former students, many now heads

of their own botanical institutions, wrote letters to Janet Klein about her husband's far-reaching vision and the impact he'd had on their lives. In all, a total of six memorial services were held to accommodate all those who loved Dr. Klein: one each in Denver, Philadelphia, Miami, and Hana, Maui, and two on Kauai, one on the hill for the Garden trustees, another down at Pump Six, where the garden crew, dressed in work clothes and boots, bowed their heads. The Hawaiian men presented Janet with elaborate orchid leis to cast on the outgoing tide, Hawaiian style.

After that tearful service, employees milled around Pump Six, not wanting to disperse. Janet Klein pulled me aside. "Lucinda, will you help me with these?" she asked, the leis in her arms. We were far from the beach, so we walked to a small bridge across the Lawai Stream that fed into the Pacific. Below us shallow water flickered over stones and shoals. "We'll toss them together," said Janet. "They'll eventually reach the sea."

We swung the leis high, then watched as they fell to the water below and crumpled against rocks. Ribbons of currents carried them away.

In the days and weeks after Dr. Klein's death, Doug Kinney took over the Garden, running it by telephone. "I'm in charge," he announced.

Bill had groomed Chipper Wichman, the young director of our Limahuli Garden on the north shore, to succeed him, pushing him to hone his management skills and connections with other botanical institutions. Chipper didn't possess a Ph.D. but brought perhaps more weighty credentials — passion, a connection to the island, and a charismatic charm that inspired great loyalty from his employees. He had inherited the one-thousand-

acre Limahuli Valley from his grandmother Juliet Rice Wichman, one of the first Garden trustees, but had felt so strongly
that it deserved to be a public institution that he donated the
property to the NTBG.

But Chipper's name wasn't even mentioned as a successor
to Bill. Instead Doug assigned Chipper to go to Maui to take
charge of the Kahanu Garden. Doug recruited the former finance director, my nemesis, to come back from the mainland to
serve as acting president. No nightmare could have been worse.
Our new president immediately took down Dr. Klein's poster
boards displaying architectural drawings that lay out the future
growth of the Garden and replaced them with charts listing
budget cuts. One by one, Klein-appointed staff were called into
closed-door meetings and fired.

"It's just business, Lucinda," explained Doug. After they
packed up their desks and departed, it was as if they had been
disappeared, never to be mentioned again. I watched each go
with a growing sense of foreboding. By chance, I witnessed
the shoddy treatment of Geoffrey Rausch, our distinguished
landscape architect. Rausch perched awkwardly on a small desk
chair in the open office area at headquarters, within a few feet of
my secretary and the two finance department assistants. The accountant-president pulled up a chair. He leaned toward Rausch.
"We're taking a close look at all of the consultants," he told the
designer. "Now what is it that you do?"

Rausch sat straight up, flinched, his already pale face turning
white. I closed my office door behind me before I heard the rest
of the dismissal. If they didn't know what the landscape architect did, we were in more trouble than I thought.

The atmosphere in the office, always somewhat sour whenever

Dr. Klein was away, grew charged with the toxic deadness that pervades an institution that has just axed a number of its workforce and the survivors ponder who's next. My experience with regime change at *The Philadelphia Inquirer* had prepared me for some of this. But the dreadful drama at the Garden was Shakespearian in its display of unmasked brutality. With astonishing speed Dr. Klein, once honored as a visionary, was now portrayed as a reckless screw-up. Supposed errors were discovered, magnified, and triumphantly exposed—aha! What bothered me most was the enjoyment.

In one of our daily phone calls, Doug told me that several weeks ago he and the accountant-president had discovered a budget deficit. "We didn't balance the budget last year as Bill Klein claimed," Doug said, with an air of mournful victory. I reeled with the news that for weeks I had been excluded from those discussions.

"How could that be?" I asked. "We raised so much money last year that we delayed a big foundation grant so we wouldn't get it until this year." I faxed him figures. After that I no longer had access to budget numbers. But the figures didn't really matter. It was all done in whispers. *Bill Klein was a big spender. He hired those outside consultants.* Hell, many of the accusations were true, anyway. He had boasted about shaking up the garden, expanding it, hiring new staff, and increasing the budget. I had no doubt that Bill Klein would have realized many of his ambitions given time. His three years had been long enough to build a new foundation but too short to complete the job. The Garden was like a rubber band snapping back into its former inertia. I sensed that it would descend into another dark era.

Yet nothing could erase a lifetime of goodwill. Bill Klein continued to walk the Garden like the ghost of good King Duncan who haunted his successor Macbeth. We remaining Klein loyalists learned to confer only when we were alone, outdoors. As I drove through the Garden grounds one day, I met foreman Scott Sloan on an empty road. We pulled our vehicles abreast and leaned out open windows, quietly appraising each other as fellow comrades. "I can't stand it," I said. "The way they're talking stink about Dr. Klein makes me sick."

"I know. He was my friend," Scott said proudly. "I feel like I've gone from having a mentor as a boss to having a *tor*-mentor." We laughed as conspirators. "It's true," Scott continued, "not all of his plans were doable and sometimes he got ahead of himself. But he had to do *something*, just to get this place moving."

Most of the time I wasn't laughing. I picked up cigarettes again, smoking when I rose in the middle of the night, panicked. I had depended too much on my relationship with Dr. Klein, failing to build alliances to protect myself. I remembered Bill's words. *Make friends, because come a hurricane, you're gonna need them.* I could feel the people on the board whom I felt were my allies dropping away, in phone calls not returned or, if they were, by their distant tones. I was outnumbered by Doug, the new president, and those who united around them. When I protested one of their new initiatives, Mike Shea, the Garden corporate counsel advised simply: Swim with them.

I didn't know where to go. There were no other jobs on the island for me. Like many of the most beautiful places on earth, Kauai was primarily a resort and retirement community. Home to the newlywed or nearly dead. I was in the middle of the Pacific. My living arrangements were akin to those of an indentured plantation worker. I lived in a Garden cottage, drove a Garden car. If they fired me, would I be thrown out of the cottage that day or would they give me a week to pack?

And so I kept my mouth shut. Every morning as I readied for work, I felt fear rising in me like a smothered scream. I looked into the bathroom mirror in my enchanting cottage and gave myself a little pep talk: *Smile on your face, back straight, act as if nothing is happening, show the flag, hide your opinions, get through the day. Model prisoner. Today, you're going to keep your job!*

Acting exhausted me. There's a violence inflicted on those who need to suppress their voice and silence their opinions. A death of self. A veil of gray depression descended, making me doubt and blame myself. At home, at dawn, I made frantic calls to old friends on the mainland. "Get out, get out!" most counseled. There were other nonprofit organizations, ones that prized fund-raising skills. Conceivably I could climb to ever-larger institutions, with ever-larger salaries. Perhaps become a director myself. The best of these jobs required passionate leadership, not just the urge to be in charge. At times, Bill Klein drove me mad with his ego and occasional pomposity, yet he had assumed the identity of the Garden. The Garden's growth was his growth; its transformation became his transformation.

I realized I could never embrace the task of presiding over an institution, though, immersing myself in administrative improvement while inspiring a collective effort. Individual work interested me more. The hunt of reporting, of crafting the results into a narrative, then getting the story out and contributing to the public debate — those were my interests. And I missed the rest of the world. I missed men. Smart men and ambitious women. Careerists who wanted to move mountains. I missed journalists, the fomenters of ideas, experimentation, and the kind of competition that spurred greater achievement. I missed talking about issues and the news of the day. I missed writing under my own name instead of the reams of letters and reports I produced anonymously. I was a journalist and needed to go back to that. Though I had grown weary of daily deadlines and the short half-life of news stories, journalism offered more choices. Magazine pieces, books, perhaps teaching. In early mornings at the cottage, a return to writing started with diary entries, sometimes no more than notes that served as warm-up exercises.

As I knew that my time in Hawaii was running out, I wanted to fill in the missing pieces in the Hawaiian plant story. I wasn't sure whether saving them was truly a lost cause. What could be done to protect the biodiversity of Hawaii, if not the rest of the planet? And why hadn't the National Tropical Botanical Garden led the charge? Keith Robinson remained a puzzle. I desperately wanted to see how he had reintroduced rare and endangered plants into the wild, succeeding when no one else could. John Rapozo had been a childhood friend of the mysterious Robinson, had even helped him carry water up at the Outlaw Plant Reserve. John volunteered to intercede and arrange a meeting with Robinson.

CHAPTER TWENTY-FOUR

Never Too Late

ARLOADS OF EAGER customers were lined up for the
volunteers' annual plant sale. A temporary nursery of canvas tents shaded potted palms, ferns, bougainvillea,
and, most in demand, one-of-a-kind anthuriums bred by Allerton Garden's master gardener, Hideo Teshima. I held up a pot
of the delicate, lipstick-pink, arrow-shaped blossoms. Before I
knew it, I had snatched several pots of anthuriums and seven
containers of ti, those fountains of red or green leaves. Then, in
a mad rush, I grabbed three palms and half a dozen ferns. John
Rapozo, unofficial foreman for the sale, piled my pots onto a
large wheelbarrow. We could barely pack all of the plants into
my car, so the palms extended out the trunk.

Suddenly, I recognized my inner urges. Spring fever. March
had arrived. In Philadelphia I would have been sowing seeds in
flats on the kitchen counter. Hawaii's seasonal changes creep in
so subtly that I failed to recognize the signs, but my body clock
registered the lengthening days. Settling in, work, and grief had
consumed so much attention that I hadn't time or energy to
start a garden at the cottage. Unsure of how much longer I'd
remain after Dr. Klein died, creating a garden seemed pointless.

But now I remembered his words: It's the nature of gardeners to take these disasters and improve on them.

Although the cottage interior had been transformed, only scraps of foundation plantings adorned its exterior. No pastel petunias, geraniums, or daffodils from my previous life here, I vowed. This was my once-in-a-lifetime chance for a tropical garden. I unfurled a coiled garden hose into undulating curves to mark new outlines for expanded beds. The circle drive seemed forlorn. Perhaps it needed a tree in the center, encircled with ferns and hot splashes of color.

On my knees, I tried to rip out a yellowing, multistemmed bamboo sprawled against the house. Then I heard the clunky chug of James's beat-up car climbing the hill to the cottage. Oh murder, he's going to be mad that I'm messing up the yard, I thought.

James shot from the car like a cannonball and charged over, glowering. "What you doing?" he asked accusingly. "That's my job. I'll do that for you. It needs a pickax." He marched to the locked toolshed at the rear of the cottage and returned with a brutal ax.

By the weekend, the bamboo had disappeared. I dug in a few hundred pounds of composted cow manure until the red Kauai dirt ran black. When shopping for ferns at a nearby nursery, on impulse I abandoned my ban on temperate zone plants and lunged for several flats of mundane but useful pastel impatiens. For the driveway circle, I bought flats of low-growing heather covered with tiny lavender flowers, and New Guinea impatiens in hot magenta, cerise, and tangerine. That afternoon I cranked up the sound system inside the cottage to blast out the window:

Wagner's *Die Walküre* and sound tracks from *South Pacific* and *The Sound of Music.* I broke open a package of new leather gardening gloves I had been hoarding. No reason to save them.

"*The hiiiillllllls are alllliiiiive with the sound of music,*" I sang as I set out the pots of fingered Laua'e ferns, interspersed with two shades of pink impatiens. I strapped on my riding helmet for protection because tall coconut palms swayed over some of the garden beds. Falling coconuts reputedly kill more people each year than sharks. Sam tried to help, rubbing against my ankles as I dug. I shooed her away. She picked herself up and moved off a few feet, then lay down and ate grass while she watched.

Preoccupation with the effort to drag a fifty-pound bag of manure or place a rock at the right angle of repose gave relief from the ever-growing office worries. Somehow *not* thinking helps to sort things out. Despite the memorial services, I hadn't yet grieved for Bill Klein. Now I knew how soldiers felt when comrades fell. You had to keep shooting and ducking before you could focus on your loss. But a garden is a good place to bury the dead. It's within the natural order for all living things to die; it allows for new growth. When I machete weeds to throw into the ravine, they decompose to a nourishing organic matter. Walt Whitman's words that all flesh is grass is a hopeful idea to a gardener.

I finished planting a sweet little patch of green ferns and pink impatiens. Then I worked again to complete a second bed. At the end of the afternoon, I hiked out the drive to get a long view, to see if the new plants provided the islands of color I sought. Not really. They'll grow quickly, I reminded myself. But a true cottage garden now swept across the length of the house in soft ovals and curves. A lake of veined caladiums and red ti surrounded the platform lanai off the back door. Green ti continued across the bedroom wing of the house, interspersed with funnels of asparagus ferns. A brazen, multicolored croton guarded the front porch. On the other side of the steps, two low-growing cycads and shooting comets of blue agapanthuses anchored a kidney-shaped bed, which then fed into a sweep of ferns and impatiens across the living room. During a time when I felt the earth shifting under me, something about literally putting down roots helped create a feeling of sanity.

Over the next few weeks, every step out the front door became a joyful occasion for inspecting progress. I congratulated myself on each new agapanthus bloom and the growing carpet of blue daze, a ground cover dotted with periwinkle blue flowers. News of my little cottage garden traveled fast among the garden staff. "I hear you are making a beautiful garden," said Eddie, one of the oldest gardeners. "I want to see it."

One evening I returned home to find eight huge lava boulders in place around the center driveway circle. I knew immediately that they had been dumped by John Rapozo and gently nudged into place with a bulldozer. Another night I found two black plastic garbage bags on the porch, filled with plugs of mondo grass, a wordless gift from the venerated Hideo, to fill in bare dirt patches.

I found more and more diversions outside the office: Not only my lifesaving little cottage garden, my research into Allerton history, and my return to writing, but also a sport that unexpectedly connected me more deeply to Hawaii than I could have imagined.

• • •

I DON'T WANT TO GET UP. It's 4:30 a.m., starless and black outside. It's probably raining at the river, anyway, and no one will show up. I don't wanna to go. Jeez, whose idea was this anyhow? Even the cat thinks it's too early. She's asleep on my feet and if I move she'll wake up and yowl.

Rousing myself to rearrange Sam, I got up and shivered into a robe, shuffled down the dark hallway to the kitchen, and switched on the small light under the stove hood. Sam didn't even bother following, she thought it so indecently early. Under a cone of light, I poured leftover coffee into a mug, put it in the microwave, punched one minute and ten seconds. Groped my way back to the bathroom. Wiggled into a Speedo bathing suit and black spandex bicycle shorts, then pulled on a sweat suit. Zapped another cup of coffee for the road, and clicked on a flashlight to guide me out the front door, down the steps to the driveway, and into the car. At this hour, only a handful of trucks and another early bird driver or two sped along Route 50 and through an empty Lihue.

Several weeks earlier at an art opening, I had met Carol Lovell, director of the Kauai Museum. She had raved about paddling with an all-women's outrigger canoe club. "We have enough to qualify for a women's master division," she said.

Wistfully I asked, "How do you manage to work it into your schedule?"

"We're on the river at five-thirty a.m.," she said.

"Five-thirty?"

As I reached the boat landing on the Wailua River, I pulled up beside four parked cars, then walked through heavily dewed grass toward silhouettes of figures, bent at the waist, stretching over legs spread wide. "Halloooooo," I called. As usual, there was no chitchat. A stately, full-figured Hawaiian woman with waist-length hair approached out of the dark. She drew me close and kissed me on the cheek, saying "Aloha" with the dignity of a Hawaiian queen. As race director for Kawaikini Canoe Club, Puna Dawson had already transformed a laid-back bunch of woman into a serious training team.

Six of us lined up along the canoe, three to each side. One, two, three, and we heaved, lifting the heavy boat out of its cradle and sliding it over a bed of old tires. Our fiberglass boat — *the vaha* — weighed four hundred pounds, much lighter than the hand-carved wooden crafts used by ancient Hawaiians. I scrambled down the riverbank into chilly water to guide the canoe. Puna directed me to sit last, in the number six seat, then hopped on behind me, astride the back of the canoe for a steering lesson. We headed upstream into blackness. After several weeks of practices I had learned the basic strokes, but steering was new. And more difficult. I tried to insert the paddle vertically into the water alongside the boat like a rudder. The boat tacked sharply from one side of the river to the other until Puna dispatched me to the number four seat while she took over. Old, teenage feelings of odd man out made me blush.

Each seat position had a job. Number six was the steersman, the captain who called which stroke to use. The strongest stroker sat in the number one seat and set the pace. The number two seat called the paddle changes. After six, eight, or twelve strokes, she yelled "Hut!" The crew responded "Ho," and pulled paddles from one side of the boat to the other, all in smooth, synchronized motion. The three and five seats provided balance, leaning out of the boat if necessary to keep it from tipping over. My seat, number four, had the least responsibility. I kept missing the beat, fumbling with the paddle.

As the sky paled to a thin wash of rose we headed downriver and took the boat out of the water. Puna looked at me appraisingly and said, "Lucinda, you're going to feel rotten for a while. The others have been paddling longer than you have. Don't beat yourself up about it."

I had never participated in women's team sports in school. But I figured I was a late bloomer anyway and now had as good a chance as any to redo my teenage years. "It's never too late to be what you might have been" was a motto for George Eliot. Why not for me? After all, the Kawaikini Canoe Club members were mostly middle-aged, and the early morning practices took place on the calm Wailua, the only navigable river in the Hawaiian Islands, instead of the undulating ocean. As I retreated, weak and marginalized at the office, my body got tougher and tougher.

One Sunday morning, Puna gathered twelve of us around her and announced, "We're going to take the boat out to the ocean." Sundays were for fun paddles that didn't begin until well past daybreak. We fell quiet. We had seen the big combers rolling in, pounding the beach.

Irene, a strong paddler, expressed what we all felt. "I don't want to go," she said. "I'm not ready. I'm afraid."

I thought Puna would insist, but instead she gathered us in a circle. "If someone speaks out against something, it may be telling us something. Some negativity could affect the enterprise. Go walk along the river under the bridge and I'll meet you on the beach."

On a sand dune with the incoming surf to her back, Puna lined us up in a row, sternly addressing us: "When you're out in a race, you're going to have to swim through water like this, so I want you to get comfortable in it." For sprints, "iron man" crews paddle the whole race themselves. But for longer distances, an escort motorboat pulls up alongside the canoe, and relief paddlers dive into the water and swim to the canoe as the tired crewmembers vault into the ocean from their seats.

"On the count of three, I want you to run into the surf and swim six strokes out, then return. One, two, three," she called, and we charged down the dune into the water, ducked under a wave, and stroked against the heavy, sucking pull. We body surfed in on a wave, then tried to dash out of the water before another surge hammered us into the sand. Puna sent us out again, this time for eight strokes. Then twelve. By sixteen, I panted. A heavy wave filled my mouth with salt water. I spit and sputtered and dragged myself out, thinking I couldn't go again. Thank God, she stopped.

"In a distance race," she told us, as we sprawled on the sand, "there will be twenty-eight changes when you'll have to jump off the escort boat and swim to the canoe, or leave the canoe and swim to the escort boat. You just did five. And look what happened. You're all exhausted. In an ocean race, you have to keep paddling after you've been in the salt water and swallowed salt."

After we stowed the canoe back on its cradle, we sat on a picnic table and listened to Puna talk about all the improvements we had made in recent weeks. We were beginning to hit the water together, she said, and we were getting stronger. We'd enter a short sprint race. After that, we could qualify for a long-distance race, the annual Molokai Channel race between the islands of Molokai and Oahu. "Forty-two miles, in a straight line, across rough water. Longer if you tack from side to side," Puna said. "Next year we'll aim for the Molokai. How many are interested?"

Every hand went up.

Puna fascinated me. She had plenty to do other than show up at 5:30 to coach a bunch of neophyte paddlers. She worked for a social agency that delivered meals to the elderly. Her five children were mostly grown, with the youngest age eighteen. But she had a goal, and it was nothing less than to make Hawaiian outrigger canoe paddling an Olympic sport. Puna took the long view and moved toward her goal like a chess player, each advance requiring years of organizing work. Like most generals, she realized that a grand plan was fine, but the battles were won in the trenches. And this particular trench was right here, at 5:30 a.m. with an unlikely group of middle-aged novices.

Puna had grown up at Kailua Beach on Oahu, her father, grandfather, and uncle all boat builders. Back then, canoes were beautiful objects of polished koa. Paddling provided entertainment for children, along with surfing, sand boarding, and fishing. Puna starting paddling in regattas at age eight, usually pressed into duty as an extra.

Men ran all the canoe clubs then. After they raced, the women fit in their sprints. "We had to fight for canoe time," she remembers fiercely. But the big events were the long-distance races — and they were only for men. Even in Hawaii, though, the rumblings of the women's movement began to shake things up. Women started agitating for their own long-distance racing.

"Women were becoming *alive,* and it all stemmed from that," Puna told me.

By the time she was twenty-four, Puna was married with two children and pregnant with a third, but still paddling. Her husband, Kalani Dawson, became assistant to the race director of the Honolulu Canoe Racing Association. Both Puna and Kalani became deeply involved in the administration and organization of racing.

Parents came to watch their children paddle; Puna and Kalani enticed the parents to start paddling themselves. Originally they did it for exercise, but the adults inevitably caught the competition bug and starting training to enter sprint regattas. Puna checked into what was necessary to make outrigger canoeing an Olympic sport. For one thing, an Olympic sport had to have participation by both sexes and all age groups. Even for consideration as an exhibition sport at the Olympics, they would have to show that at least thirty-eight countries participated in the sport. Puna saw that the only venue that could draw that many other countries was the legendary Molokai Channel crossing that drew paddlers from as far away as Tahiti and Java. By counting over a span of years, they could show that teams from enough countries had raced the Molokai.

Women started to secure their own funding, paddling became a bigger and bigger sport, and, at the 1990 Los Angeles Summer Olympics, outrigger canoeing debuted as an exhibition sport. There are still hurdles to overcome for full Olympic competition status — international regulations have yet to be adopted for boat design and equipment. Just as Puana was making progress, her husband, Kalani, was transferred to Kauai.

Paddling interest on Kauai was low. Puna and Kalani saw that their task was to prod Kauai's lackadaisical canoe clubs into races.

The Kawaikini Canoe Club members had never entered a race. They were known for showing up once a week, on Sunday, for a desultory run up the river followed by beer. But the new members brought competitive spirit and a rigorous practice schedule. Carol, the lanky director of the Kauai Museum, acted as our team captain. She was a handsome woman with white streaks in her short wavy hair, a natural athlete, diplomat, and leader. She enlisted her scrappier sister, Irene, who sang in a Hawaiian band and arranged flowers at the trendy Pacific Café. Both sisters were married to fishermen. Their friend Angie was another key member, loud and boisterous, who sometimes brought her beautiful teenage daughter to paddle. Though often wisecracking, Angie could also be found sweeping the boat landing. "That's part of clubbing, too," she said.

Several doctors joined in order to squeeze in exercise before reporting to duty at Wilcox Memorial Hospital and quickly became a divisive presence. The local women contended that the doctors never helped with the fund-raising necessary to buy the canoes and rigging. Dr. Karen showed up for early morning practice but rarely said a word. Dr. Mary was the most outgoing, our Miss Congeniality, although she didn't realize she branded herself a recent import by showing up at practices in her Mercedes and inviting the club to her swanky mini-mansion overlooking the river. Dr. Ellen was a relative youngster at thirty-five, and the most aggressive, with a combative air not disguised by a tousled mass of blond curls. Beth, a nurse, was the only regular under thirty. A steady presence with good humor, she had broad, powerful shoulders and a dark blue medallion design tattooed in the middle of her back. Martha, another nurse, was local and sometimes brought her boyfriend, Brian, a fisherman who also acted as assistant coach.

But as we progressed together, this early morning crew became a force, attending the monthly club meetings and insisting on a racing schedule. A revolution had occurred in Kawaikini Canoe Club and I became a part of it.

CHAPTER TWENTY-FIVE

Obake

*B*EFORE I KNEW it, spring turned into summer. I was still hanging on at the Garden, faking it, but my spirits had started to revive. One Saturday after a late ride with Bo, I returned to the pasture after a harvest moon had risen. Hungry, I decided to stop at the Big Save grocery. As I got out of the car, I heard a high-pitched singing in Japanese, accompanied by a steady boom of a bass drum. The Bon Dance in Koloa.

Although I wore riding clothes—a jean shirt over black stretch riding pants and cowboy boots, all streaked with red dirt stains—I crossed the road to join the fair at the Koloa Jodo Mission. Paper lanterns bobbed along spokes strung from a central post, from which big speakers broadcast the harsh nasal tones of Japanese singing. Every August, Buddhist missions all over the island held ritual dances to grieve lost loved ones and bid them a return to the spiritual world.

About fifty women in their best kimonos moved together in intricate steps, each waving a white handkerchief, a symbol of a departed soul. *Obake,* or ghosts, they called them. One tall, slender woman, probably seventy, was dressed in brilliant red silk tied with a pale pink obi. She turned her face upward with the joy of movement, dancing with grace, her arms and feet swinging in long-memorized patterns. Other dancers sneaked glances at neighbors to follow the steps, but she knew them, unerringly. A few small girls in tiny kimonos pranced amid the other dancers, improvising with unrestrained energy.

At the snack booths, men turned out hot "flying saucer" sandwiches by slapping bread into round, black iron holders, then spooning in a spicy hamburger mixture. Closing the holder sealed the crusts and nipped off the edges, making little round bread pockets, grilled over hot flames. Delicious. After consuming two, I headed for the Okinawa doughnut booth for a paper bag of the deep-fried delights. I remembered that Bill Klein had introduced them to me, saying, "You can tell they're good when the paper bag is soaked with grease."

The fair lasted two nights and would end with a ceremonial good-bye to the spirits that both honored the dead and subtly instructed the grieving that it was time to resume their lives. I went inside the temple to buy a ghost ship, a small wooden boat with a paper sail to shield a candle flame. I wrote three names on a slip of paper and tucked it behind the sail. Dad. Mom. Bill.

Doug Kinney had finally found a new Garden director, a botany professor. The professor had never run a botanical garden, nor expressed any interest in the art or demands of one. I feared for the worst.

If I didn't get out I would shrink into a gutless wimp.

Ever since the Berlin Wall fell in 1989, I had been intrigued by stories of American journalists who traveled to Iron Curtain countries to help build a free press. At the time, I could never afford to take time off from the weekly paycheck that paid my mortgage and bills. But when I left the Garden, I would be cut loose again from any obligations. I filled out an application for a Knight International Press Fellowship, run by a Washington, D.C., organization that sent reporters and editors abroad in sort of a journalistic Peace Corps. What is your preferred destination? the application asked. Eastern Europe, I wrote. Expect hardship conditions, they warned. Pay was low. I wouldn't hear whether I was accepted for another month or two, but I had made my decision. Tomorrow I would call Doug. I was beginning another journey whose destination was not yet revealed.

I wasn't afraid. In Philadelphia, I had allowed myself to be diminished by others. How small my visions for myself had been then, how limited my imagination of what possibilities lay before me. I felt solid within now and could move on my own power to protect myself, without the deus ex machina that had brought me to Kauai.

Yet I no longer wanted to make long-term plans, nor try to design my fate. Life can change in a second. If you let it. The essence of grace was to live within the mysteries, accept the uncertainties, and greet whatever develops.

The next night a crowd gathered on the rock pier at Kukuiula Harbor in Poipu to observe the final act of the Bon ceremony. A phalanx of young men in swimsuits carried on their shoulders three flat-bottomed rowboats, each holding hundreds of ghost ships, candles all lit. The men swam the boats out beyond the wave break to tie them to a small outboard craft. The silent crowd watched. The outboard motor hummed, then shifted into higher gear as it moved off, trailing a wake of dancing, flickering candle flames. As the boats moved further and further out to sea, the outline of the outboard disappeared into darkness. We could make out only the glimmering lights.

And then the flames no longer advanced with purpose. They drifted, bobbing on the waves. The motorboat had let them go.

IN THE END, Doug graciously allowed me to live at my cottage for a few months after I quit. I left campaign plans, drafts for the end-of-year fund appeals, the last newsletter, and a script for a video about the Garden, which I knew would never be completed without Dr. Klein but agreed to write anyway. In return, I unrolled into the luxury of having days to myself to fill with hours at the laptop in the sunlit cottage, unrushed rides through the hills with Bo, and, of course, canoeing.

Outrigger canoeing history captured me. It wasn't just because I could participate; the canoes were intrinsic to Hawaiian life, responsible for the settling of the Hawaiian Islands in the first place. Polynesians had invented the double-hulled voyaging canoe for their vast organized migrations that began two thousand years ago in Samoa and thrusted north and went to unknown Pacific islands. Expert navigators, they memorized the seasonal changes of the sun and stars and learned to discern distant land from ocean waves and flotsam and jetsam. They studied bird migration. The Pacific golden plover, among other birds, arrived each fall on wind currents from the unknown north. The tiny bird tarried a few days, then flew off to the south, bound for islands whose distance the early Polynesians had already measured. So more islands must lie northward, they concluded.

For everyday life the Polynesians paddled lightweight, shallow fishing canoes that skimmed the surface of their calm ocean lagoons. But settlers in the Hawaiian Islands needed a new sort of fishing canoe if they wanted to eat. Unlike most of Oceania, the Hawaiian Islands lie in the middle of deep ocean trenches, without rings of coral reefs to protect them from the most violent storms or to create many shallows full of fish. The Hawaiians needed heavier canoes to pierce the treacherous surf and yet also navigate close to the shorelines of rocky cliffs. They built heavier and more deeply drawing boats, fitted with one-piece hulls, higher surf guards, and simplified outriggers.

The end product, the Hawaiian canoe, "may well be the most versatile and seaworthy rough water craft ever designed or built by any culture in any time," contended the celebrated paddler and canoe historian Tommy Holmes. (The need for these rough-water canoes was particularly evident on Kauai, where a harbor dock that could meet and off-load ships was not built until 1962. Up until then, sugarcane had to be cabled out to ships. Locals in canoes met seaplanes to ferry smaller cargo ashore.)

Like Dr. Klein, I was beginning to see the history of plant life and the study of botany as the root (sorry, can't help myself!) behind all human achievement. And in Hawaii, the root that became critical to development of the sturdy Hawaiian canoe was attached to the koa tree. *Acacia koa.* The new Hawaiians surely must have fallen to their knees in astonishment and gratitude when they explored the Islands' interiors and discovered immense forests of tall native hardwood trees that reached one hundred feet into the air. Circumferences spanned as many as thirty-six feet. Whole villages of one hundred men and more would decamp to the interior to fell one of the giant trees, rough out a dugout, then drag the ten-ton canoe down to the coast. At the time koa covered many of the Islands, the most populous tree second only to ohia. After five centuries of plunder, only a small fraction remain, a testament to the continued modern demand for koa art frames, furniture, and even wall paneling.

Early European explorers envied the speed, maneuverability, and seaworthiness of the Hawaiian watercraft. "One man will sometimes paddle a single canoe faster than a good boat's crew could row a whaleboat," wrote one eighteenth-cenury British captain. Yet despite their canoes' obvious advantages, the Hawaiians nearly abandoned them after they saw tall ships. Only ten years after Cook's arrival, King Kamehameha entreated American and British captains for ships' carpenters so they could build their own Western-style brigs. By the 1840s the Hawaiian "navy consisted of decked vessels . . . armed schooners of from twenty to a hundred tons," according to nineteenth-century explorer George Simpson. What little enthusiasm for canoe racing that survived was effectively smothered by zealous missionaries to whom the gambling element, so much a part of the canoe race, was utterly sinful.

In 1875, King David Kalakaua, who was dedicated to reviving traditional Hawaiian water sports, set aside his birthday, November 16, as the date for an annual regatta. Men and women alike—even royalty—joined in. A number of clubs came into existence during Kalakaua's reign, but when he died, water sports again went into decline. Not until the 1930s did a local group of paddlers with Hawaiian, Japanese, and Portuguese ancestry in South Kona begin building canoes exclusively for racing.

When famed paddler A. E. "Toots" Minvielle first called for a race of the treacherous Molokai Channel, forty miles from Molokai to Waikiki, not even his own canoe club, the Outrigger Canoe Club in Honolulu, supported him. They feared it too long, too dangerous, and too impractical. That was 1939. He continued to lobby, finally persuading three clubs to enter the first race thirteen years later.

AS EARLY MORNING canoe practices continued, I began to realize that team spirit would determine whether we would ever race. Our first test came when Puna approached us one morning about catering a traditional luau for a young Japanese couple who wanted to celebrate the first birthday of their daughter, a big occasion in the islands.

"We could earn some of the money to pay for racing entry fees, shipping the canoe to other islands, and hiring an escort boat," Puna told us.

The local women all knew what to do. Staging a luau is as much a part of their repertoire as putting on a Thanksgiving turkey dinner is for women in the rest of the country. Preparations consumed the better part of a week.

When I arrived at Carol Lovell's house, stacks of aluminum trays and cook pots filled the small kitchen and spilled out into the living room. Her five-year-old grandson and three of his coconspirators ran in and out between our legs. Outside on the deck, Carol's sister, Irene, emptied gallon bags of concentrated purple paste into a huge pail at a laundry sink. She added water, then mixed the concoction with one assured hand, scooping and pulling, until it became smooth and ropey. "Some people can't do it, their poi has lumps in it," she said. "Hawaiians don't like lumps in their poi."

Neither Carol nor Irene would trust us *haoles* with any important tasks, so we got the grunt work. We scooped poi into Dixie cups, added a few drops of water to keep it moist, wiped the cup clean, then covered it with a plastic top. "Water keeps it sour," Irene told us. "Hawaiians like it sour, so it's almost furry on top. I like it real sour," she continued. "One of my favorite dinners is a can of sardines mixed with shoyu sauce, a little sesame oil, and fresh poi on top." Just the thought made my tongue recoil.

For two long days we worked. Carol's family already had its own *imu* pit that dominated their small backyard like an open grave. Mary and Ellen hauled pine logs to stoke up the fire, while Beth, Irene, and others chopped onions, olives, and boiled potatoes for potato and macaroni salads, staples of a modern luau. Carol's fisherman husband, Sol, diced fifteen pounds of fresh marlin for *poke,* then mixed it with flecks of seaweed. Grandpa Lovell made long rice in huge aluminum pots at his house next door. Irene and Carol scraped salmon into mushy pulp for the *lomi-lomi.* A neighbor stretched fishing line between her hands and used it to cut small cubes of *kulolo,* a sticky cake of dark purple taro and coconut, similar in richness and texture to marzipan.

The *imu* fire still raged after several hours, heating bowling-ball-sized lava rocks until they burned an incandescent red. When the flames banked down into coals, the men lined huge wire pans with aluminum foil to hold a hundred-pound pig, headless and quartered. They added six turkeys wrapped in foil, as well as sweet potatoes and vats of rice for rice pudding— other modern luau accoutrements. The men pulled the wire cages onto the fire and covered them with a fragrant layer of split banana stalks. To get them evenly spread apart, they had to step on the coals. As they walked on fire in heavy boots, billowing clouds of heat and smoke cloaked them.

We laid fans of ti leaves over the pit in an overlapping design. Quickly, six men pulled a sheet of plastic over it all, then rushed to shovel cold ashes and dirt all along the edges, sealing in heat and steam. They all looked at one another, about to congratulate themselves, when Sol hit himself on the head with the heel of a hand. "The bags! We forgot the bags!"

Nearby a pile of wet burlap bags lay untouched. Frantically, the crew shoveled the dirt away, struggling through the heat and smoke to pull away the plastic. They arranged the bags, then reclosed the pit to steam overnight. "What did the Hawaiians do before they had plastic?" I teased Sol.

"That's a good question," he said.

The next morning we returned at dawn to uncover the pit. The men pulled the smoked meat off the bone and carried big trays to long tables set up in the open carport. Six of us paddlers, dressed in aprons over our shorts, worked quickly with tongs to remove all gristle, bone, and skin, shredding the meat into fine pieces. We diverted crispy pigskin and crackling outer meat to a special pan. Irene carried it over to Grandpa Lovell's house, a trail of kids behind her, all begging. I followed, too, and we gorged ourselves on it before Grandma Lovell took it. "We'll chop it up for *saimin*," she said.

We worked all day, then rushed home to change into our Kawaikini pink and blue team T-shirts, ready to report for duty at our clients' house. We helped the young mother decorate picnic tables with balloons and stuffed animals in honor of the birthday girl, who toddled around in a red and white kimono. As guests arrived, a five-piece band played Hawaiian songs. A curtain strung between two palms served as a "fish pond" for kids to troll for a gift. Doughnuts dangled on strings for a messy doughnut-eating contest.

In the carport, Mary dished kalua pig and turkey while Ellen manned the poi cups and long rice. Beth, the youngest team member, distributed *lomi-lomi* salmon and marlin *poke*. My job was to dish out the salads, as well as a bowl of precious *opihi*—meat from tiny periwinkles picked from rocks, as prized as Beluga caviar and almost as expensive.

Every time we sensed that no one could see us, Beth and I pounced on the food, stuffing ourselves on tender, smoky pork and turkey, free from fat and gristle. "That's how it's supposed to be," Carol informed me. Even so, I declined the special treat of *lomi-lomi* salmon mixed with poi. As the guests finished their last helpings, we scrubbed dishes and packaged copious leftovers into big Ziploc plastic bags. Part of the tradition, Puna insisted, included sending relatives home with leftovers.

One of the doctors, Karen, had failed to show for any of the preparations over the two days. But at the end of the event, she appeared in jeans to help clean up. "I've been on call all weekend," she explained.

One paddler went to hug Sol and thank him for all the work he did.

"It's what makes a family," he said.

CHAPTER TWENTY-SIX

Renegade Plant Rescuer

WITH SOME ANXIETY, I drove through the cane fields to reach a rundown, ramshackle house. A once-grand portico sagged forlornly over a parked Oldsmobile Cutlass Supreme Oldsmobile with three flat tires and a registration sticker that had expired two years ago. Keith Robinson's mother, Helen, wore the vacant smile and quizzical expression of advanced senility as she wandered around the front yard. Her sweater bagged and had been buttoned crookedly. "In case you haven't guessed, there isn't a lot of money left," Keith said quietly, as we loaded his truck. He set down on its seat his food for the day: a half loaf of store white bread and three bags of potato chips.

"Aren't you bringing water, Keith? I have two quarts in my backpack."

"No, ma'am. I usually work the whole day without water." The pickup truck rattled and jostled us harshly as we left the cane plains and climbed through scruffy dry forest. Robinson reached around behind his seat. "Oh, gee," he said with elaborate nonchalance, "I forgot my shoulder holster and pistol. Normally I carry weapons as a matter or course. Particularly when taking a woman up to the preserve."

"Why is that?"

"Might run into outlaws, bad guys, marijuana growers," he said brusquely. After an hour we reached an isolated spot in the west side's backcountry, eleven miles above Waimea. He put on his trademark Kelly-green construction hardhat. On foot, he led me across a narrow concrete dam over a ditch and up a hill to an unmarked clearing, then stopped.

"Welcome to the Kauai Outlaw Preserve," he said with a sardonic grin.

As promised, John Rapozo had arranged an initial meeting for me with Robinson a week before. I knew it was a chance for Robinson to decide whether I was trustworthy. When he picked me up in his battered pickup, I was surprised by his nondescript looks: thin, very pale, with gray hair clipped short around a receding hairline. I insisted he call me by name rather than the *ma'am* he kept using, but he shook his head earnestly. "It's my upbringing, ma'am. I've been taught to treat ladies with respect." Inside the truck, where my legs would have rested, were newspapers, crumbled bags, empty soda cans, and about fifty pounds of other trash. I edged onto the seat with my knees under my chin, then tried to brace myself against the jarring, bumpy ride of a truck whose shocks had long been shot. He didn't need much prompting to start what became an all-day monologue. Before he would take me to the preserve, he said, he needed to educate me about "realities."

We drove up the Waimea Canyon Road to the mountains, Robinson talking a mile a minute. "First thing you have to understand is that the environmental movement is based on massive lies," he lectured. "The eco-Nazis are perfecting a fiction that Hawaii's native species can be saved. But native plants are biologically incompetent. They're far less efficient than nonnative species in extracting nutrients and water from the soil. They recover much slower from grazing than nonnative species. They cannot compete for sunlight. Their seed dispersal systems are far poorer. Their root systems are a lot shallower. They lack the internal mechanisms that nonnative species have, such as resistance to disease or lack of rainfall."

Yet while Robinson harshly recited the botanical deficiencies of Hawaiian plants, he was still devoting his life to trying to save them. Why? I asked. He shook his head, chuckling, as if bemused at his own folly in a noble yet doomed mission. "It's the way I was brought up," he says. "To take care of the land."

It's not the first time a Robinson has tried to stage a last stand against the intrusion of civilization. Since his great-great-great-grandmother Eliza Sinclair bought the island of Niihau in 1868, the Sinclairs and their descendants, the Gay and Robinson families, have tried to preserve it as the last pure settlement of Hawaiian life. Often called the Forbidden Island, Niihau still harbors about two hundred Hawaiians who live without cars and only a few electric generators. It's the last place on earth where the native Hawaiian language is still spoken daily. Visitors are not allowed unless invited, and any resident who chooses to leave may never come back. The Robinson stewardship has been both praised for preserving a last scrap of authentic antique culture and condemned as feudal dictatorship, a remnant of colonial society, rife with abuse.

Ever since the Sinclair family acquired Niihau, the island has been as much albatross as prize. The widowed Mrs. Sinclair, then sixty-two, and her large family arrived in Hawaii from New Zealand in 1868 looking for a new place to settle. King

Kamehameha V offered them Niihau, the small island that lay seventeen miles northwest of Kauai. The king demanded ten thousand dollars, and they paid it in gold. No one told the Sinclairs that the island had received record high rainfalls the previous two years. After the family settled on Niihau, the lush green meadows quickly returned to their usual state of drought, and the freshwater lakes dried up into brackish mudflats.

After only a few years, the Sinclairs moved to the west side of Kauai. The children married into the local gentry and soon acquired thousands of acres of land for their ranches and sugar plantation. But they never let go of Niihau, raising cattle on the island and using it as a summer retreat. For more than one hundred years, the Robinsons employed the entire Niihau population on its ranch, carrying them even when there was no work during frequent droughts. Residents continued to live, for no charge, in modest houses. A supply ship provided erratic transport to and from the island. The Robinsons also supplied free health care of a sort, free beef and mutton, and some supplies. But in return, they lay down the law, demanding that no Niihauans speak to outsiders about the family and their affairs and that residents follow "moral behavior" or face expulsion.

Keith's father, Aylmer Robinson, also instilled a strict Christian faith in his sons. Keith spent much of his boyhood on isolated Niihau. "In your business life, you were sober and wise," he remembered. "In your personal life, you didn't attend wild parties and you didn't associate with people who did."

Keith's paranoia about a government takeover of his nursery has some historic basis in fact. In the 1960s, the Hawaiian state government had succeded in appropriating hundreds of acres of Robinson land in the Kalalau Valley for a state park on Kauai's north shore. Then in the 1970s, the government proposed to start condemnation proceedings in order to turn Niihau island into a national park. As the Hawaiian activist movement has grown, Hawaiians have increasingly called for the Robinsons to give Niihau to the residents.

When Keith and his brother, Bruce, were born, the extended Robinson family owned nearly a third of Kauai. Keith says the family has spent millions to support Niihau. That, plus inheritance and land taxes, he says, have left much of the family nearly broke. The Robinsons had hoped to sell several thousand acres on Kauai's north shore, but then the state blocked that possibility by zoning the land for conservation use.

Keith began his endangered plant nursery in 1986 with the idea of reestablishing the native flora as a model to be duplicated throughout Hawaii. He dreamed that he could convert some of the family's unprofitable agricultural land to high-quality ecotourism. For the past seventeen years, he's worked as a commercial fisherman, but spends most of his energy on his plant preserve. Except for caring for his mother, there was nothing else. "I don't have any wife or children. I'm not particularly enjoying life," he told me, "and I have nothing to look forward to."

WHEN WE FINALLY ARRIVED at the Outlaw Preserve, I wasn't prepared for how extensive it was. Nor how camouflaged. No one except a plant expert would recognize it as a treasure trove of rarities. Robinson's domain was an untamed, weedy place. Waist-high yellowing brush and grasses grew everywhere in a meadow as dry as a tinderbox. Trees and shrubs contained in wire pens strained to escape, like zoo animals in cages. A flowering yellow hibiscus trumpeted over the grass. Fan palms of varying heights bobbed up and down. Although Robinson continued to address me as "Ma'am," with courtly politeness, he seemed ready to erupt.

"There's going to be nothing pretty here," he said grimly. "Nothing fun. This is reality. This is what the eco-Nazis don't tell you about. The work that needs to be done to keep these endangered species alive is slave labor." Although many of the species grew from seeds he had collected—questionably—from state land, he never really risked prosecution. State and federal foresters respected Robinson's work so much that they sometimes slipped him rare seeds, a fact that Keith quietly admitted.

Now, sweat darkened the back of his polyester denim-colored shirt. Big, hand-sewn stitches—obviously his own work—held together a tear on the upper left sleeve. My eyes kept returning to that puckered patch, as if secret evidence of Robinson's fragile vulnerability despite his hard bluster.

"Oh my," he worried as he bent over a hibiscus that had withered in the brutal heat. "Everything is showing stress." A recent drought had dried up Kauai, particularly on the west side, forcing Keith to carry more water for a longer time than he had in the past. "How the devil am I going to carry the equivalent of three drums of water every day at the age of fifty-seven?" he asked, beseeching the heavens.

Robinson led me through his wonderland of specimens. Here he was king and protector, gathering lonely sole survivors, or pairs like Noah, that he coaxed to develop seed. He reeled off each plant's Latin botanical name with the familiarity of a grandfather. *Kokia kauaiensis,* a native hibiscus that grows only in the mountains of Kauai. *Munroidendron racemosum,* the Waimea Canyon variety. "Only five or six trees have ever been seen," he said. "I discovered the first one around 1982. The parent tree was killed by a falling boulder, but now I have several growing, from seed." Other miracles included a a native plumeria and a huge native palm, *Pritchardia aylmer-robinsonii*, from Niihau.

"NTBG has nothing like this," he said with disgust. "Those air-conditioned bureaucrats there don't know that this kind of work exists."

Robinson walked back to the truck. He shouldered an empty fifty-five-gallon plastic drum, carried it fifteen yards to the dam, lugged it across, then up the hill to the preserve. Back and forth, back and forth, he carried drums, wire, and long iron poles. He could have saved himself enormous effort just by parking the truck closer to the dam and unloading it there. Drawing water one bucket at a time from the ditch was equally laborious.

"Keith, couldn't you rig up an electric pump and hose to make an irrigation system?" I asked, careful to phrase it as diplomatically as possible.

He shook his head dismissively. "There is no cost efficient way to do it."

I'm not sure a harder way to water plants existed. As he carried water, he ranted and fumed. Mosquitoes, thick and buzzing everywhere, bit all the way through my long-sleeved shirt. I rolled up a sleeve and found a dime-sized welt that itched and prickled in the heat. The sun beat down unrelentingly on our heads and backs.

As we hiked higher up the mountain, we approached a rocky stream, shrunk to a yard wide. Despite his earlier bravado about not ever drinking water, he lay on a flat rock, stretched his neck out, and put his lips to the muddy stream, the only pristine, drinkable natural water in Hawaii, he claimed. He drank long and hard. "My, that was good," he said, smacking his lips.

We continued to pass his caches of water and supplies. In a forest glen, he unpacked a rusted coffee can of crystallized blue fertilizer. Like a cook measuring salt, he took a tiny pinch from it and sprinkled it at the base of several trees and shrubs. "You have to put this fertilizer on a certain distance from the trunk, put in only a certain amount," he explained.

"How did you learn to get these plants to grow in the wild?" I asked.

He answered with an impatient snort. "Lady, this isn't the wild. I'm standing over these plants every five minutes with water and fertilizer. Yeah, I've licked it, but only because of fantastic amounts of hard labor." He removed his hard hat and, using it as a dipper, scooped up water from a drum. Ever so slowly he poured the water down the stalks of his penned beauties. The water mixed with the perspiration in his hat so that he literally gave the sweat of his brow to the endeavor. A tenderness cleared all the furies from his visage as he poured a steady stream, seemingly willing it to be absorbed down to the roots.

"Keith," I asked neutrally, "why did you never forge ties with the National Tropical Botanical Garden? It seems like it would make such a natural partnership. Steve Perlman and Ken Wood explore the remote reaches of Hawaii's mountaintops to bring back seeds, Kerin propagates them in the Garden nursery, and you plant them back into the countryside."

To my surprise, he answered calmly. From the beginning, he said, he planned his preserve as a mid-elevation level nursery for NTBG's seedlings. Robinson said he worked with several of the early botanists at the Garden, but they were fired. Then, "it became a twittering fairy festival," he snorted. "The tiptoe boys. They made a few overtures but I had nothing to do with them." The current crew at the Garden acted snobbishly to him, he said.

Then Robinson's brother, Bruce, caught Garden field collector Ken Wood trespassing and marched him to the Waimea Police Station. "Wood had been pretending to be buddies," Robinson remembered acidly. "I had given him a lot of stuff. Really rare stuff from Robinson land. When I got to the police station, Wood *laughed* at me. He told me, 'This became necessary because you are such a selfish person.' I got really mad. A police sergeant had to come between us. He thought I was going to take a swing."

Similar alliances and friendships with Oahu botanists Keith Woolliams from Waimea Botanical Garden and Charlie Lamoureux at Lyon Arboretum also dissolved in storms of perceived betrayal.

"What do you think about when you're up here?" I asked.

"Think and you go crazy," he said. "Mostly, I'm planning work. Many times I'm thinking bitterly about the government and how they're not doing the work I'm doing. I'm getting real resentful about that." I rested on a mossy rock. Sweat soaked my own shirt, even in the shade. I wilted in the midday heat. I noticed a pile of stuff under a tarp and asked him what it was.

"I backpacked in five thousand pounds of concrete and now I have to bring in another five thousand pounds," he said.

"Why?"

"To make a base for the composting toilet." He pointed a few yards away to a large square mound the size of an outhouse, covered with blue plastic tarp.

I was confused. "Who's going to use it?" I questioned.

He explained impatiently that it was part of his plan to use the preserve for ecotourism. The shrouded toilet made the skin on my scalp prickle. What motivates a man to break his back carrying materials to build a toilet up a steep trail and deep into the woods for nonexistent tourists? Assuming that he could ever organize such a thing, assuming that he could ever talk to tourists in civil terms, assuming they would want to ride an hour up a bumpy road, shimmy across a narrow dam, and hike up here, a toilet might not be the first thing they would need.

As Keith spooned hatfuls of water on his specimens, I thought of the other petty wars that raged in this elusive paradise, this Garden of Eden. Many of these plantsmen and plantswomen got along better with plants than with people.

Robinson and I hiked another hour and a half uphill as he repeated his now-common refrain. "I will destroy my preserve rather than let the government get its hands on it. I would rather die than let them take over." He seemed to believe that the most serious threat had come a few years earlier when the U.S. Fish and Wildlife Service listed a rare tree, *Caesalpinia kavaiensis,* on its endangered species list and proposed a recovery plan to save its habitat. Only one specimen of the tree grew on Kauai—in the middle of Robinson's preserve. When he read the plan, he concluded that the Feds intended to seize his Outlaw Preserve.

Robinson's face paled with exertion. As we reached the edge of a clearing, he walked over to a charred, blackened tree trunk that stood about twelve feet high. I saw that this dead tree was his Boston Tea Party; his Waco, Texas; his Ruby Ridge. He encircled the remains of *Caesalpinia kavaiensis* with one hand and intoned, "Once it was a flowering tree. The last of its gene pool.

They were warned. They published the plan anyway. What I created, I can destroy. Anytime you feel like taking this place, bring in the Army. They won't even see me in the hills with my sniper scope."

LATER I TRACKED DOWN the facts about the federal plan to "take over" the Outlaw Plant Preserve.

Early botanists had first discovered Robinson's tree, *Caesalpinia kavaiensis,* on Kauai in 1860, when it spread widely in upland forests. By the time the federal government began listing endangered species in Hawaii in the 1980s, the population of the dense-wood tree had dwindled to forty-two known specimens. Eleven grew on Oahu, and another thirty in North Kona on the Big Island. Only single trees grew on Lanai and Kauai.

The government's draft plan for *Caesalpinia kavaiensis* called for establishment of new populations of the rare tree. The plan recommended "Secure habitat of current populations and manage threats." That was what led Keith Robinson to conclude that the feds were trying to take over his land.

"It was a semantic disconnect," said U.S. Fish and Wildlife Service botanist John Fay when I reached him in his Washington, D.C., office. "That's not what we meant, but that's how Keith took it. I explained to him at great length that we would not take his land, and we were never going to take his land, but he couldn't see it that way. He was stockpiling arms to fight a government takeover."

Keith apparently never read the sentence on page fifty-one of the sixty-four-page plan that mentioned him specifically, although not by name: "The landowner's current program of rare plant conservation should be supported and assisted."

Robinson and Fay, as it turns out, were longtime friends. Fay had begun his botany career at the then–Pacific Tropical Botanical Garden in the early 1970s. Later, he joined the Fish and Wildlife Service, eventually serving as consulting botanist when the government listed the spotted owl as endangered, setting off a colossal battle with the lumber companies in the Pacific Northwest. When Robinson first decided to start his preserve, he paid Fay to fly back to Kauai to advise him.

I asked Fay, "Are you aware that he burned his *Caesalpinia* tree to deliver a warning to the government?"

Fay sighed with resignation. "No. I recall him threatening to torch the whole place. Keith is paranoid. I'm not a psychologist, but I'd describe it as unfounded apprehension, which is what paranoia is. It fits the Robinson family's view of life."

But even the burned tree does not stop Fay from admiring Keith. Although the two have quarreled and Keith wouldn't speak to him for years at a time, Fay has since returned several times to the preserve. "I couldn't in my wildest imagination have predicted what would happen there," said Fay. "It's remarkable in almost every way. The preserve has the appearance of a regenerative native Hawaiian forest. Nobody has ever seen that before. Some things are from Maui and the Big Island, so it isn't completely authentic, but the gestalt of the place is 'Here you've got a forest composed of native, rare, Hawaiian plants.' It is how the land would have looked one thousand years ago."

Fay thinks that Robinson loves his plants too much to have really burned his last specimen of *Caesalpinia*. Perhaps, he suggested with hope, in a corner of the preserve there are one or two others, unlabeled, unmarked, thriving in anonymity.

CHAPTER TWENTY-SEVEN

Saying Good-Bye to a Garden

WITH GREAT POMP and circumstance, a ceremonial Hawaiian blessing, and the unveiling of a gift shop, the little sugar shack opened to the public. Mike Faye had woven his magic, and now the cottage's pistachio-green wood sides and gingerbread touches drew visitors in droves. I was proud—few fund-raisers manage to see a project from start to finish.

I had sworn not to do any more gardening at my own plantation but couldn't help adding a new plant here and there. Gardeners can never really stop. I had always known the cottage was never mine to keep, but it had been a source of pride. Wanting to leave it in prime condition, I shined the floors and washed the windows. Living in the little cottage had extinguished a need for a bigger house. I never once missed the three stories of my Philadelphia house, nor its formal dining room. The happiness doctors—the Ph.D. psychologists who track and analyze what it takes to make a modern American happy these days—will tell you that the big house will do virtually nothing to increase your well-being. I can subscribe to that.

Outside, the driveway circle, now ringed in jagged lava boulders thanks to John Rapozo, was filled with hot-colored impatiens and lavender-studded heather. But it lacked a centerpiece. There was only one choice. While the oak or elm defines most of America, the palm symbolizes the tropics. "Few people ever forget the first sight of a palm-tree of any species," wrote Isabella Bird.

At Kauai Nursery in Lihue, Steve, one of the nursery's landscape designers, drove me in an electric golf car to the back nurseries to make a selection. I dismissed the Manila palms, the nursery's biggest sellers, as too common, although their shiny green shanks were attractive straight poles, topped by a symmetrical crown of feather fronds. I also worried that the big fan palms would present too much sail to the wind in the exposed plateau of the driveway.

Steve steered me down a row of triangle palms, whose bases, not surprisingly, are formed by three flat sides. The trunks reached only about four feet high, but the wide-spreading fronds of silvery blue reached another twelve feet into the air and rustled against one another with an almost imperceptible click-click-click. For a semi-reasonable sum, I could acquire one of medium maturity, which Steve, with a little prodding, said would include free delivery. I told him confidently that I would have the eighteen-inch hole dug and ready.

The next Saturday I approached the driveway circle, shovel ready. I swung back high, then hit the dirt, penetrating a mere two inches. Again with more force, I had the same result. For half an hour I worked, my hair tied up in a bandanna, my shoes and pants getting more and more stained with red dirt. Each shovel blow dislodged a scant cup of hard-packed clay, a legacy from the years of pineapple farming on the property. I was a prisoner, trying to tunnel out through concrete dirt, one teaspoon at a time.

To soften the soil, I filled the shallow depression I had dug with several inches of water. Fifteen minutes later the water had not fully seeped into the ground, a disquieting signal that I had to shovel through even more densely packed clay.

Over the next three days I intermittently continued to dig and finally succeeded in making an eighteen-inch-deep hole. When Steve arrived with the palm on the back of his pickup truck, I proudly told him the hole I dug was plenty deep. No, it's not, he grunted.

With easy strokes he took the shovel and sliced through another foot of earth. Steve was clearly a professional and gave a treatise on palm planting as we worked. He scuffed up the sides of the hole a bit, so that the roots would spread and not be confined in an underground clay chamber. I sprinkled small amounts of granular fertilizer into the hole and on the surrounding dirt. Steve deftly lowered the palm into place, then mixed piles of earth and humus for backfill. For the final smoothing, he handled a rake like a blackjack dealer, grading the soil surface, constructing a little saucer well to capture water.

"These roots really need watering in the next two weeks. Don't count on rainfall," he instructed. As he packed up his tools, I stumbled over an offer to tip him. He shook his head.

"Well, now we've planted a palm together," I said. "Thank you."

With luck, the palm will grow to sway over another generation of gardeners. It was a way to leave something behind, a benediction of gratitude. The last months had held more for me than I could have imagined for myself. Adversity leads to happiness, if not too crushing. I had found peace here at the cottage, and that's what I took with me. And I had devised my own maxim: The way to say good-bye to a garden is to improve it.

FORTY YEARS AGO Robert Allerton's last act of generosity was a gift of one million dollars to the newly formed Pacific Tropical Botanical Garden, thus creating a new institution to showcase and study Hawaii's unique flora. At the age of ninety-two, Robert slipped and broke a leg; he died a few days later on December 22, 1964.

John Allerton inherited Lawai-Kai, Robert's art collection, his personal effects, and two million dollars. Robert gave away the bulk of his money to a charitable trust, because the income taxes for John would have consumed most of it. To this day, one-third of the income on that trust is annually donated to the Honolulu Academy of the Arts and two-thirds to the Art Institute of Chicago.

The absolute decorum dictated by Robert relaxed. Servants sometimes walked around the house naked. John soon discovered that he did not have the money to support the lifestyle to which he had become accustomed. Still, John made a habit of walking through Allerton Garden every day, especially in late afternoon, chatting with Steve Perlman, who lived in the chalet near Pump Six for some of those years, and asking about Steve's cat or a new bunch of kittens. By the early 1980s he was growing infirm and often preferred a golf cart.

In a document dated May 6, 1968, John Allerton made a promise to other Garden trustees. "After you have acquired at least two hundred acres of land adjacent to Lawai-Kai to be used for the botanical garden I will create an irrevocable declaration of trust and will transfer to this trust all of Lawai-Kai." Garden leaders celebrated jubilantly. Allerton Garden would soon be theirs—land, title, money, everything. John hosted a luau at Lawai-Kai for the dedication ceremony. In coming years, John helped the new garden staff lay out its first trails and gardens.

I kept looking for the secret, the reason why the botanical garden never excelled, never fulfilled its promise. What I heard was the same old story. No earth-shaking secret. Just ordinary, run-of-the mill, undistinguished human nature: inertia, lack of ambition, lack of vision, lack of leadership. Young scientists hired by the new botanical garden fell under the spell of Allerton Garden. They felt a thrilling responsibility to help create the jewel of tropical research. After short tenures, they left, embittered. The first two directors had taken some important steps but were never able to lead the institution into serious scientific endeavors or even envision, much less perform, the groundwork needed to operate a true public garden. Dr. Klein had begun to change all that. Mightily. But I could see that the garden could easily revert into obscurity.

As John Allerton aged, he retreated more and more into his grand beach house. When he died of heart failure on September 1, 1985, at eighty-six years old, the botanical garden leaders assumed they would finally assume ownership of Allerton Garden. John's will came as a shock. After twenty years of coy, veiled promises, he did, in fact, deed the Allerton property to a charitable trust as he had stated he would do—but not to the National Tropical Botanical Garden. Instead, Allerton Garden, along with its multimillion-dollar endowment, went to a private trust administered by the First National Bank of Chicago. The bank contracted with NTBG to manage Allerton Garden but would always retain ownership and control. Although NTBG was furious, they shouldn't have been surprised — in his last years John Allerton had expressed continued unhappiness at their lack of progress.

Soon after John's death, his Chicago attorney and the manager of the Allerton Trust for First National Bank of Chicago boarded a helicopter. They scattered John's ashes over Lawai-Kai on the outgoing tide. Just as John had done for Robert sixteen years earlier.

In an instant, the ocean swallowed the tiny cinder specks.

"LET US LIVE," I said in a low voice.

"Let them find us," offered Beth.

On the morning of race day, a dozen canoes in brightly colored racing rigs lay beached at the Waimea town pier. Angry gray swells rolled in. Beth, looking buff in a two-piece suit that showed off her tattooed back, chugged water from a wide-mouth plastic bottle. She and I made repeated trips to the bathroom, probably more out of nerves than need. Other Kawaikini Canoe Club members had shown up to cheer us on.

A bearded paddler in surfing jams, the race organizer, called for a group prayer. About seventy-five paddlers made a circle and held hands. "We want to welcome the Kawaikini Canoe Club to their first appearance at this race," he said. We smiled shyly. As the circle broke, Beth and I agreed quietly that we needed the prayers.

Puna had borrowed a sleek blue and yellow racing canoe from the Hanalei Canoe Club to give us a fighting chance. We walked out on the wooden pier to watch the men, first to race. The starting horn blew. Eight boats shot forward, strong and fast. They mounted swells, swooped down water mountains, and disappeared from sight. They rounded the first buoy, then set off for the second. They returned to the finish line, stroking hard.

Now the women's race was to begin. We gathered excitedly around the beached outrigger, ready to push it into the water. Puna told us to rest our hands on the gunnels and bow our heads. She chanted in Hawaiian but also spoke in English, "When you are out there, there will be a time when you ask yourselves why you are doing this. Remember, you are doing it because you are empowered Hawaiian women, doing Hawaiian things." *Right. Empowered Hawaiian women.* We pounded the gunnels with our fists, then shouted in unison, "Kawaikini!"

I tore off my T-shirt as we strode into the water, rushed the *vaha* through the breaking surf, and scrambled into the boat. A strong wave knocked my left thigh hard against the gunnel, shooting pains down my leg. I had to lift it into the boat with two hands. I zipped up the blue racing cover around me guiltily; I didn't want the others to know.

We arrived first at the starting buoy. A novice's mistake, we soon learned. Another team wedged itself between our boat and the buoy, pushing us to a rear position. Then another boat squeezed in, separating us even further from the buoy and putting us behind all the other boats. Paddlers all around us whooped war cries when the starting horn blared. We stroked hard but couldn't move forward. One boat rammed our right side. Boats to our left cut in front of us. Paddles, canoes, and arms locked together in a squirming mass. The pack broke free, surging far ahead of us before we even had begun to paddle.

Our lightweight *vaha* was tippy and seemed to lift out of the water at the slightest wave. Dark water sucked below.

One, two, three, four, five, six, seven, eight, nine, ten, eleven, twelve. Hut!

Ho!

We neared the first buoy, but the other boats had all rounded it and were already headed for the second marker.

"It takes a lot of guts to be last," I yelled.

We made for the second buoy. Faster, faster, the paddles whirled.

. . . nine, ten, eleven, twelve, Hut!

All the other canoes were racing back to the finish line by the time we rounded the second turning point. A green and white canoe trailed behind the frontrunners. We sensed a chance to beat it!

. . . four, five, six, Hut!

We dug into the water, our hands covered with ocean. We neared the finishing line. Seven miles of paddling, and we could do it. Mary, who hadn't said a word the entire race, now shouted, "If there's one thing we're going to do, we're going to look strong when we cross that line."

We pulled hard. We yee-hawed and whooped. We passed the finish line and held our paddles high.

Dead last.

THE NEXT DAY I finished packing. There wasn't much left—the furniture had already been carted away and put into storage. I would fly to Budapest carrying only what could fit into the same three suitcases I had brought with me when I arrived. Sam would live with friends. Val and I had sold Bo to a time-share salesman. Although I had reveled in living in the plantation cottage with its grand expanse of property, I didn't need to ever own another house or let real estate hold me back.

Throughout my stay on Kauai I had felt I was on a parallel journey with so many other travelers who enter a strange land, meet guides and foes, then return, much wiser, to the wider world. I'd never aspire to the extremes undertaken by Isabella Bird, nor her decades of rootlessness. But I did aim for her free-legged air and her break from societal and self-imposed boundaries. For Robert and John Allerton, Hawaii was their final destination and retreat. For Isabella and me, it was a beginning.

A chrysalis.

*A*FTER FLYING TO Budapest so long ago, I did live a nomadic life for several years, training journalists throughout Eastern and Central Europe and Africa. I loved the work. While I never slept in a camel's tent, I stayed in enough former Communist hotels to develop a loathing for Stalinist design and its discomforts.

I'm thankful for the career reverses I've staggered through, because without them I'd never have gone on any of those excursions. As I work at my desk now, the computer screen saver flashes through a slide show of photos taken in Hawaii, Botswana, Kosovo, Prague, and elsewhere. I remember when I thought my life was over in Philadelphia and think, *Look at all that's happened since then!*

In a perhaps apocryphal story, when my hero Carl Jung met someone who had just been fired, the great psychologist would say, "Congratulations, something exciting is going to happen to you." And when Jung met someone who had just been promoted, he'd offer his condolences.

When I watch colleagues who have climbed career ladders with steady progress and seldom a misstep, it does seem that there is a certain predictability, a safeness . . . and a lack of imagination.

I avoided returning to the Garden for years. As I feared, it entered another bleak period. The new management fired or forced out everyone in the Plant Conservation Department, until only Steve Perlman was left, a staff of one. Rick Hanna, curator of Allerton Garden history as well as the library, was prohibited from researching anything to do with Robert and John Allerton.

At long last, the board of trustees revolted at all the turmoil and ineptitude. Chipper Wichman, the likable and visionary director of Limahuli Garden on the north shore and then Kahanu on Maui, was appointed CEO and executive director to lead the whole National Tropical Botanical Garden empire. As Chipper had worked or hiked with many of the Garden staff, he drew on deep friendships and a mutual respect. Now the Garden seems in better shape than ever. A new world-class nursery and greenhouse as first envisioned by Dr. Klein has opened, with state-of-the-art timed irrigation, misting, and temperature controls. For the first time, the Garden can replicate mid-elevation and mountain climates. Chipper rehired many of the fired scientists and increased the Conservation Department to almost three dozen staff members, who cultivate an ever-growing number of endangered plants.

The National Tropical Botanical Garden has assumed its responsibility as the most advanced and largest plant-rescue operation in the Hawaiian Islands.

Chipper persuaded Warren Wagner of the Smithsonian to spend a year at the Garden as a visiting scientist; he also hired Dave Burney, the fervent paleoecologist who had excavated at

Mahaulepu, to oversee ecological restorations. Ten-foot-tall native plants now fill the Mahaulepu cave. Burney's also turned the gorgeous Lawai-Kai at the Allerton estate into a native beach plant restoration.

To my surprise and delight, Chipper asked me to give a lecture at the Garden on Allerton history — the real history of how and why they left Chicago to settle, happily, in this remote valley.

In another of Chipper's miracles, Keith Robinson gave a talk to the Garden's class of student interns. Keith enjoyed it so much that he sat on a stone wall outside for an hour, talking to the admiring students.

On my lecture visit, I finally persuaded Steve Perlman to take me along on a field collecting expedition. We slipped and slid in the cool waters of a small stream tributary in the upper Limahuli Valley, on a mission to collect seeds from the elusive white-flowering *Hibiscus waimeae,* subspecies *hannerae.* Botanists reported this endangered plant extinct until the 1970s when Steve and Chipper discovered fifty plants here and in the neighboring Hanakapiai Valley. Although the hibiscus produces thousands of blooms, it doesn't develop much fruit. Birds, rats, slugs, borers, and weevils gobble the few seed capsules that do appear. It's a tough world out there if you are the last of your species, not very fertile, and your offspring are all consumed by terrors.

Steve collected enough of its seeds last year to propagate seventy seedlings in the nursery. A restoration crew carefully airlifted them by helicopter up the mountain and camped out for three days to transplant them. So far, nearly every single one survives.

As he led the way through the jungle terrain, I noticed that Steve has aged along with the rest of us. After a prolonged recovery from a rare blood cancer that almost killed him, he has whiter hair. If anything, the near-death experience only increased his resolve to botanize more of the Pacific islands before the native flora is wiped out.

After a decade of grimy weed-whacking, chainsawing of big trees, and backbreaking brush clearing, some footholds have been gained in the Limahuli Valley. Restoration efforts are concentrated on a modest twelve acres in the lower valley and another five in the upper—a mere 1.7 percent of the entire one-thousand-acre preserve.

Success is measured one plant at a time.

"We shouldn't lose any of these species. But as far as saving the forest, that's a more dismal picture." Steve says bluntly. Restoring entire forests, he predicts, will take hundreds of years of determined effort.

"The key is to start with something good," Steve says. "Constructing a forest from scratch is really impossible." That's why he is so excited about Chipper's plan to fence the Upper Limahuli Valley to keep roaming pigs and goats out. More than 90 percent native, the upper forest is among the most pristine in the state. By fencing it, reintroducing some of the plants that used to grow there, and watching over it, there is a likely chance that the valley can stay that way.

We couldn't find the rare hibiscus that day. But as we walked down through the valley, Steve pointed out some of the treasures that grow in Limahuli. His beloved *Brighamia* dot the landscape by the dozens. Fewer than ten plants of *Schiedea kauaiensis* continue to grow in the wild; here several examples thrive. Another rare hibiscus, *Hibiscadelphus distans,* had nearly died out in its habitat, the Waimea Canyon. Steve and Chipper had collected some of its seeds in 1990, and so it also lives here, protection against the day when it will completely die out in the wild.

The work he and the others do is Herculean by any standard. Helicoptering fences and men to mountain summits, snaring and hunting animals: It's much slower and more difficult than what is now possible in the laboratory, where scientists can make endless clones from snips of a plant, then use tissue culture to produce thousands of sprouts. Those methods produce plants with a reduced gene pool, but at least it's a way to keep a species alive, barricaded in the botanical garden, our Noah's Ark.

Neither god nor beast but somewhere in between, species *Homo sapiens* has used its higher intelligence to dominate the plant and animal kingdoms. And in doing so, has abused the planet. Perhaps God banished Adam and Eve from the Garden of Eden for this exploitation — not for the theft of an apple but for their failure to tend the orchard, to replenish the earth's bounty and to protect it. Dr. Klein liked to say that gardens are for growing people, but we must not forget: People are for growing gardens.

ACKNOWLEDGMENTS

SOME OF MY most evocative childhood memories come from my mother's backyard garden. Her magenta peonies provided deep shade for our dog, while grape-colored lilacs filled the house with scent. She grew a brown iris—she called it root beer—which I've been looking for ever since. The bleeding hearts, columbine, and virtually all of Mom's garden plantings began as tubers and divisions from Grandma's garden on the other side of Minneapolis.

So when the gardening bug bit me later in life, I realized that I descend from a long line of gardeners. Unconsciously I tried to duplicate the sweet smells and visions of those Minnesota gardens. I also aimed to match the New England perennial borders tended by my mother-in-law, Lucette Liebig, not only a master gardener but a master chef. "Gardens take a lot of time, and a lot of mistakes," Lucette instructed.

She could have been talking about writing a book. Although this project required many hours with the seat of the pants applied to the seat of the chair, it was not a solitary act. All of the writers I've read, worked with, revered, conversed with, and consulted are with me when I write. Writing a first book required learning a literary style as well as how to find an agent and publisher. I'm not sure which took longer.

By GOOD FORTUNE I was referred by writer Peggy Anderson to agent Fredrica Friedman, who took a chance on a first-time author, as did my editor Amy Gash and the rest of the crew at Algonquin Books. I was lucky to have such smart women on this project, who insisted on rewriting and rewriting. Amy helped me find the core of the book and bring it to conclusion. I'm grateful to Michelle Daniel for her high standard of copyediting. Several people read relevant excerpts and provided guidance and corrections, including Janet Klein, Steve Perlman, David Burney, and Warren Wagner. I am grateful for their help, but any mistakes are my own.

Early readers included writer and editor colleagues Jonathan Neuman, Patsy McLaughlin, Gioia Diliberto, Charles Layton, and Mary Walton, all of whom helped me focus. My friend Julia Cass was a constant sounding board who read several drafts. As she was working on her own book during the same time, we encouraged each other during the ups and downs.

I am ever grateful to Dr. William Klein for rescuing me with an out-of-the-blue job offer, and for his dependable friendship. On Kauai the Klein family extended their welcome—particularly Janet and her daughter Melissa, a fellow horse rider. Several friends offered me their houses to stay in on Kauai: Diane Forsyth, Janet Klein, Anne O'Malley, Judy and Doug Bean. Fran and the late Diego McConkey hired me as cat-sitter for several extended stays in their fabulous oceanfront condo that provided time for research and writing. Best job I ever had. Michael and Betsy Claffey lent me their cottage in County

Cork, Ireland, for a six-week writing retreat. My sister, Libby, and her husband, Max, allowed me to use their Milan apartment as a base during my year in eastern Europe. My cousins Bill and Gerry Epmeier in Chicago, as well as the late Ihma Epmeier, my aunt and a formidable pioneer and gardener in her own right, were hosts during my lengthy Chicago research. Mathea Allansmith invited me to stay with her in London, where I began to research Isabella Bird. The folks at the International Center for Journalists in Washington, D.C., granted me two fellowships: a Knight International Press Fellowship and the McGee Journalism Fellowship for Southern Africa. Both allowed for some writing time while teaching, as well as breathing space for reflection and redirection.

I kept notes as I experienced the events depicted in this memoir. Memory was also aided by dozens of interviews with those involved, and by others who shared with me recollections of the early days of Allerton Garden. In real life, many things happen all at once; to separate them out into a linear narrative, I found I had to make some minor adjustments in timing of events. All names are real, except, of course, for Cal, as well as the Miami doctor.

Many people dredged up recollections of their stays at the National Tropical Botanical Garden and consented to interviews. The list is long, and I fear I will omit an important name, but I will attempt to list the primary interviews here. Special thanks go to Rick Hanna, collector of Allertonia and a frequent resource. Field collector Steve Perlman and botanist David Lorence were always ready to answer my plant questions. I thank David Penhallow, a prominent Kauai figure and actor who was the stand-in for Lieutenant Cable in the 1957 filming of *South Pacific*.

It was David who told me that a scene representing Bali Hai was filmed in Allerton Garden. He also remembered for me his visits to the Allerton estate and an evening costume party. Former NTBG board member John Plews recalled his early days at the estate, accompanying his mother, Edith Plews, to discuss Red Cross business with Robert Allerton during World War II. Derral Herbst shared with me his recollections of late evening talks with John Gregg Allerton. Hideo Teshima allowed me to garden with him in Allerton Garden a couple of mornings and recalled his time with the Allertons, as did his brother, Joe, his sister, Masaki, and his wife, Nancy. Geoffrey Chauncey at the University of Chicago and Chad Heap, now at George Washington University, shared with me their research and pointed me to Special Collections at the University of Chicago Regenstein Library. Dr. Heap's University of Chicago Ph.D. thesis on the Pansy Craze of the 1930s was a particularly valuable resource. Dick Babcock, editor of *Chicago Magazine,* encouraged me by publishing a longer version of my Chicago chapter. The late John Rapozo, and his wife, Florence, gave information, dinners, and friendship.

For help with history about the Allertons and the National Tropical Botanical Garden, I interviewed David Chang, James Elder, Steve Frowline, Hobey and Nancy Goodale, Woody Hume, Doug and Liz Kinney, the late Charles Lamoreaux, Mateo Lettunich, Scot Medbury, Kerin Lilleeng-Rosenberger, Francis Lono, Geoffrey Rausch, Adam and Lianne Rose, Michael Shea, Scott Sloan, William Theobald, Chipper and Hau'oli Wichman, Keith Woolliams, and Ken Wood. Also helpful were former Allerton estate lawyer Robert Joynt and former Robert Allerton attorney Frank Bixby.

Thanks to Keith Robinson for a memorable trip to his

12

Outlaw Plant Preserve and John Fay at the U.S. Fish and Wildlife Service. Also thanks to Michael Faye for sharing the history of plantation cottages and to Puna Dawson for outrigger canoe history. Thanks also to Alan Wong and his kitchen staff for allowing me to watch them cook.

In Illinois, I am grateful to Etta Arntzen, David Bowman, and Jerry Soesbe at Allerton Park for their interviews and their guidance on source material.

Thanks also go to all my friends on Kauai and elsewhere who encouraged me during this long project and on all the adventures and mishaps of life in general. You are too numerous to list, but know that you are dear to me. I am grateful to have worked with Gene Roberts and the rest of our generation at *The Philadelphia Inquirer* when journalism excellence and experimentation were the norm. The *Inquirer* provided a home and a place to grow up journalistically—a process I'm still completing. Thanks also to the National Tropical Botanical Garden staff and trustees, past and current, for preserving the Garden and all its satellites as the national treasures they truly are.

A note on Hawaiian language: the current use of diacritical marks for Hawaiian words remains uneven in adoption, but loaded with political significance. In Hawaii, two diacritical marks are used—the *'okina* glottal stop, similar to the sound between the syllables of "oh-oh," and the *kahako* macron, which lengthens and adds stress to the marked vowel. For greater reading ease and consistency, I have most often chosen to forego use of these marks, but mean no disrespect to the native language tradition.

Archival research was conducted at the State of Hawaii Library, the National Tropical Botanical Garden library, the

Kauai Historical Society, the Kauai Public Libraries, the Art Institute of Chicago, the Chicago Historical Society, the Newberry Library in Chicago, the Piatt County Historical Society in Illinois, the Allerton Park estate, the Allerton archives at the University of Illinois at Urbana-Champaign, the British Library, and the Library of Congress.

I remain indebted to the people of Kauai for welcoming me.

Lucinda Fleeson
Washington, D.C.

SELECTED READINGS

Barr, Pat. *A Curious Life for a Lady: The Story of Isabella Bird, a Remarkable Victorian Traveller,* Doubleday & Co., New York, 1970.

Bird, Isabella L. *Six Months in the Sandwich Islands: Among Hawaii's Palm Groves, Coral Reefs, and Volcanoes,* Mutual Publishing, Honolulu, 1998. First printed in 1881 by Putnam's Sons, New York, and in 1875 by John Murray, London.

Burney, Lida Pigott, and David A. Burney. "Charcoal Stratigraphies for Kauai and the Timing of Human Arrival," *Pacific Science,* Vol. 57, No. 2, April 2003.

Carlquist, Sherwin. *Island Biology,* Columbia University Press, New York, 1974.

Cook, Chris, editor. *A Kauai Reader: The Exotic Literary Heritage of the Garden Island,* Mutual Publishing, Honolulu, 1995.

Cook, Chris. *The Kauai Movie Book,* Mutual Publishing, Honolulu, 1996.

Fleeson, Lucinda. "The Gay Thirties in Chicago," *Chicago Magazine,* November 2005. (On the web at www.chicagomag.com/Chicago -Magazine/November-2005/The-Gay-30S/.)

Heap, Chad. *Slumming: Sexual and Racial Encounters in American Nightlife, 1885–1940,* University of Chicago Press, Chicago, 2009.

Joesting, Edward. *Kauai: The Separate Kingdom,* University of Hawaii Press and Kauai Museum Association, Ltd., Honolulu, 1984.

Kimura, Bert Y., and Kenneth M. Nagata. *Hawaii's Vanishing Flora,* Oriental Publishing Co., Honolulu, 1980.

Laudan, Rachel. *The Food of Paradise: Exploring Hawaii's Culinary Heritage*, University of Hawaii Press, Honolulu, 1996.

Linder, H. Peter. "Inferring Evolutionary History without Fossils: Evolution of Diversity: the Cape Flora," *Trends in Plant Science*, Vol. 10, No. 11, November 2005.

London, Jack. *Stories of Hawaii*, edited by A. Grove Day, Mutual Publishing, Honolulu, 1984.

Low, Lieutenant Charles R. *Captain Cook's Three Voyages Round the World, with a Sketch of his Life*, George Routledge & Sons, 1876.

Merwin, W. S. *The Folding Cliffs: A Narrative of 19th-Century Hawaii*, Alfred Knopf, New York, 1998.

Meyen, Dr. F. J. F. *A Botanist's Visit to Oahu in 1831*, Press Pacifica, Kailua, Hawaii, 1981.

Sohmer, S. H., and R. Gustafson. *Plants and Flowers of Hawaii*, University of Hawaii Press, Honolulu, 1987.

Twain, Mark. *Mark Twain in Hawaii: Roughing It In The Sandwich Islands, Hawaii in the 1860s*, edited by A. Grove Day, Mutual Publishing, Honolulu, 1990.

Wagner, Warren L., and V. A. Funk, editors. *Hawaiian Biogeography: Evolution on a Hot Spot Archipelago*, Smithsonian Institution Press, Washington, D.C., 1995.

ROY MORRIS

Lucinda Fleeson is director of the Hubert Humphrey Fellowship Program at the Philip Merrill College of Journalism at the University of Maryland. A reporter at the *Philadelphia Inquirer* for many years, she has received an Arthur Rouse Award for Press Criticism, a McGee Journalism Fellowship in Southern Africa, a Knight International Press Fellowship, and a Nieman Fellowship at Harvard. Before settling in Washington, D.C., she lived in Philadelphia, Boston, New York, Budapest, Botswana, and most notably, Kauai.